305.896 D816n 2007
Du Bois, W. E. B. (William
Edward Burghardt), 1868-1963
The Negro

WITHDRAWN

D1171269

The Negro

THE OXFORD W. E. B. DU BOIS

Henry Louis Gates, Jr., Editor

The Suppression of the African Slave-Trade to the United States
of America: 1638–1870
  Introduction: Saidiya Hartman

The Philadelphia Negro: A Social Study
  Introduction: Lawrence Bobo

The Souls of Black Folk
  Introduction: Arnold Rampersad

John Brown
  Introduction: Paul Finkelman

Africa, Its Geography, People and Products
Africa—Its Place in Modern History
  Introductions: Emmanuel Akyeampong

Black Reconstruction in America
  Introduction: David Levering Lewis

Black Folk: Then and Now
  Introduction: Wilson J. Moses

Dusk of Dawn
  Introduction: Kwame Anthony Appiah

The World and Africa
Color and Democracy: Colonies and Peace
  Introductions: Mahmood Mamdani and *Gerald Horne*

In Battle for Peace: The Story of My Eighty-third Birthday
  Introduction: Manning Marable

The Black Flame Trilogy: Book One
The Ordeal of Mansart
  Introduction: Brent Edwards
  Afterword: Mark Sanders

The Black Flame Trilogy: Book Two
Mansart Builds a School
  Introduction: Brent Edwards
  Afterword: Mark Sanders

The Black Flame Trilogy: Book Three
Worlds of Color
  Introduction: Brent Edwards
  Afterword: Mark Sanders

Autobiography of W. E. B. Du Bois
  Introduction: Werner Sollors

The Quest of the Silver Fleece
  Introduction: William L. Andrews

The Negro
  Introduction: John K. Thornton

Darkwater: Voices from Within the Veil
  Introduction: Evelyn Brooks Higginbotham

Gift of Black Folk: The Negroes in the Making of America
  Introduction: Glenda Carpio

Dark Princess: A Romance
  Introduction: Homi K. Bhabha

THE NEGRO

W. E. B. Du Bois

Series Editor, Henry Louis Gates, Jr.

Introduction by John K. Thornton

305
.896
D816n
2007

WITHDRAWN

10/07

OXFORD
UNIVERSITY PRESS

CUYAHOGA COMMUNITY COLLEGE
EASTERN CAMPUS LIBRARY   NOV   2 2007

For Cornel West

OXFORD
UNIVERSITY PRESS

Oxford University Press, Inc., publishes works that further
Oxford University's objective of excellence in research,
scholarship, and education.

Oxford   New York
Auckland   Cape Town   Dar es Salaam   Hong Kong   Karachi
Kuala Lumpur   Madrid   Melbourne   Mexico City   Nairobi
New Delhi   Shanghai   Taipei   Toronto

With offices in
Argentina   Austria   Brazil   Chile   Czech Republic   France   Greece
Guatemala   Hungary   Italy   Japan   Poland   Portugal   Singapore
South Korea   Switzerland   Thailand   Turkey   Ukraine   Vietnam

Copyright © 2007 by Oxford University Press

Published by Oxford University Press, Inc.
198 Madison Avenue, New York, NY 10016
www.oup.com

Oxford is a registered trademark of Oxford University Press

All rights reserved. No part of this publication may be reproduced,
stored in a retrieval system, or transmitted, in any form or by any means,
electronic, mechanical, photocopying, recording, or otherwise,
without the prior permission of Oxford University Press.

Library of Congress Cataloging-in-Publication Data is available.

ISBN: 9780195311808 (Series)
ISBN: 9780195325768 (Volume)

1 3 5 7 9 8 6 4 2

Printed in the United States of America
on acid-free paper

TO

A FAITHFUL HELPER

M. G. A.

Contents

MAPS

The Black Letters on the Sign:
W. E. B. Du Bois and the Canon

"... the slave master had a direct interest in discrediting the personality of those he held as property. Every man who had a thousand dollars so invested had a thousand reasons for painting the black man as fit only for slavery. Having made him the companion of horses and mules, he naturally sought to justify himself by assuming that the negro was not much better than a mule. The holders of twenty hundred million dollars' worth of property in human chattels procured the means of influencing press, pulpit, and politician, and through these instrumentalities they belittled our virtues and magnified our vices, and have made us odious in the eyes of the world. Slavery had the power at one time to make and unmake Presidents, to construe the law, and dictate the policy, set the fashion in national manners and customs, interpret the Bible, and control the church; and, naturally enough, the old masters set themselves up as much too high as they set the manhood of the negro too low. Out of the depths of slavery has come this prejudice and this color line. It is broad enough and black enough to explain all the malign influences which assail the newly emancipated millions to-day.... The office of color in the color line is a very plain and subordinate one. It simply advertises the objects of oppression, insult, and persecution. It is not the maddening liquor, but the black letters on the sign telling the world where it may be had ... Slavery, stupidity, servility, poverty, dependence, are undesirable conditions. When these shall cease to be coupled with color, there will be no color line drawn."

—FREDERICK DOUGLASS, "The Color Line," 1881.

William Edward Burghardt Du Bois (1868–1963) was the most prolific and, arguably, the most influential African American writer of his generation. The novelist and poet James Weldon Johnson (1871–1938) once noted the no single work had informed the shape of the African American literary tradition, except perhaps *Uncle Tom's Cabin*, than had Du Bois's seminal collection of essays *The Souls of Black Folk* (1903). While trained as a sociologist at Berlin and as a historian at Harvard, Du Bois was fearless in the face of genre—even when some of the genres that he sought to embrace did not fully embrace him in return. Du Bois published twenty-two single-author works, twenty-one in his lifetime (his *Autobiography*, edited by his friend and literary executor, Herbert Aptheker, would not be published until

1968). A selection of his greatest works, *An ABC of Color: Selections from over a Half Century of the Writings of W. E. B. Du Bois*, appeared in 1963, the year he died. And while these books reflect a wide variety of genres—including three widely heralded and magisterial books of essays published in 1903, 1920, and 1940 (*The Souls of Black Folk, Darkwater: Voices from within the Veil*, and *Dusk of Dawn: An Essay toward an Autobiography of a Race Concept*), one biography, five novels, a pioneering sociological study of a black community, five books devoted to the history of Africa, three historical studies of African American people, among others—Du Bois was, in the end, an essayist, an essayist of the first order, one of the masters of that protean form that so attracted Du Bois's only true antecedent, Frederick Douglass (1818–1895) as well as Du Bois's heir in the history of the form, James Baldwin (1924–1987). (Baldwin, like Du Bois, would turn repeatedly to fiction, only to render the form as an essay.)

Du Bois, clearly, saw himself as a man of action, but a man of action who luxuriated within a verdant and fecund tropical rainforest of words. It is not Du Bois's intoxication with words that marks his place in the history of great black public intellectuals—persons of letters for whom words are a vehicle for political action and their own participation in political movements. After all, one need only recall Du Bois's predecessor, Frederick Douglass, or another of his disciples, Martin Luther King Jr. for models in the African American tradition of leaders for whom acting and speaking were so inextricably intertwined as to be virtually coterminous; no, the novelty of Du Bois's place in the black tradition is that he wrote himself to a power, rather than spoke himself to power. Both Douglass and King, for all their considerable literary talents, will be remembered always for the power of their oratory, a breathtaking power exhibited by both. Du Bois, on the other hand, was not a great orator; he wrote like he talked, and he talked like an extraordinarily well-educated late Anglo-American Victorian, just as James Weldon Johnson did; no deep "black" stentorian resonances are to be found in the public speaking voices of either of these two marvelous writers. Booker T. Washington (1856–1915) spoke in a similar public voice.

First and last, W. E. B. Du Bois was a writer, a writer deeply concerned and involved with politics, just as James Baldwin was; as much as they loved to write, Douglass and King were orators, figures fundamentally endowed with a genius for the spoken word. Even Du Bois's colleague, William Ferris, commented upon this anomaly in Du Bois's place in the tradition, at a time (1913) when he had published only five books: "Du Bois," Ferris wrote, "is one of the few men in history who was hurled on the throne of leadership by the dynamic force of the written word. He is one of the few writers who leaped to the front as a leader and became the head of a popular movement through impressing his personality upon men by means of a book" ("The African Abroad," 1913). Despite the fact that Du Bois by this time had published his Harvard doctoral dissertation in history, *The Suppression of the African Slave-Trade* (1896), his sociological study, *The Philadelphia Negro* (1899), *The Souls of Black Folk* (1903), the sole biography that he would publish, *John Brown* (1909), and his first of five novels, *The Quest of the Silver Fleece* (1911), Ferris attributed Du Bois's catapult to leadership to one book and one book alone, *The Souls of Black Folk*. Indeed, it is probably true that had Du Bois published this book alone, his place in the canon of African American literature would have been secure, if perhaps not as fascinating!

The Souls of Black Folk, in other words, is the one book that Du Bois wrote which most of us have read in its entirety. It is through *The Souls of Black Folk* that we center Du Bois's place in the literary canon; it is through *Souls* that we structure the arc of his seven decade career as a man of letters. There are many good reasons for the centrality of this magical book to Du Bois's literary career, but it is also the case that the other works that comprise Du Bois's canon deserve fresh attention as a whole. And it is for this reason that my colleagues and I have embarked upon this project with Oxford University Press to reprint Du Bois's single-authored texts, and make them available to a new generation of readers in a uniform edition. The only other attempt to do so—Herbert Aptheker's pioneering edition of Du Bois's complete works, published in 1973—is, unfortunately, long out of print.

The Souls of Black Folk is such a brilliant work that it merits all of the attention that it has been given in the century since it was published. In April 1903, a thirty-five-year-old scholar and budding political activist published a 265 page book subtitled "Essays and Sketches," consisting of thirteen essays and one short story, addressing a wide range of topics, including the story of the freed slaves during Reconstruction, the political ascendancy of Booker T. Washington, the sublimity of the spirituals, the death of Du Bois's only son Burghardt, and lynching. Hailed as a classic even by his contemporaries, the book has been republished in no fewer than 120 editions since 1903. In fact, it is something of a rite of passage for younger scholars and writers to publish their take on Du Bois's book in new editions aimed at the book's considerable classroom market.

Despite its fragmentary structure, the book's disparate parts contribute to the sense of a whole, like movements in a symphony. Each chapter is pointedly "bicultural," prefaced by both an excerpt from a white poet and a bar of what Du Bois names "The Sorrow Songs" ("some echo of haunting melody from the only American music which welled up from black souls in the dark past.") Du Bois's subject was, in no small part, the largely unarticulated beliefs and practices of American Negroes, who were impatient to burst out of the cotton fields and take their rightful place as Americans. As he saw it, African American culture in 1903 was at once vibrant and disjointed, rooted in an almost medieval agrarian past and yet fiercely restive. Born in the chaos of slavery, the culture had begun to generate a richly variegated body of plots, stories, melodies, and rhythms. In *The Souls of Black Folk*, Du Bois peered closely at the culture of his kind, and saw the face of black America. Actually, he saw two faces. "One ever feels his two-ness—an American, a Negro," Du Bois wrote. "Two souls, two thoughts, two unreconciled strivings; two warring ideals in one dark body, whose dogged strength alone keeps it from being torn asunder." He described this condition as "double consciousness," and his emphasis on a fractured psyche made *Souls* a harbinger of the modernist movement that would begin to flower a decade or so later in Europe and in America.

Scholars, including Arnold Rampersad, Werner Sollors, Dickson Bruce, and David Levering Lewis, have debated the origins of Du Bois's use of the concept of "double consciousness," but what's clear is that its roots are multiple, which is appropriate enough, just as it is clear that the source of one of Du Bois's other signal metaphors—"the problem of the twentieth-century is the problem of the color line"—came to him directly from Frederick Douglass's essay of that title. Du Bois had studied in Berlin during a Hegel revival, and Hegel, famously, had written on the relationship between master and bondsman, whereby each defines himself through the recognition of the other. But the concept comes up, too, in Emerson, who wrote in 1842 of the split between our reflective self, which wanders through the realm of ideas, and the active self, which dwells in the here and how, a tension that recurs throughout the Du Bois oeuvre: "The worst feature of this double consciousness is that the two lives, of the understanding and of the soul, which we lead, really show very little relation to each other."

Even closer to hand was the term's appearance in late-nineteenth-century psychology. The French psychologist, Alfred Binet, writing in his 1896 book, *On Double Consciousness*, discusses what he calls "bipartititon," or "the duplication of consciousness": "Each of the consciousnesses occupies a more narrow and more limited field than if there existed one single consciousness containing all the ideas of the subject." William James, who taught Du Bois at Harvard, talked about a "second personality" that characterized "the hypnotic trance." When Du Bois transposed this concept from the realm of the psyche to the social predicament of the American Negro, he did not leave it unchanged. But he shared with the psychologists the notion that double consciousness was essentially an affliction. "This American world," he complained, yields the Negro "no true self-consciousness, but only lets him see himself through the revelation of the other world. It is a peculiar sensation, this double-consciousness, this sense of always looking at one's self through the eyes of others, of measuring one's soul by the tape of a world that looks on in amused contempt and pity." Sadly, "the double life every American Negro must live, as a Negro and as an American," leads inevitably to "a painful self-consciousness, an almost morbid sense of personality and a moral hesitancy which is fatal to self-confidence." The result is "a double life, with double thoughts, double duties and double social classes," and worse, "double words and double ideas," which "tempt the mind to pretense or revolt, hypocrisy or to radicalism." Accordingly, Du Bois wanted to make the American Negro whole; and he believed that only desegregation and full equality could make this psychic integration possible.

And yet for subsequent generations of writers, what Du Bois cast as a problem was taken to be the defining condition of modernity itself. The diagnosis, one might say, outlasted the disease. Although Du Bois would publish twenty-two books, and thousands of essays and reviews, no work of his has done more to shape an African American literary history than *The Souls of Black Folk*, and no metaphor in this intricately layered book has proved more enduring than that of double consciousness, including Du Bois's other powerfully resonating metaphors, that of "the veil" that separates black America from white America, and his poignant revision of Frederick Douglass's metaphor of "the color line," which Du Bois employed in that oft-repeated sentence, "The problem of the twentieth-century is the problem of the color line"—certainly his most prophetic utterance of many.

Like all powerful metaphors, Du Bois's metaphor of double consciousness came to have a life of its own. For Carl Jung, who visited the United States in the heyday of the "separate but equal" doctrine, the shocking thing wasn't that black culture was not equal, the shocking thing was that is was not separate! "The naïve European," Jung wrote, "thinks of America as a white nation. It is not wholly white, if you please; it is partly colored," and this explained, Jung continued, "the slightly Negroid mannerisms of the American." "Since the Negro lives within your cities and even within your houses," Jung continued, "he also lives within your skin, subconsciously." It wasn't just that the Negro was an American, as Du Bois would note, again and again, but that the American was, inevitably and inescapably, a Negro. The bondsman and the slave find their identity in each other's gaze: "two-ness" wasn't just a black thing any longer. As James Baldwin would put it, "Each of us, helplessly and forever, contains the other—male in female, female in male, white in black, black in white."

Today, talk about the fragmentation of culture and consciousness is a commonplace. We know all about the vigorous intermixing of black culture and white, high culture and low—from the Jazz Age freneticism of what the scholar Ann Douglass calls "mongrel Manhattan" to Hip Hop's hegemony over American youth in the late-twentieth and early-twenty-first centuries. Du Bois yearned to make the American Negro one, and lamented that he was two. Today, the ideal of wholeness has largely been retired. And cultural multiplicity is no longer seen as the problem, but as a solution—a solution to the confines of identity itself. Double consciousness, once a disorder, is now the cure. Indeed, the only complaint we moderns have is that Du Bois was too cautious in his accounting. He'd conjured "two souls, two thoughts two unreconciled strivings." Just two, Dr. Du Bois, we are forced to ask today? Keep counting.

And, in a manner of speaking, Du Bois did keep counting, throughout the twenty two books that comprise the formal canon of his most cogent thinking. The hallmark of Du Bois's literary career is that he coined the metaphors of double-consciousness and the veil—reappropriating Frederick Douglass's seminal definition of the semi-permeable barrier that separates and defines black-white racial relations in America as "the color line"—to define the place of the African American within modernity. The paradox of his career, however, is that the older Du Bois became, the more deeply he immersed himself in the struggle for Pan-Africanism and decolonization against the European colonial powers, and an emergent postcolonial "African" or "Pan-Negro" social and political identity—culminating in his own life in his assumption of Ghanaian citizenship in 1963. And the "blacker" that his stand against colonialism became, the less "black," in a very real sense, his analysis of what he famously called "The Negro Problem" simultaneously became. The more "African" Du Bois became, in other words, the more cosmopolitan his analysis of the root causes of anti-black and -brown and -yellow racism and colonialism became, seeing the status of the American Negro as part and parcel of a larger problem of international economic domination, precisely in the same way that Frederick Douglass rightly saw the construction of the American color line as a function of, and a metaphor for, deeper, structural, economic relations—"not the maddening liquor, but the black letters on the sign telling the world where it may be had," as Douglass so thoughtfully put it. The Negro's being-in-the-world, we might say, became ever more complex for Du Bois the older he grew, especially as the Cold War heated up and the anti-colonial movement took root throughout Africa and the Third World.

Ironically, Du Bois himself foretold this trajectory in a letter he wrote in 1896, reflecting on the import of his years as a graduate student at Friedrich Wilhelm University in Berlin: "Of the greatest importance was the opportunity which my *Wanderjahre* [wander years] in Europe gave of looking at the world as a man and not simply from a narrow racial and provincial outlook." How does the greatest black intellectual in the twentieth century—"America's most conspicuously educated Negro," as Werner Sollors puts it in his introduction to Du Bois's *Autobiography* in this series—make the rhetorical turn from defining the Negro American as a metaphor for modernity, at the turn of the century, to defining the Negro—at mid-century—as a metonym of a much larger historical pattern of social deviance and social dominance that had long been central to the fabric of world order, to the fabric of European and American domination of such a vast portion of the world of color? If, in other words, the Negro is America's metaphor for Du Bois in 1903, how does America's history of black-white relations become the metaphor of a nefarious pattern of economic exploitation and dominance by the end of Du Bois's life, in 1963? Make no mistake about it: either through hubris or an uncanny degree of empathy, or a mixture of both, throughout his life, W. E. B. Du Bois saw his most naked and public ambitions as well as his most private and intimate anxieties as representative of those of his countrymen, the American Negro people. Nevertheless, as he grew older, the closer he approached the end of his life, Du Bois saw the American Negro as a metaphor for class relations within the wider world order.

In order to help a new generation of readers to understand the arc of this trajectory in Du Bois's thinking, and because such a large part of this major thinker's oeuvre remains unread, Oxford University Press and I decided to publish in a uniform edition the twenty-one books that make up Du Bois's canon and invited a group of scholars to reconsider their importance as works of literature, history, sociology, and political philosophy. With the publication of this series, Du Bois's books are once again in print, with new introductions that analyze the shape of his career as a writer, scholar, and activist.

Reading the canon of Du Bois's work in chronological order, a certain allegorical pattern emerges, as Saidiya Hartman suggests in her introduction to *The Suppression of the African Slave-Trade*. Du Bois certainly responded immediately and directly to large historical events through fierce and biting essays that spoke adamantly and passionately to the occasion. But he also used the themes of his books to speak to the larger import of those events in sometimes highly mediated ways. His first book, for example, proffers as its thesis, as Hartman puts it, a certain paradox: "the slave trade flourished under the guise of its suppression," functioning legally for twenty years following the Compromise of the Federal Convention of 1787 and "illegally for another half century." Moreover, Du Bois tackles this topic at precisely the point in American history when Jim Crow segregation is becoming formalized through American law in the 1890s, culminating in 1896 (the year of the publication of his first book) with the infamous *Plessy v. Ferguson* "separate but equal" decision of the Supreme Court—exactly twenty years following the end of Reconstruction. Three years later, as Lawrence Bobo shows, Du Bois publishes *The Philadelphia Negro* in part to detail the effects of the "separate but equal" doctrine on the black community.

Similarly, Du Bois's biography of John Brown appeared in the same year as a pioneering band of blacks and whites joined together to form the National Association for the Advancement of Colored People (NAACP), the organization that would plot the demise of legal segregation through what would come to be called the Civil Rights Movement, culminating in its victory over de jure segregation in the Supreme Court's *Brown v. Board of Education* decision, which effectively reversed the *Plessy* decision, and in the Civil Rights Act of 1964 and the Voting Rights Act of 1965. John Brown, for Du Bois, would remain the emblem of this movement.

Likewise, Du Bois's first novel, *The Quest of the Silver Fleece*, published just two years following his biography of John Brown, served as a subtle critique both of an unreflective assimilationist ideology of the early NAACP through its advocacy of "a black-owned farming cooperative in the heart of the deep South," as William Andrews puts it, just as it surely serves as a critique of Booker T. Washington's apparently radical notion that economic development for the newly freed slaves could very well insure political equality in a manner both irresistible and inevitable, an argument, mind you, frequently made today under vastly different circumstances about the role of capitalism in Du Bois's beloved Communist China.

Du Bois registers his critique of the primitivism of the Harlem Renaissance in *The Gift of Black Folk*, as Glenda Carpio cogently argues, by walking "a tightrope between a patriotic embrace of an America in which African American culture has become an inextricable part and an exhortation of the rebellion and struggle out of which that culture arose." In response to the voyeurism and faddishness of Renaissance Harlem, Du Bois harshly reminds us that culture is a form of labor, too, a commodity infinitely exploitable, and that the size of America's unprecedented middle class can be traced directly to its slave past: "It was black labor that established the modern world commerce which began first as a commerce in the bodies of the slaves themselves and was the primary cause of the prosperity of the first great commercial cities of our day"—cities such as New York, the heart of the cultural movement that some black intellectuals passionately argued could very well augur the end of racial segregation throughout American society, or at least segregation between equal classes across the color line.

Paul Finkelman, in his introduction to *John Brown*, quotes the book's first line: "The mystic spell of Africa is and ever was over all America." If that is true, it was also most certainly the case for Du Bois himself, as John Thornton, Emmanuel Akyeampong, Wilson J. Moses, and Mahmood Mamdani show us in their introductions to five books that Du Bois published about Africa, in 1915, 1930, 1939, and 1947. Africa, too, was a recurring metaphor in the Duboisian canon, serving variously as an allegory of the intellectual potential of persons of African descent; as John K. Thornton puts it, "What counted was that African

history had movement and Africans were seen as historical actors and not simply as stolid recipients of foreign techniques and knowledge," carefully "integrating ancient Egypt into *The Negro* as part of that race's history, without
having to go to the extreme measure of asserting that somehow the Egyptians
were biologically identical to Africans from further south or west." The history
of African civilization, in other words, was Du Bois's ultimate argument for the
equality of Americans white and black.

Similarly, establishing his scholarly mastery of the literature of African history also served Du Bois well against ideological rivals such as Marcus Garvey,
who attacked Du Bois for being "too assimilated," and "not black enough."
Du Bois's various studies of African history also served as a collective text for
the revolutions being formulated in the forties and fifties by Pan-African
nationalists such as Kwame Nkrumah and Jomo Kenyatta, who would lead
their nations to independence against the European colonial powers. Du Bois
was writing for them, first as an exemplar of the American Negro, the supposed
vanguard of the African peoples, and later, and more humbly, as a follower of
the African's lead. As Wilson J. Moses notes, Du Bois once wrote that "American
Negroes of former generations had always calculated that when Africa was
ready for freedom, American Negroes would be ready to lead them. But the
event was quite opposite." In fact, writing in 1925 in an essay entitled "Worlds
of Color," an important essay reprinted as "The Negro Mind Reaches Out" in
Alain Locke's germinal anthology *The New Negro* (as Brent Staples points out in
his introduction to Du Bois's fifth novel, *Worlds of Color*, published just two
years before he died), Du Bois had declared that "led by American Negroes, the
Negroes of the world are reaching out hands toward each other to know, to
sympathize, to inquire." And, indeed, Du Bois himself confessed at his ninety-
first birthday celebration in Beijing, as Moses notes, that "once I thought of you
Africans as children, whom we educated Afro-Americans would lead to liberty.
I was wrong." Nevertheless, Du Bois's various books on Africa, as well as his
role as an early theorist and organizer of the several Pan-African Congresses
between 1900 and 1945, increasingly underscored his role throughout the first
half of the century as the father of Pan-Africanism, precisely as his presence and
authority within such civil rights organizations as the NAACP began to wane.

Du Bois's ultimate allegory, however, is to be found in *The Black Flame Trilogy*,
the three novels that Du Bois published just before repatriating to Ghana, in
1957, 1959, and 1961. The trilogy is the ultimate allegory in Du Bois's canon
because, as Brent Edwards shows us in his introductions to the novels, it is a fictional representation of the trajectory of Du Bois's career, complete with several
characters who stand for aspects of Du Bois's personality and professional life,
including Sebastian Doyle, who "not only studied the Negro problem, he
embodied the Negro problem. It was bone of his bone and flesh of his flesh. It
made his world and filled his thought," as well as Professor James Burghardt,
trained as a historian at Yale and who taught, as Du Bois had, at Atlanta
University, and who believed that "the Negro problem must no longer be
regarded emotionally. It must be faced scientifically and solved by long, accu-
rate and intense investigation. Moreover, it was not one problem, but a series of

problems interrelated with the social problems of the world. He laid down a program of study covering a hundred years."

But even more important than these allegorical representations of himself, or early, emerging versions of himself, Du Bois used *The Black Flame* novels to underscore the economic foundation of anti-black racism. As Edwards notes, "The real villain," for Du Bois, "is not an individual Southern aristocrat or racist white laborer, but instead capitalism itself, especially in the corporate form that has dominated the economic and social landscape of the world for more than a century," which underscores Du Bois's ideological transformations from an integrationist of sorts to an emergent mode of African American, first, and then Pan-Africanist cultural nationalism, through socialism, landing squarely in the embrace of the Communist Party just two years before his death.

Despite this evolution in ideology, Mansart, Du Bois's protagonist in the triology, ends his series of intellectual transformations precisely where Du Bois himself began as he embarked upon his career as a professor just a year after receiving his Harvard PhD in 1895. In language strikingly familiar to his statement that the time he spent in Berlin enabled him to look "at the world as a man and not simply from a narrow racial and provincial outlook," Du Bois tells us in the final volume of the trilogy that Mansart "began to have a conception of the world as one unified dwelling place. He was escaping from his racial provincialism. He began to think of himself as part of humanity and not simply as an American Negro over against a white world." For all of his ideological permutations and combinations, in other words, W. E. B. Du Bois—formidable and intimidating ideologue and ferocious foe of racism and colonialism—quite probably never veered very far from the path that he charted for himself as a student, when he fell so deeply in love with the written word that he found himself, inevitably and inescapably, drawn into a life-long love affair with language, an affair of the heart to which he remained faithful throughout an eighty-year career as a student and scholar, from the time he entered Fisk University in 1885 to his death as the Editor of "The Encyclopedia Africana" in 1963. And now, with the publication of the Oxford W. E. B. Du Bois, a new generation of readers can experience his passion for words, Du Bois's love of language purely for its own sake, as well as a conduit for advocacy and debate about the topic that consumed him his entire professional life, the freedom and the dignity of the Negro.

◆ ◆ ◆

The first volume in the series is Du Bois's revised dissertation, and his first publication, entitled *The Suppression of the African Slave-Trade to the United States of America*. A model of contemporary historiography that favored empiricism over universal proclamation, *Suppression* reveals the government's slow movement toward abolition as what the literary scholar Saidiya Hartman calls in her introduction "a litany of failures, missed opportunities, and belated acts," in which a market sensibility took precedence over moral outrage, the combination of which led to the continuation of the Atlantic slave trade to the United States until it was no longer economically beneficial.

Lawrence D. Bobo, one of the foremost urban sociologists working today, argues in his introduction to *The Philadelphia Negro: A Social Study* (1899), that Du Bois was not only an innovative historian, as Hartman properly identifies him, but also a groundbreaking social scientist whose study of Philadelphia displays "the most rigorous and sophisticated social science of its era by employing a systematic community social survey method." Although it was well reviewed at its publication—which coincided with the advent of the field of urban sociology—*The Philadelphia Negro* did not become the subject of significant scholarly attention until the 1940s, and has become, since then, a model for the study of black communities.

The distinguished scholar of black literature and culture, Arnold Rampersad, calls *The Souls of Black Folk* "possibly the most important book ever penned by a black American"—an assertion with which I heartily agree. A composite of various essays, subjects, and tones, *Souls* is both very much of its time, and timeless. It contributed to the American lexicon two terms that have been crucial for more than a century in understanding the African American experience: the "color line" and "double consciousness." For Rampersad, that we have learned so much about both issues since Du Bois first wrote, but have not made either irrelevant to our twenty-first century experience is, in a real way, our scholarly blessing and burden.

Abandoning the scholarly and empirical prowess so vividly on display in *Suppression* and *Philadelphia Negro*, Du Bois meant his biography of John Brown to be not a work of scholarship but rather one "about activism, social consciousness, and the politics of race," argues the legal historian Paul Finkelman in his introduction to *John Brown* (1909). The only biography in Du Bois's vast oeuvre, the book grew out of his participation in the Niagara Movement's meeting at Harpers Ferry in 1906 (an event the centenary of which I had the good fortune to celebrate), and—with the myth of John Brown taking precedence at times over the facts of his life—marks Du Bois's transition from professional academic to full-time activist.

There was not a genre that Du Bois did not attempt in his long career as a writer. After the John Brown biography, Du Bois turned to the novel. In his introduction to *The Quest of the Silver Fleece* (1911), Du Bois's first novel, the literary historian William Andrews looks beyond the Victorian diction and sometimes purple prose to see a work that is the "most noteworthy Great *African American* Novel of its time." *Quest* is a "Southern problem" novel writ large on a national and even mythic canvas, and one that is ultimately radical in its endorsement of strong black womanhood, equality and comradeship between the sexes, and, in Du Bois's words, "a bold regeneration of the land," which for Andrews means a hitherto-unheard-of proposed economic alliance between poor blacks and poor whites in the rural South.

Moving from a national to an international canvas, Du Bois published *The Negro* (1915), more than half of which is devoted to African history. In this way, John K. Thornton argues in his introduction, Du Bois firmly grounded for an educated lay readership the history of African Americans in the history of Africa. Drawing on the emergent disciplines of anthropology and linguistics and including, even sketchily, accounts of what would now be called Diaspora communities in the Caribbean and Latin America, *The Negro* is important in that it presents, in Thornton's words, "African history [as having] movement and Africans . . . as historical actors and not simply as stolid recipients of foreign techniques and knowledge."

Dismissed by some critics and lauded by others as the "militant sequel" to *The Souls of Black Folk, Darkwater: Voices from Within the Veil* (1920) appeared in a world radically transformed by the ravages of World War I. In addition to these international upheavals, and to the "crossing and re-crossing" of the color line engendered by the war, the historian Evelyn Brooks Higginbotham tells us in her magisterial introduction to this volume that blacks at home in the U.S. faced major changes and relocations. The Great Migration was in full swing when Du Bois wrote *Darkwater*, and the change in the center of black life is reflected in the change of scene to the North, a far, urban cry from the rural setting of most of *Souls*. If *Souls* saw the American landscape in black and white, Higginbotham finds that *Darkwater* is like chiaroscuro, the painting technique developed by artists of the Italian Renaissance: "Du Bois, like these Renaissance painters, moves beyond the contouring line of the two-dimensional and introduces depth and volume through his representation of color—through his contrast and shading of white and various darker peoples." Higginbotham goes on to say that "Du Bois continually undermines the fixedness of racial boundaries and subverts the visual coherence of racial identities to an extent that cannot be accidental." The Du Bois who emerges in *Darkwater* is increasingly a citizen of the world, whose gaze may be fixed on his native land but whose understanding of that land is inextricably bound to the larger world around him.

The Gift of Black Folk (1924) had an odd genesis as part of the Knights of Columbus's series on "Racial Contributions to the United States." In her introduction, Glenda Carpio notes that Du Bois's celebration of black accomplishments did not turn away from the bitter history of slavery that spawned them: these were not gifts always rendered freely, Carpio points out. Though less substantial than many of his other works, and primarily a catalog of black accomplishments across different fields, *Gift* is notable for the complex ways Du Bois links African American contributions in the arenas of labor, war, church and social life, fraternal organizations, and especially the arts, by both women and men, to the bitter history of slavery.

Homi Bhabha sees *The Dark Princess* (1928) as another odd work, a "Bollywood-style Bildungsroman," in which the race-man Mathew Towns teams with Kautilya, the "dark Princess of the Tibetan Kingdom of Bwodpur," to combat international colonialism in the struggle for global emancipation. But in this somewhat messy novel, which renders the international scenes with a Zolaesque precision, Bhabha detects a serious philosophical purpose: to elaborate on the "rule of juxtaposition" (first defined in *Darkwater*), which "creat[es] an enforced intimacy, an antagonistic proximity, that defines the color-line as it runs across the uncivil society of the nation."

Du Bois moved from the esoteric exercise of *The Dark Princess* to a more accessible form for his next publications, *Africa, Its Geography, People and Products*, and

Africa—Its Place in Modern History (1930). Published as Blue Books for the educated lay reader by E. Haldeman-Julius of Girard, Kansas, the two volumes are,
for the African historian and African Emmanuel Akyeampong, remarkably use-
ful and trenchant. The first volume is a relatively straightforward analysis of
Africa's geography, climate, and environment, and the impact these physical factors have had on the development of African civilization. The second volume,
which seeks "to place the continent at the very center of ancient and modern history," is more polemical, with economics cited as the central motivating factor
behind modern colonialism and the slave trade.

The anger that was evident in the second of the two Blue Books came to full
flower in *Black Reconstruction* (1935), a sweeping corrective to contemporary his-
tories of the Reconstruction era, which (white) historians had shaped with the
view of blacks as inadequate to the task of capitalizing on the freedom that emancipation had given them, and black history as "separate, unequal, and irrelevant,"
in the words of Du Bois's Pulitzer Prize-winning biographer, David Levering
Lewis. Inspired by *The Gift of Black Folk* and from Du Bois's own withdrawal of his
article on the Negro in the *Encyclopedia Britannica*, which demanded an excision of
"a paragraph on the positive Reconstruction role of black people," *Black Reconstruction* provided original interpretations of black labor's relation to industrial
wealth and, most radically, of the *agency* of black people in determining their lives
after the Civil War. In his introduction, Lewis contends, rightly, that the books
marks a progression in Du Bois's thought, from his early faith in academic knowledge and empiricism as a cure-all for the nation's problems, to the "more effective
strategy of militant journalism informed by uncompromising principles and vital
social science."

Wilson J. Moses presents *Black Folk Then and Now* (1939) as a midway point
between *The Negro* (1915) and *The World and Africa* (1946). While all three volumes
sought to address the entire span of black history, the special mandate of *Black
Folk* was to "correct the omissions, misinterpretations, and deliberate lies that
[Du Bois] detected in previous depictions of the Negro's past." In this volume, he
went back to the original Herodotus and provided his own translation, which led
him to affirm, with other black writers, that the Egyptians were, indeed, black (a
conclusion he had resisted earlier in his career). But even in this work, with such
evidence of his intellectual background on display, Du Bois is less interested in
intellectual history than in social history. Even as he tracks developments in the
United States, the Caribbean, Latin America, Du Bois neglects the Pan-African
movement and his own involvement in it.

Du Bois's autobiography, on the other hand, shows a man far more interested
in writing about his intellectual journey than his personal or social life. The
philosopher Anthony Appiah, in his subtle introduction to *Dusk of Dawn*, tells us
that Du Bois was famous for nothing so much as his accomplishments as an intellectual and a writer; his institutional affiliations (with the NAACP, with the Pan-
African Congress) were fleeting, and his internal contradictions were vexing (he
was both a committed Socialist and a committed elitist). The aim of this account,
like so much of Du Bois's other work, was to address the problem of the color line,
and he presents his distinguished, singular life as emblematic of that problem,
and himself as hopeful for its solution.

At the time he rejoined the NAACP to oversee its global programming in 1944, Du Bois was prepared to dedicate himself completely to the abolition of colonialism, which he saw as the driving force behind all global conflicts. What was remarkable about his anti-colonialism was, as Gerald Horne rightly points out in his introduction to *Color and Democracy* (1946), Du Bois's inclusion of Asia, and particularly Japan, in the discussion. As fertile ground for colonial enterprises, Asia yielded still more evidence of the "inviolate link between color and democracy."

Color continued to preoccupy Du Bois, and in The World and Africa, he attempted to correct the ways in which color (black) had affected history. Mahmood Mamdani tells us in his introduction that Du Bois's motivation in writing this somewhat hasty volume was to tell the story of "those left out of recorded history" and to challenge, in effect, "an entire tradition of history-writing . . . modern European historiography." Du Bois was aware that this was just a beginning to a much larger project, to connect the history of Europe that dominated the academic discipline of history to events and progress in the world at large, including Africa.

In Battle for Peace: The Story of My 83rd Birthday features an embattled Du Bois enduring prosecution by (and eventually winning acquittal from) the federal government whose indictment of him as an unregistered agent for the Soviet Union was, according to Manning Marable, a trumped-up means by which to discredit the great black leader and frighten his fellow supporters of international peace into silence. It worked, at least in part: while Du Bois drew support from many international associations, the NAACP essentially abandoned him. Ten years later, in 1961, Du Bois would permanently leave the United States for Ghana.

Brent Hayes Edwards in his introduction calls the *Black Flame* trilogy of novels Du Bois's most neglected work. Written in the last few years of life, *The Ordeal of Mansart* (1957), *Mansart Builds a School* (1959), and *Worlds of Color* (1961) follow the life of Manuel Mansart from his birth in 1876 (the last year of Reconstruction) to his death in 1956, a period which spans his rise from a noted but provincial Southern educator to a self-educating citizen of the world of color. With its alternating apocalyptic and utopian tone, its depiction of real historical figures and events, and its thoughtful "animation of economic history and especially labor history," the *Black Flame* trilogy offers, according to Edwards, "the clearest articulation of Du Bois's perspective at the end of his life, and his reflections on an unparalleled career that had stretched from Reconstruction through the Cold War."

Du Bois was a largely marginalized figure in the last decade of his life, and his work published at that time, most notably the *Black Flame* trilogy, went into the critical and cultural abyss. Mark Sanders suggests that the "invisibility" of the trilogy, then and now, can be explained by an evolution in literary "taste" in the 1950s, wrought by new trends in literary criticism and magazine culture, the emergence of the Civil Rights Movement, and Du Bois's own development. Even if we have rejected in many real ways the ethos of the 1950s, for Sanders, our prescriptions for taste still owe a great deal to that decade.

Werner Sollors finds "four major narrative strains" in the posthumously published *Autobiography of W. E. B. Du Bois* (1968): the personal (including "startling" sexual revelations from the famously staid Du Bois); the academic, editorial, and organizational, in which his work is fully explored, and the political is always personal even while science and reason are held to be the solution to the race problem; the Communist, first as interested onlooker and then as Party member; and the elderly, in which an old man takes stock of contemporary youth culture with something of a jaundiced eye. Sollors suggests that far from being disjointed, the various strands of the *Autobiography* are united by Du Bois's ongoing quest for recognition. I would argue that there is nothing pathetic in this quest; it is simply the desire for respect from the society (black and white) that Du Bois spent his long life trying to understand.

Henry Louis Gates, Jr.
Cambridge, Massachusetts
December 7, 2006

Introduction

John K. Thornton, Boston University

The Negro was originally published in 1915 in the Home University of Modern Knowledge, a series of books intended by the editors to be an introduction to topics that might increase the knowledge of people who lacked a college education but were interested in self-education. From the start, however, *The Negro* was a great deal more to Du Bois than simply an introduction to the study of African American affairs, and it is not surprising that *The Negro* became one of the most important introductory books for the next two generations. It became an introduction not just to African American affairs, but also to the history of the larger black world, the Pan-African world that Du Bois had already been promoting for some time. In this respect *The Negro* was much more a manifesto than a handy book of facts.

For Du Bois, *The Negro* was his first extended work on African history, and that more than half the book was dedicated to purely African history reflects the importance that Du Bois placed on vindicating and reevaluating Africa in both the history of African Americans and world history. Though Du Bois wrote an extensive chapter on African Americans, in many respects he was only updating and condensing work that he had been doing for twenty years—first in the earlier issues of the Atlanta University Studies, which he had been editing since 1896 (eighteen issues of which had appeared by the time that *The Negro* appeared), and then in his masterwork on the African American condition, *Souls of Black Folk* (1903).

Du Bois was not the first African American writer to take on Africa: for half a century before him, a number of others had sought to depict the continent in a more positive light. Some had pointed out the role of Ethiopia in the Bible, others had used travelers' accounts to reveal an Africa possessing a higher level of civilization than was described in the racist diatribes of the day. But Du Bois was certainly the first to take a comprehensive view of the continent—a view that was based on the scholarly literature of the time—and the first to include all parts of the New World.

In order to understand the significance of Du Bois's project with regard to African history, it is worth considering not only that African history was not widely known in Du Bois's day, but that it had been dropped from American education only a few years earlier. At the start of the nineteenth century, Americans had learned of faraway places and of modern history from travelers' accounts, or collections of them, popular in the eighteenth and early nineteenth centuries. These accounts often devoted as much as a quarter of their pages to Africa and presented factual data, remarkably evenhandedly, based on eyewitness testimony. An informed American merchant of 1850 probably knew more of African history than even modern-day university graduates know.

But when Du Bois was growing up in rural Massachusetts, higher education was being revolutionized by a new curriculum modeled on the German university program. Within twenty years this new curriculum had taken over most of the colleges and universities that provided academic education for the mercantile and political elite. If the earlier curriculum had included a great deal of quality information on Africa, the new curriculum had virtually nothing, thanks to the racist attitude engendered by colonial occupation in Africa and by disenfranchisement in the United States. Even as colleges and universities offered modern history and geography for the first time, they completely excluded Africa from it, and in a short time, whatever practical knowledge that American elites once had of Africa was lost. There was a definite need for an accessible source of up-to-date information to replace it.

To write the portions of The Negro that are about Africa, Du Bois drew on the emerging anthropological and linguistic literature by writers such as the liberal Englishman Harry Johnson, as well as on that of recent travelers such as the Germans Heinrich Barth and Leo Frobenius. All the while, however, Du Bois made use of his sources with an eye to presenting the Africans in a favorable light and to endowing their history with the characteristics of other continental regions.

Du Bois was clearly not concerned with making a detailed and careful study of the source material to produce a well-grounded synthesis; the format of the publication and the lack of time available precluded such a study. As a result, the scholarship of the African portions, though generally acceptable for the times, was often sketchy and speculative. What counted was showing that African history had movement and that Africans were historical actors and were not simply stolid recipients of foreign techniques and knowledge. Much of the movement was in the march of races here and there across the continent. Thus Du Bois describes the indigenous Negro civilizations of Yoruba and Benin encountering the Mediterranean race, the resulting mix eventuating in the empire of the Western Sudan. Elsewhere he describes Egyptians facing "strong continuous pressure from the wild and unruly Negro tribes of the Upper Nile Valley."

Like many early twentieth-century versions of world history, Du Bois's made much use of the concept of races, but he was careful to define the Negro race broadly, and to insist that the American definition of "Negro"—a definition that included in the race all mixed groups—was held to. So Du Bois had no difficulty in integrating ancient Egypt into The Negro as part of the race's history, without having to go to the extreme measure of asserting that somehow the Egyptians were biologically identical to Africans from farther south or west.

Du Bois had written his PhD thesis on the slave trade, and the slave trade played a crucial role in the historical development of Africa in *The Negro*. A long and passionate chapter on the slave trade connects the trade's horrors to the decline of higher civilization in Africa, as well as to Africa's apparent backwardness in Du Bois's own day.

In keeping with his desire to ensure that the history of African Americans be anchored firmly in a revised and revitalized history of Africa, Du Bois made sure to include the Caribbean and Latin America in his survey. His coverage of these areas was cursory, but the inclusion itself was more important than the details of the history. In any case, Du Bois was too much of a scholar to drift too far from the documented facts, even if his study did not delve very deep.

In spite of its shortcomings as a work of scholarship, *The Negro* succeeded remarkably well. It was one of Du Bois's most sought-after works, even years later, and Du Bois thought enough of the project of writing the history of Africa to attempt it two more times, first in *Black Folk, Then and Now* (1939) and again in *The World in Africa* (1946). *The World in Africa* superseded *The Negro* as Du Bois's contribution to Pan-African history, yet *The Negro* still remained in his monumental unfinished project *Encyclopedia Africana*.

Preface

The time has not yet come for a complete history of the Negro peoples. Archæological research in Africa has just begun, and many sources of information in Arabian, Portuguese, and other tongues are not fully at our command; and, too, it must frankly be confessed, racial prejudice against darker peoples is still too strong in so-called civilized centers for judicial appraisement of the peoples of Africa. Much intensive monographic work in history and science is needed to clear mooted points and quiet the controversialist who mistakes present personal desire for scientific proof.

Nevertheless, I have not been able to withstand the temptation to essay such short general statement of the main known facts and their fair interpretation as shall enable the general reader to know as men a sixth or more of the human race. Manifestly so short a story must be mainly conclusions and generalizations with but meager indication of authorities and underlying arguments. Possibly, if the Public will, a later and larger book may be more satisfactory on these points.

W. E. BURGHARDT DU BOIS

New York City, February 1, 1915.

The Negro

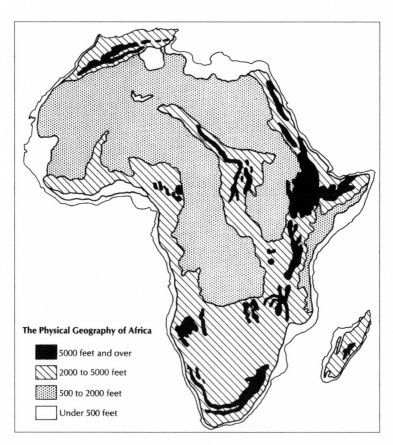

The Physical Geography of Africa

CHAPTER I

◆

Africa

"Behold!
The Sphinx is Africa. The bond
Of Silence is upon her.
Old And white with tombs, and rent and shorn;
With raiment wet with tears and torn,
And trampled on, yet all untamed."

MILLER

Africa is at once the most romantic and the most tragic of continents. Its very names reveal its mystery and wide-reaching influence. It is the "Ethiopia" of the Greek, the "Kush" and "Punt" of the Egyptian, and the Arabian "Land of the Blacks." To modern Europe it is the "Dark Continent" and "Land of Contrasts"; in literature it is the seat of the Sphinx and the lotus eaters, the home of the dwarfs, gnomes, and pixies, and the refuge of the gods; in commerce it is the slave mart and the source of ivory, ebony, rubber, gold, and diamonds. What other continent can rival in interest this Ancient of Days?

There are those, nevertheless, who would write universal history and leave out Africa. But how, asks Ratzel, can one leave out the land of Egypt and Carthage? and Frobenius declares that in future Africa must more and more be regarded as an integral part of the great movement of world history. Yet it is true that the history of Africa is unusual, and its strangeness is due in no small degree to the physical peculiarities of the continent. With three times the area of Europe it has a coast line a fifth shorter. Like Europe it is a peninsula of Asia, curving southwestward around the Indian Sea. It has few gulfs, bays, capes, or islands. Even the rivers, though large and long, are not means of communication with the outer world, because from the central high plateau they plunge in rapids and cataracts to the narrow coastlands and the sea.

The general physical contour of Africa has been likened to an inverted plate with one or more rows of mountains at the edge and a low coastal belt. In the south the central plateau is three thousand or more feet above the sea, while in the north it is a little over one thousand feet. Thus two main divisions of the continent are easily distinguished: the broad northern rectangle, reaching down as

1

far as the Gulf of Guinea and Cape Guardafui, with seven million square miles; and the peninsula which tapers toward the south, with five million square miles.

Four great rivers and many lesser streams water the continent. The greatest is the Congo in the center, with its vast curving and endless estuaries; then the Nile, draining the cluster of the Great Lakes and flowing northward "like some grave, mighty thought, threading a dream"; the Niger in the northwest, watering the Sudan below the Sahara; and, finally, the Zambesi, with its greater Niagara in the southeast. Even these waters leave room for deserts both south and north, but the greater ones are the three million square miles of sand wastes in the north.

More than any other land, Africa lies in the tropics, with a warm, dry climate, save in the central Congo region, where rain at all seasons brings tropical luxuriance. The flora is rich but not wide in variety, including the gum acacia, ebony, several dye woods, the kola nut, and probably tobacco and millet. To these many plants have been added in historic times. The fauna is rich in mammals, and here, too, many from other continents have been widely introduced and used.

Primarily Africa is the Land of the Blacks. The world has always been familiar with black men, who represent one of the most ancient of human stocks. Of the ancient world gathered about the Mediterranean, they formed a part and were viewed with no surprise or dislike, because this world saw them come and go and play their part with other men. Was Clitus the brother-in-law of Alexander the Great less to be honored because he happened to be black? Was Terence less famous? The medieval European world, developing under the favorable physical conditions of the north temperate zone, knew the black man chiefly as a legend or occasional curiosity, but still as a fellow man—an Othello or a Prester John or an Antar.

The modern world, in contrast, knows the Negro chiefly as a bond slave in the West Indies and America. Add to this the fact that the darker races in other parts of the world have, in the last four centuries, lagged behind the flying and even feverish footsteps of Europe, and we face to-day a widespread assumption throughout the dominant world that color is a mark of inferiority.

The result is that in writing of this, one of the most ancient, persistent, and widespread stocks of mankind, one faces astounding prejudice. That which may be assumed as true of white men must be proven beyond peradventure if it relates to Negroes. One who writes of the development of the Negro race must continually insist that he is writing of a normal human stock, and that whatever it is fair to predicate of the mass of human beings may be predicated of the Negro. It is the silent refusal to do this which has led to so much false writing on Africa and of its inhabitants. Take, for instance, the answer to the apparently simple question "What is a Negro?" We find the most extraordinary confusion of thought and difference of opinion. There is a certain type in the minds of most people which, as David Livingstone said, can be found only in caricature and not in real life. When scientists have tried to find an extreme type of black, ugly, and woolly-haired Negro, they have been compelled more and more to limit his home even in Africa. At least nine-tenths of the African people do not at all conform to this type, and the typical Negro, after being denied a dwelling place in the Sudan, along the Nile, in East Central Africa, and in South Africa, was finally given a very small country between the Senegal and the Niger, and even there was found to give trace of many stocks. As Winwood Reade says, "The typical Negro is a rare variety even among Negroes."

As a matter of fact we cannot take such extreme and largely fanciful stock as typifying that which we may fairly call the Negro race. In the case of no other race is so narrow a definition attempted. A "white" man may be of any color, size, or facial conformation and have endless variety of cranial measurement and physical characteristics. A "yellow" man is perhaps an even vaguer conception.

In fact it is generally recognized to-day that no scientific definition of race is possible. Differences, and striking differences, there are between men and groups of men, but they fade into each other so insensibly that we can only indicate the main divisions of men in broad outlines. As Von Luschan says, "The question of the number of human races has quite lost its *raison d'être* and has become a subject rather of philosophic speculation than of scientific research. It is of no more importance now to know how many human races there are than to know how many angels can dance on the point of a needle. Our aim now is to find out how ancient and primitive races developed from others and how races changed or evolved through migration and inter-breeding."[1]

The mulatto (using the term loosely to indicate either an intermediate type between white and black or a mingling of the two) is as typically African as the black man and cannot logically be included in the "white" race, especially when American usage includes the mulatto in the Negro race.

It is reasonable, according to fact and historic usage, to include under the word "Negro" the darker peoples of Africa characterized by a brown skin, curled or "frizzled" hair, full and sometimes everted lips, a tendency to a development of the maxillary parts of the face, and a dolichocephalic head. This type is not fixed or definite. The color varies widely; it is never black or bluish, as some say, and it becomes often light brown or yellow. The hair varies from curly to a wool-like mass, and the facial angle and cranial form show wide variation.

It is as impossible in Africa as elsewhere to fix with any certainty the limits of racial variation due to climate and the variation due to intermingling. In the past, when scientists assumed one unvarying Negro type, every variation from that type was interpreted as meaning mixture of blood. To-day we recognize a broader normal African type which, as Palgrave says, may best be studied "among the statues of the Egyptian rooms of the British Museum; the larger gentle eye, the full but not over-protruding lips, the rounded contour, and the good-natured, easy, sensuous expression. This is the genuine African model." To this race Africa in the main and parts of Asia have belonged since prehistoric times.

The color of this variety of man, as the color of other varieties, is due to climate. Conditions of heat, cold, and moisture, working for thousands of years through the skin and other organs, have given men their differences of color. This color pigment is a protection against sunlight and consequently varies with the intensity of the sunlight. Thus in Africa we find the blackest men in the fierce sunlight of the desert, red pygmies in the forest, and yellow Bushmen on the cooler southern plateau.

Next to the color, the hair is the most distinguishing characteristic of the Negro, but the two characteristics do not vary with each other. Some of the blackest of the Negroes have curly rather than woolly hair, while the crispest, most closely curled hair is found among the yellow Hottentots and Bushmen. The difference between the hair of the lighter and darker races is a difference of degree, not of kind, and can be easily measured. If the hair follicles of a Chinaman, a European, and a Negro are cut across transversely, it will be found that the diameter of the first is 100 by 77 to 85, the second 100 by 62 to 72, while that of the Negro is 100 by 40 to 60. This elliptical form of the Negro's hair causes it to curl more or less tightly.

There have been repeated efforts to discover, by measurements of various kinds, further and more decisive differences which would serve as really scientific determinants of race. Gradually these efforts have been given up. To-day we realize that there are no hard and fast racial types among men. Race is a dynamic and not a static conception, and the typical races are continually changing and developing, amalgamating and differentiating. In this little book, then, we are studying the history of the darker part of the human family, which is separated from the rest of mankind by no absolute physical line, but which nevertheless forms, as a mass, a social group distinct in history, appearance, and to some extent in spiritual gift.

We cannot study Africa without, however, noting some of the other races concerned in its history, particularly the Asiatic Semites. The intercourse of Africa with Arabia and other parts of Asia has been so close and long-continued that it is impossible to-day to disentangle the blood relationships. Negro blood certainly appears in strong strain among the Semites, and the obvious mulatto groups in Africa, arising from ancient and modern mingling of Semite and Negro, has given rise to the term "Hamite," under cover of which millions of Negroids have been characteristically transferred to the "white" race by some eager scientists.

The earliest Semites came to Africa across the Red Sea. The Phœnicians came along the northern coasts a thousand years before Christ and began settlements which culminated in Carthage and extended down the Atlantic shores of North Africa nearly to the Gulf of Guinea.

From the earliest times the Greeks have been in contact with Africa as visitors, traders, and colonists, and the Persian influence came with Cambyses and others. Roman Africa was bounded by the desert, but at times came into contact with the blacks across the Sahara and in the valley of the Nile. After the breaking up of the Roman Empire the Greek and Latin Christians filtered through Africa, followed finally by a Germanic invasion in 429 A.D.

In the seventh century the All-Mother, Asia, claimed Africa again for her own and blew a cloud of Semitic Mohammedanism all across North Africa, veiling the dark continent from Europe for a thousand years and converting vast masses of the blacks to Islam. The Portuguese began to raise the veil in the fifteenth century, sailing down the Atlantic coast and initiating the modern slave trade. The Spanish, French, Dutch, and English followed them, but as traders in men rather than explorers.

The Portuguese explored the coasts of the Gulf of Guinea, visiting the interior kingdoms, and then passing by the mouth of the Congo proceeded southward. Eventually they rounded the Cape of Good Hope and pursued their explorations as far as the mountains of Abyssinia. This began the modern exploration of Africa, which is a curious fairy tale, and recalls to us the great names of Livingstone, Burton, Speke, Stanley, Barth, Schweinfurth, and many others. In this way Africa has been made known to the modern world.

The difficulty of this modern lifting of the veil of centuries emphasizes two physical facts that underlie all African history: the peculiar inaccessibility of the continent to peoples from without, which made it so easily possible for the great human drama played here to hide itself from the ears of other worlds; and, on the other hand, the absence of interior barriers—the great stretch of that central plateau which placed practically every budding center of culture at the mercy of barbarism, sweeping a thousand miles, with no Alps or Himalayas or Appalachians to hinder.

With this peculiarly uninviting coast line and the difficulties in interior segregation must be considered the climate of Africa. While there is much diversity and many salubrious tracts along with vast barren wastes, yet, as Sir Harry Johnston well remarks, "Africa is the chief stronghold of the real Devil—the reactionary forces of Nature hostile to the uprise of Humanity. Here Beelzebub, King of the Flies, marshals his vermiform and arthropod hosts—insects, ticks, and nematode worms—which more than in other continents (excepting Negroid Asia) convey to the skin, veins, intestines, and spinal marrow of men and other vertebrates the microorganisms which cause deadly, disfiguring, or debilitating diseases, or themselves create the morbid condition of the persecuted human being, beasts, bird, reptile, frog, or fish."[2] The inhabitants of this land have had a sheer fight for physical survival comparable with that in no other great continent, and this must not be forgotten when we consider their history.

NOTES

1. Von Luschan: in *Inter-Racial Problems*, p. 16.
2. Johnston: *Negro in the New World*, pp. 14–15.

CHAPTER II

◆

The Coming of Black Men

The movements of prehistoric man can be seen as yet but dimly in the uncertain mists of time. This is the story that to-day seems most probable: from some center in southern Asia primitive human beings began to differentiate in two directions. Toward the south appeared the primitive Negro, long-headed and with flattened hair follicle. He spread along southern Asia and passed over into Africa, where he survives to-day as the reddish dwarfs of the center and the Bushmen of South Africa.

Northward and eastward primitive man became broader headed and straight-haired and spread over eastern Asia, forming the Mongolian type. Either through the intermingling of these two types or, as some prefer to think, by the direct prolongation of the original primitive man, a third intermediate type of human being appeared with hair and cranial measurement intermediate between the primitive Negro and Mongolian. All these three types of men intermingled their blood freely and developed variations according to climate and environment.

Other and older theories and legends of the origin and spread of mankind are of interest now only because so many human beings have believed them in the past. The biblical story of Shem, Ham, and Japheth retains the interest of a primitive myth with its measure of allegorical truth,[1] but has, of course, no historic basis.

The older "Aryan" theory assumed the migration into Europe of one dominant Asiatic race of civilized conquerors, to whose blood and influence all modern culture was due. To this "white" race Semitic Asia, a large part of black Africa, and all Europe was supposed to belong. This "Aryan" theory has been practically abandoned in the light of recent research, and it seems probable now that from the primitive Negroid stock evolved in Asia the Semites either by local variation or intermingling with other stocks; later there developed the Mediterranean race, with Negroid characteristics, and the modern Negroes. The blue-eyed, light-haired Germanic people may have arisen as a modern variation of the mixed peoples produced by the mingling of Asiatic and African elements. The last word on this development has not yet been said, and there is still much to learn and explain; but it is certainly proved to-day beyond doubt that the so-called Hamites of Africa, the brown and black curly and frizzly-haired inhabitants of North and East Africa, are not "white" men if we draw the line between white and black in any logical way.

The primitive Negroid race of men developed in Asia wandered eastward as well as westward. They entered on the one hand Burmah and the South Sea Islands, and on the other hand they came through Mesopotamia and gave curly hair and a Negroid type to Jew, Syrian, and Assyrian. Ancient statues of Indian divinities show the Negro type with black face and close-curled hair, and early Babylonian culture was Negroid. In Arabia the Negroes may have divided, and one stream perhaps wandered into Europe by way of Syria. Traces of these Negroes are manifest not only in skeletons, but in the brunette type of all South Europe. The other branch proceeded to Egypt and tropical Africa. Another, but perhaps less probable, theory is that ancient Negroes may have entered Africa from Europe, since the most ancient skulls of Algeria are Negroid.

The primitive African was not an extreme type. One may judge from modern pygmy and Bushmen that his color was reddish or yellow, and his skull was sometimes round like the Mongolian. He entered Africa not less than fifty thousand years ago and settled eventually in the broad region between Lake Chad and the Great Lakes and remained there long stretches of years.

After a lapse of perhaps thirty thousand years there entered Africa a further migration of Asiatic people, Negroid in many characteristics, but lighter and straighter haired than the primitive Negroes. From this Mediterranean race was developed the modern inhabitants of the shores of the Mediterranean in Europe, Asia, and Africa and, by mingling with the primitive Negroes, the ancient Egyptians and modern Negroid races of Africa.

As we near historic times the migrations of men became more frequent from Asia and from Europe, and in Africa came movements and minglings which give to the whole of Africa a distinct mulatto character. The primitive Negro stock was "mulatto" in the sense of being not widely differentiated from the dark, original Australoid stock. As the earlier yellow Negro developed in the African tropics to the bigger, blacker type, he was continually mingling his blood with similar types developed in temperate climes to sallower color and straighter hair.

We find therefore, in Africa to-day, every degree of development in Negroid stocks and every degree of intermingling of these developments, both among African peoples and between Africans, Europeans, and Asiatics. The mistake is continually made of considering these types as transitions between absolute Caucasians and absolute Negroes. No such absolute type ever existed on either side. Both were slowly differentiated from a common ancestry and continually remingled their blood while the differentiating was progressing. From prehistoric times down to to-day Africa is, in this sense, primarily the land of the mulatto. So, too, was earlier Europe and Asia; only in these countries the mulatto was early bleached by the climate, while in Africa he was darkened.

It is not easy to summarize the history of these dark African peoples, because so little is known and so much is still in dispute. Yet, by avoiding the real controversies and being unafraid of mere questions of definition, we may trace a great human movement with considerable definiteness.

Three main Negro types early made their appearance: the lighter and smaller primitive stock; the larger forest Negro in the center and on the west coast, and the tall, black Nilotic Negro in the eastern Sudan. In the earliest times we find the Negroes in the valley of the Nile, pressing downward from the interior. Here they mingled with Semitic types, and after a lapse of millenniums there arose from this mingling the culture of Ethiopia and Egypt, probably the first of higher human cultures.

To the west of the Nile the Negroes expanded straight across the continent to the Atlantic. Centers of higher culture appeared very early along the Gulf of Guinea and curling backward met Egyptian, Ethiopian, and even European and Asiatic influences about Lake Chad. To the southeast, nearer the primitive seats of the earliest African immigrants and open to Egyptian and East Indian influences, the Negro culture which culminated at Zymbabwe arose, and one may trace throughout South Africa its wide ramifications.

All these movements gradually aroused the central tribes to unrest. They beat against the barriers north, northeast, and west, but gradually settled into a great southeastward migration. Calling themselves proudly La Bantu (The People), they grew by agglomeration into a warlike nation, speaking one language. They eventually conquered all Africa south of the Gulf of Guinea and spread their influence to the northward.

While these great movements were slowly transforming Africa, she was also receiving influences from beyond her shores and sending influences out. With mulatto Egypt black Africa was always in closest touch, so much so that to some all evidence of Negro uplift seem Egyptian in origin. The truth is, rather, that Egypt was herself always palpably Negroid, and from her vantage ground as almost the only African gateway received and transmitted Negro ideals.

Phœnician, Greek, and Roman came into touch more or less with black Africa. Carthage, that North African city of a million men, had a large caravan trade with Negroland in ivory, metals, cloth, precious stones, and slaves. Black men served in the Carthaginian armies and marched with Hannibal on Rome. In some of the North African kingdoms the infiltration of Negro blood was very large and kings like Massinissa and Jugurtha were Negroid. By way of the Atlantic the Carthaginians reached the African west coast. Greek and Roman influences came through the desert, and the Byzantine Empire and Persia came into communication with Negroland by way of the valley of the Nile. The influence of these trade routes, added to those of Egypt, Ethiopia, Benin, and Yoruba, stimulated centers of culture in the central and western Sudan, and European and African trade early reached large volume.

Negro soldiers were used largely in the armies that enabled the Mohammedans to conquer North Africa and Spain. Beginning in the tenth century and slowly creeping across the desert into Negroland, the new religion found an already existent culture and came, not a conqueror, but as an adapter and inspirer. Civilization received new impetus and a wave of Mohammedanism swept eastward, erecting the great kingdoms of Melle, the Songhay, Bornu, and the Hausa states. The older Negro culture was not overthrown, but, like a great wedge, pushed upward and inward from Yoruba, and gave stubborn battle to the newer culture for seven or eight centuries.

Then it was, in the fifteenth century, that the heart disease of Africa developed in its most virulent form. There is a modern theory that black men are and always have been naturally slaves. Nothing is further from the truth. In the ancient world Africa was no more a slave hunting ground than Europe or Asia, and both Greece and Rome had much larger numbers of white slaves than of black. It was natural that a stream of black slaves should have poured into Egypt, because the chief line of Egyptian conquest and defense lay toward the heart of Africa. Moreover, the Egyptians, themselves of Negro descent, had not only Negro slaves but Negroes among their highest nobility and even among their Pharaohs. Mohammedan conquerors enslaved peoples of all colors in Europe, Asia, and Africa, but eventually their empire centered in Asia and Africa and their slaves came principally from these countries. Asia submitted to Islam except in the Far East, which was self-protecting. Negro Africa submitted only partially, and the remaining heathen were in small states which could not effectively protect themselves against the Mohammedan slave trade. In this wise the slave trade gradually began to center in Africa, for religious and political rather than for racial reasons.

The typical African culture was the culture of family, town, and small tribe. Hence domestic slavery easily developed a slave trade through war and commerce. Only the integrating force of state building could have stopped this slave trade. Was this failure to develop the great state a racial characteristic? This does not seem a fair conclusion. In four great centers state building began in Africa. In Ethiopia several large states were built up, but they tottered before the onslaughts of Egypt, Persia, Rome, and Byzantium, on the one hand, and finally fell before the turbulent Bantu warriors from the interior. The second attempt at empire building began in the southeast, but the same Bantu hordes, pressing now slowly, now fiercely, from the congested center of the continent, gradually overthrew this state and erected on its ruins a series of smaller and more transient kingdoms.

The third attempt at state building arose on the Guinea coast in Benin and Yoruba. It never got much beyond a federation of large industrial cities. Its expansion toward the Congo valley was probably a prime cause of the original Bantu movements to the southeast. Toward the north and northeast, on the other hand, these city-states met the Sudanese armed with the new imperial Mohammedan idea. Just as Latin Rome gave the imperial idea to the Nordic races, so Islam brought this idea to the Sudan.

In the consequent attempts at imperialism in the western Sudan there arose the largest of the African empires. Two circumstances, however, militated against this empire building: first, the fierce resistance of the heathen south made war continuous and slaves one of the articles of systematic commerce. Secondly, the highways of legitimate African commerce had for millenniums lain to the north. These were suddenly closed by the Moors in the sixteenth century, and the Negro empires were thrown into the turmoil of internal war.

It was then that the European slave traders came from the southwest. They found partially disrupted Negro states on the west coast and falling empires in the Sudan, together with the old unrest of over-population and migration in the valley of the Congo. They not only offered a demand for the usual slave trade, but they increased it to an enormous degree, until their demand, added to the demand of the Mohammedan in Africa and Asia, made human beings the highest priced article of commerce in Africa. Under such circumstances there could be but one end: the virtual uprooting of ancient African culture, leaving only misty reminders of the ruin in the customs and work of the people. To complete this disaster came the partition of the continent among European nations and the modern attempt to exploit the country and the natives for the economic benefit of the white world, together with the transplanting of black nations to the new western world and their rise and self-assertion there.

NOTES

1. Ham is probably the Egyptian word "Khem" (black), the native name of Egypt. In the original myth Canaan and not Ham was Noah's third son.

    The biblical story of the "curse of Canaan" (Genesis IX, 24–25) has been the basis of an astonishing literature which has to-day only a psychological interest. It is sufficient to remember that for several centuries leaders of the Christian Church gravely defended Negro slavery and oppression as the rightful curse of God upon the descendants of a son who had been disrespectful to his drunken father! Cf. Bishop Hopkins: *Bible Views of Slavery*, p. 7.

CHAPTER III

---◆---

Ethiopia and Egypt

Having viewed now the land and movements of African people in main outline, let us scan more narrowly the history of five main centers of activity and culture, namely: the valleys of the Nile and of the Congo, the borders of the great Gulf of Guinea, the Sudan, and South Africa. These divisions do not cover all of Negro Africa, but they take in the main areas and the main lines in development.

First, we turn to the valley of the Nile, perhaps the most ancient of known seats of civilization in the world, and certainly the oldest in Africa, with a culture reaching back six or eight thousand years. Like all civilizations it drew largely from without and undoubtedly arose in the valley of the Nile, because that valley was so easily made a center for the meeting of men of all types and from all parts of the world. At the same time Egyptian civilization seems to have been African in its beginnings and in its main line of development, despite strong influences from all parts of Asia. Of what race, then, were the Egyptians? They certainly were not white in any sense of the modern use of that word—neither in color nor physical measurement, in hair nor countenance, in language nor social customs. They stood in relationship nearest the Negro race in earliest times, and then gradually through the infiltration of Mediterranean and Semitic elements became what would be described in America as a light mulatto stock of Octoroons or Quadroons. This stock was varied continually; now by new infiltration of Negro blood from the south, now by Negroid and Semitic blood from the east, now by Berber types from the north and west.

Egyptian monuments show distinctly Negro and mulatto faces. Herodotus, in an incontrovertible passage, alludes to the Egyptians as "black and curly-haired"[1]—a peculiarly significant statement from one used to the brunette Mediterranean type; in another passage, concerning the fable of the Dodonian Oracle, he again alludes to the swarthy color of the Egyptians as exceedingly dark and even black. Æschylus, mentioning a boat seen from the shore, declares that its crew are Egyptians, because of their black complexions.

Modern measurements, with all their admitted limitations, show that in the Thebaid from one-seventh to one-third of the Egyptian population were Negroes, and that of the predynastic Egyptians less than half could be classed as non-Negroid. Judging from measurements in the tombs of nobles as late as the eighteenth dynasty, Negroes form at least one-sixth of the higher class.[2]

Such measurements are by no means conclusive, but they are apt to be under rather than over statements of the prevalence of Negro blood. Head measurements of Negro Americans would probably place most of them in the category of whites. The evidence of language also connects Egypt with Africa and the Negro race rather than with Asia, while religious ceremonies and social customs all go to strengthen this evidence.

The ethnic history of Northeast Africa would seem, therefore, to have been this: predynastic Egypt was settled by Negroes from Ethiopia. They were of varied type: the broad-nosed, woolly-haired type to which the word "Negro" is sometimes confined; the black, curly-haired, sharper featured type, which must be considered an equally Negroid variation. These Negroes met and mingled with the invading Mediterranean race from North Africa and Asia. Thus the blood of the sallower race spread south and that of the darker race north. Black priests appear in Crete three thousand years before Christ, and Arabia is to this day thoroughly permeated with Negro blood. Perhaps, as Chamberlain says, "one of the prime reasons why no civilization of the type of that of the Nile arose in other parts of the continent, if such a thing were at all possible, was that Egypt acted as a sort of channel by which the genius of Negro-land was drafted off into the service of Mediterranean and Asiatic culture."[3]

To one familiar with the striking and beautiful types arising from the mingling of Negro with Latin and Germanic types in America, the puzzle of the Egyptian type is easily solved. It was unlike any of its neighbors and a unique type until one views the modern mulatto; then the faces of Rahotep and Nefert, of Khafra and Amenemhat I, of Aahmes and Nefertari, and even of the great Ramessu II, become curiously familiar.

The history of Egypt is a science in itself. Before the reign of the first recorded king, five thousand years or more before Christ, there had already existed in Egypt a culture and art arising by long evolution from the days of paleolithic man, among a distinctly Negroid people. About 4777 B.C. Aha-Mena began the first of three successive Egyptian empires. This lasted two thousand years, with many Pharaohs, like Khafra of the Fourth Dynasty, of a strongly Negroid cast of countenance.

At the end of the period the empire fell apart into Egyptian and Ethiopian halves, and a silence of three centuries ensued. It is quite possible that an incursion of conquering black men from the south poured over the land in these years and dotted Egypt in the next centuries with monuments on which the full-blooded Negro type is strongly and triumphantly impressed. The great Sphinx at Gizeh, so familiar to all the world, the Sphinxes of Tanis, the statue from the Fayum, the statue of the Esquiline at Rome, and the Colossi of Bubastis all represent black, full-blooded Negroes and are described by Petrie as "having high cheek bones, flat cheeks, both in one plane, a massive nose, firm projecting lips, and thick hair, with an austere and almost savage expression of power."[4]

Blyden, the great modern black leader of West Africa, said of the Sphinx at Gizeh: "Her features are decidedly of the African or Negro type, with 'expanded nostrils.' If, then, the Sphinx was placed here—looking out in majestic and mysterious silence over the empty plain where once stood the great city of Memphis in all its pride and glory, as an 'emblematic representation of the king'—is not the inference clear as to the peculiar type or race to which that king belonged?"[5]

The middle empire arose 3064 B.C. and lasted nearly twenty-four centuries. Under Pharaohs whose Negro descent is plainly evident, like Amenemhat I and III and Usertesen I, the ancient glories of Egypt were restored and surpassed. At the same time there is strong continuous pressure from the wild and unruly Negro tribes of the upper Nile valley, and we get some idea of the fear which they inspired throughout Egypt when we read of the great national rejoicing which followed the triumph of Usertesen III (c. 2660–22) over these hordes. He drove them back and attempted to confine them to the edge of the Nubian Desert above the Second Cataract. Hemmed in here, they set up a state about this time and founded Nepata.

Notwithstanding this repulse of black men, less than one hundred years later a full-blooded Negro from the south, Ra Nehesi, was seated on the throne of the Pharaohs and was called "The king's eldest son." This may mean that an incursion from the far south had placed a black conqueror on the throne. At any rate, the whole empire was in some way shaken, and two hundred years later the invasion of the Hyksos began. The domination of Hyksos kings who may have been Negroids from Asia[6] lasted for five hundred years.

The redemption of Egypt from these barbarians came from Upper Egypt, led by the mulatto Aahmes. He founded in 1703 B.C. the new empire, which lasted fifteen hundred years. His queen, Nefertari, "the most venerated figure of Egyptian history,"[7] was a Negress of great beauty, strong personality, and of unusual administrative force. She was for many years joint ruler with her son, Amenhotep I, who succeeded his father.[8]

The new empire was a period of foreign conquest and internal splendor and finally of religious dispute and overthrow. Syria was conquered in these reigns and Asiatic civilization and influences poured in upon Egypt. The great Tahutmes III, whose reign was "one of the grandest and most eventful in Egyptian history,"[9] had a strong Negroid countenance, as had also Queen Hatshepsut, who sent the celebrated expedition to reopen ancient trade with the Hottentots of Punt. A new strain of Negro blood came to the royal line through Queen Mutemua about 1420 B.C., whose son, Amenhotep III, built a great temple at Luqsor and the Colossi at Memnon.

The whole of the period in a sense culminated in the great Ramessu II, the oppressor of the Hebrews, who with his Egyptian, Libyan, and Negro armies fought half the world. His reign, however, was the beginning of decline, and foes began to press Egypt from the white north and the black south. The priests transferred their power at Thebes, while the Assyrians under Nimrod overran Lower Egypt. The center of interest is now transferred to Ethiopia, and we pass to the more shadowy history of that land.

The most perfect example of Egyptian poetry left to us is a celebration of the prowess of Usertesen III in confining the turbulent Negro tribes to the territory below the Second Cataract of the Nile. The Egyptians called this territory Kush, and in the farthest confines of Kush lay Punt, the cradle of their race. To the ancient Mediterranean world Ethiopia (i.e., the Land of the Black-faced) was a region of gods and fairies. Zeus and Poseidon feasted each year among the "blameless Ethiopians," and Black Memnon, King of Ethiopia, was one of the greatest of heroes.

"The Ethiopians conceive themselves," says Diodorus Siculus (Lib. III), "to be of greater antiquity than any other nation; and it is probable that, born under the sun's path, its warmth may have ripened them earlier than other men. They suppose themselves also to be the inventors of divine worship, of festivals, of solemn assemblies, of sacrifices, and every religious practice. They affirm that the Egyptians are one of their colonies."

The Egyptians themselves, in later days, affirmed that they and their civilization came from the south and from the black tribes of Punt, and certainly "at the earliest period in which human remains have been recovered Egypt and Lower Nubia appear to have formed culturally and racially one land."[10]

The forging ahead of Egypt in culture was mainly from economic causes. Ethiopia, living in a much poorer land with limited agricultural facilities, held to the old arts and customs, and at the same time lost the best elements of its population to Egypt, absorbing meantime the oncoming and wilder Negro tribes from the south and west. Under the old empire, therefore, Ethiopia remained in comparative poverty, except as some of its tribes invaded Egypt with their handicrafts.

As soon as the civilization below the Second Cataract reached a height noticeably above that of Ethiopia, there was continued effort to protect that civilization against the incursion of barbarians. Hundreds of campaigns through thousands of years repeatedly subdued or checked the blacks and brought them in as captives to mingle their blood with the Egyptian nation; but the Egyptian frontier was not advanced.

A separate and independent Ethiopian culture finally began to arise during the middle empire of Egypt and centered at Nepata and Meroe. Widespread trade in gold, ivory, precious stones, skins, wood, and works of handicraft arose.[11] The Negro began to figure as the great trader of Egypt.

This new wealth of Ethiopia excited the cupidity of the Pharaohs and led to aggression and larger intercourse, until at last, when the dread Hyksos appeared, Ethiopia became both a physical and cultural refuge for conquered Egypt. The legitimate Pharaohs moved to Thebes, nearer the boundaries of Ethiopia, and from here, under Negroid rulers, Lower Egypt was redeemed.

The ensuing new empire witnessed the gradual incorporation of Ethiopia into Egypt, although the darker kingdom continued to resist. Both mulatto Pharaohs, Aahmes and Amenhotep I, sent expeditions into Ethiopia, and in the latter's day sons of the reigning Pharaoh began to assume the title of "Royal Son of Kush" in some such way as the son of the King of England becomes the Prince of Wales.

Trade relations were renewed with Punt under circumstances which lead us to place that land in the region of the African lakes. The Sudanese tribes were aroused by these and other incursions, until the revolts became formidable in the fourteenth century before Christ.

Egyptian culture, however, gradually conquered Ethiopia where her armies could not, and Egyptian religion and civil rule began to center in the darker kingdom. When, therefore, Shesheng I, the Libyan, usurped the throne of the Pharaohs in the tenth century B.C., the Egyptian legitimate dynasty went to Nepata as king priests and established a theocratic monarchy. Gathering strength, the Ethiopian kingdom under this dynasty expanded north about 750 B.C. and for a century ruled all Egypt.

The first king, Pankhy, was Egyptian bred and not noticeably Negroid, but his successors showed more and more evidence of Negro blood—Kashta the Kushite, Shabaka, Tarharqa, and Tanutamen. During the century of Ethiopian rule a royal son was appointed to rule Egypt, just as formerly a royal Egyptian had ruled Kush. In many ways this Ethiopian kingdom showed its Negro peculiarities: first, in its worship of distinctly Sudanese gods; secondly, in the rigid custom of female succession in the kingdom, and thirdly, by the election of kings from the various royal claimants to the throne. "It was the heyday of the Negro. For the greater part of the century. . . . Egypt itself was subject to the blacks, just as in the new empire the Sudan had been subject to Egypt."[12]

Egypt now began to fall into the hands of Asia and was conquered first by the Assyrians and then by the Persians, but the Ethiopian kings kept their independence. Aspeluta, whose mother and sister are represented as full-blooded Negroes, ruled from 630 to 600 B.C. Horsiatef (560–525 B.C.) made nine expeditions against the warlike tribes south of Meroe, and his successor, Nastosenen (525–500 B.C.) was the one who repelled Cambyses. He also removed the capital from Nepata to Meroe, although Nepata continued to be the religious capital and the Ethiopian kings were still crowned on its golden throne.

From the fifth to the second century B.C. we find the wild Sudanese tribes pressing in from the west and Greek culture penetrating from the east. King Arg-Amen (Ergamenes) showed strong Greek influences and at the same time began to employ the Ethiopian speech in writing and used a new Ethiopian alphabet.

While the Ethiopian kings were still crowned at Nepata, Meroe gradually became the real capital and supported at one time four thousand artisans and two hundred thousand soldiers. It was here that the famous Candaces reigned as queens. Pliny tells us that one Candace of the time of Nero had had forty-four predecessors on the throne, while another Candace figures in the New Testament.[13]

It was probably this latter Candace who warred against Rome at the time of Augustus and received unusual consideration from her formidable foe. The prestige of Ethiopia at this time was considerable throughout the world. Pseudo-Callisthenes tells an evidently fabulous story of the visit of Alexander the Great to Candace, Queen of Meroe, which nevertheless illustrates her fame: Candace will not let him enter Ethiopia and says he is not to scorn her people because they are black, for they are whiter in soul than his white folk. She sent him gold, maidens, parrots, sphinxes, and a crown of emeralds and pearls. She ruled eighty tribes, who were ready to punish those who attacked her.

The Romans continued to have so much trouble with their Ethiopian frontier that finally, when Semitic mulattoes appeared in the east, the Emperor Diocletian invited the wild Sudanese tribe of Nubians (Nobadæ) from the west to repel them. These Nubians eventually embraced Christianity, and northern Ethiopia came to be known in time as Nubia.

The Semitic mulattoes from the east came from the highlands bordering the Red Sea and Asia. On both sides of this sea Negro blood is strongly in evidence, predominant in Africa and influential in Asia. Ludolphus, writing in the seventeenth century, says that the Abyssinians "are generally black, which [color] they most admire." Trade and war united the two shores, and merchants have passed to and fro for thirty centuries.

In this way Arabian, Jewish, Egyptian, Greek, and Roman influences spread slowly upon the Negro foundation. Early legendary history declares that a queen, Maqueda, or Nikaula of Sheba, a state of Central Abyssinia, visited Solomon in 1050 B.C. and had her son Menelik educated in Jerusalem. This was the supposed beginning of the Axumite kingdom, the capital of which, Axume, was a flourishing center of trade. Ptolemy Evergetes and his successors did much to open Abyssinia to the world, but most of the population of that day was nomadic. In the fourth century Byzantine influences began to be felt, and in 330 St. Athanasius of Alexandria consecrated Fromentius as Bishop of Ethiopia. He tutored the heir to the Abyssinian kingdom and began its gradual christianization. By the early part of the sixth century Abyssinia was trading with India and Byzantium and was so far recognized as a Christian country that the Emperor Justinian appealed to King Kaleb to protect the Christians in southwestern Arabia. Kaleb conquered Yemen in 525 and held it fifty years.

Eventually a Jewish princess, Judith, usurped the Axumite throne; the Abyssinians were expelled from Arabia, and a long period begins when as Gibbon says, "encompassed by the enemies of their religion, the Ethiopians slept for nearly a thousand years, forgetful of the world by whom they were forgotten." Throughout the middle ages, however, the legend of a great Christian kingdom hidden away in Africa persisted, and the search for Prester John became one of the world quests.

It was the expanding power of Abyssinia that led Rome to call in the Nubians from the western desert. The Nubians had formed a strong league of tribes, and as the ancient kingdom of Ethiopia declined they drove back the Abyssinians, who had already established themselves at Meroe.

In the sixth century the Nubians were converted to Christianity by a Byzantine priest, and they immediately began to develop. A new capital, Dongola, replaced Nepata and Meroe, and by the twelfth century churches and brick dwellings had appeared. As the Mohammedan flood pressed up the Nile valley it was the Nubians that held it back for two centuries.

Farther south other wild tribes pushed out of the Sudan and began a similar development. Chief among these were the Fung, who fixed their capital at Senaar, at the junction of the White and Blue Nile. When the Mohammedan flood finally passed over Nubia, the Fung diverted it by declaring themselves Moslems. This left the Fung as the dominant power in the fifteenth century from the Three Cataracts to Fazogli and from the Red Sea at Suakin to the White Nile. Islam then swept on south in a great circle, skirted the Great Lakes, and then curled back to Somaliland, completely isolating Abyssinia.

Between the thirteenth and sixteenth centuries the Egyptian Sudan became a congeries of Mohammedan kingdoms with Arab, mulatto, and Negro kings. Far to the west, near Lake Chad, arose in 1520 the sultanate of Baghirmi, which reached its highest power in the seventh century. This dynasty was overthrown by the Negroid Mabas, who established Wadai to the eastward about 1640. South of Wadai lay the heathen and cannibals of the Congo valley, against which Islam never prevailed. East of Wadai and nearer the Nile lay the kindred state of Darfur, a Nubian nation whose sultans reigned over two hundred years and which reached great prosperity in the early seventeenth century under Soliman Solon.

Before the Mohammedan power reached Abyssinia the Portuguese pioneers had entered the country from the east and begun to open the country again to European knowledge. Without doubt, in the centuries of silence, a civilization of some height had flourished in Abyssinia, but all authentic records were destroyed by fire in the tenth century. When the Portuguese came, the older Axumite kingdom had fallen and had been succeeded by a number of petty states.

The Sudanese kingdoms of the Sudan resisted the power of the Mameluke beys in Egypt, and later the power of the Turks until the nineteenth century, when the Sudan was made nominally a part of Egypt. Continuous upheaval, war, and conquest had by this time done their work, and little of ancient Ethiopian culture survived except the slave trade.

The entrance of England into Egypt, after the building of the Suez Canal, stirred up eventually revolt in the Sudan, for political, economic, and religious reasons. Led by a Sudanese Negro, Mohammed Ahmad, who claimed to be the Messiah (Mahdi), the Sudan arose in revolt in 1881, determined to resist a hated religion, foreign rule, and interference with their chief commerce, the trade in slaves. The Sudan was soon aflame, and the able mulatto general, Osman Digna, aided by revolt among the heathen Dinka, drove Egypt and England out of the Sudan for sixteen years. It was not until 1898 that England reëntered the Sudan and in petty revenge desecrated the bones of the brave, even if misguided, prophet.

Meantime this Mahdist revolt had delayed England's designs on Abyssinia, and the Italians, replacing her, attempted a protectorate. Menelik of Shoa, one of the smaller kingdoms of Abyssinia, was a shrewd man of predominantly Negro blood, and had been induced to make a treaty with the Italians after King John had been killed by the Mahdists. The exact terms of the treaty were disputed, but undoubtedly the Italians tried by this means to reduce Menelik to vassalage. Menelik stoutly resisted, and at the great battle of Adua, one of the decisive battles of the modern world, the Abyssinians on March 1, 1896, inflicted a crushing defeat on the Italians, killing four thousand of them and capturing two thousand prisoners. The empress, Taitou, a full-blooded Negress, led some of the charges. By this battle Abyssinia became independent.

Such in vague and general outline is the strange story of the valley of the Nile—of Egypt, the motherland of human culture and

"That starr'd Ethiop Queen that strove
To set her beauty's praise above
The sea nymphs."

NOTES

1. "αὐτός δὲ εἴκασα τῆδε καὶ ὅτε μελάγχροές εἰσι καὶ οὐλότριχες." Liber II, Cap. 104.
2. Cf. Maciver and Thompson: *Ancient Races of the Thebaid.*
3. *Journal of Race Development*, I, 484.
4. Petrie: *History of Egypt*, I, 51, 237.
5. *From West Africa to Palestine*, p. 114.
6. Depending partly on whether the so-called Hyksos sphinxes belong to the period of the Hyksos kings or to an earlier period (cf. Petrie, I, 52–53, 237). That Negroids largely dominated in the early history of western Asia is proven by the monuments.
7. Petrie: *History of Egypt*, II, 337.
8. Chamberlain: *Journal of Race Development*, April, 1911.
9. Petrie: *History of Egypt*, II, 337.
10. Reisner: *Archeological Survey of Nubia*, I, 319.
11. Hoskins declares that the arch had its origin in Ethiopia.
12. Maciver and Wooley: *Areika*, p. 2.
13. Acts VIII, 27.

CHAPTER IV

◆

The Niger and Islam

The Arabian expression "Bilad es Sudan" (Land of the Blacks) was applied to the whole region south of the Sahara, from the Atlantic to the Nile. It is a territory some thirty-five hundred miles by six hundred miles, containing two million square miles, and has to-day a population of perhaps eighty million. It is thus two-thirds the size of the United States and quite as thickly settled. In the western Sudan the Niger plays the same role as the Nile in the east. In this chapter we follow the history of the Niger.

The history of this part of Africa was probably something as follows: primitive man, entering Africa from Arabia, found the Great Lakes, spread in the Nile valley, and wandered westward to the Niger. Herodotus tells of certain youths who penetrated the desert to the Niger and found there a city of black dwarfs. Succeeding migrations of Negroes and Negroids pushed the dwarfs gradually into the inhospitable forests and occupied the Sudan, pushing on to the Atlantic. Here the newcomers, curling northward, met the Mediterranean race coming down across the western desert, while to the southward the Negro came to the Gulf of Guinea and the thick forests of the Congo valley. Indigenous civilizations arose on the west coast in Yoruba and Benin, and contact of these with the Mediterranean race in the desert, and with Egyptian and Arab from the east, gave rise to centers of Negro culture in the Sudan at Ghana and Melle and in Songhay, Nupe, the Hausa states, and Bornu.

The history of the Sudan thus leads us back again to Ethiopia, that strange and ancient center of world civilization whose inhabitants in the ancient world were considered to be the most pious and the oldest of men. From this center the black originators of African culture, and to a large degree of world culture, wandered not simply down the Nile, but also westward. These Negroes developed the original substratum of culture which later influences modified but never displaced.

We know that Egyptian Pharaohs in several cases ventured into the western Sudan and that Egyptian influences are distinctly traceable. Greek and Byzantine culture and Phœnician and Carthaginian trade also penetrated, while Islam finally made this whole land her own. Behind all these influences, however, stood from the first an indigenous Negro culture. The stone figures of Sherbro, the megaliths of Gambia, the art and industry of the west coast are all too deep and original evidences of civilization to be merely importations from abroad.

Nor was the Sudan the inert recipient of foreign influence when it came. According to credible legend, the "Great King" at Byzantium imported glass, tin, silver, bronze, cut stones, and other treasure from the Sudan. Embassies were sent and states like Nupe recognized the suzerainty of the Byzantine emperor. The people of Nupe especially were filled with pride when the Byzantine people learned certain kinds of work in bronze and glass from them, and this intercourse was only interrupted by the Mohammedan conquest.

To this ancient culture, modified somewhat by Byzantine and Christian influences, came Islam. It approached from the northwest, coming stealthily and slowly and being handed on particularly by the Mandingo Negroes. About 1000–1200 A.D. the situation was this: Ghana was on the edge of the desert in the north, Mandingoland between the Niger and the Senegal in the south and the western Sahara, Djolof was in the west on the Senegal, and the Songhay on the Niger in the center. The Mohammedans came chiefly as traders and found a trade already established. Here and there in the great cities were districts set aside for these new merchants, and the Mohammedans gave frequent evidence of their respect for these black nations.

Islam did not found new states, but modified and united Negro states already ancient; it did not initiate new commerce, but developed a widespread trade already established. It is, as Frobenius says, "easily proved from chronicles written in Arabic that Islam was only effective in fact as a fertilizer and stimulant. The essential point is the resuscitative and invigorative concentration of Negro power in the service of a new era and a Moslem propaganda, as well as the reaction thereby produced."[1]

Early in the eighth century Islam had conquered North Africa and converted the Berbers. Aided by black soldiers, the Moslems crossed into Spain; in the following century Berber and Arab armies crossed the west end of the Sahara and came to Negroland. Later in the eleventh century Arabs penetrated the Sudan and Central Africa from the east, filtering through the Negro tribes of Darfur, Kanem, and neighboring regions. The Arabs were too nearly akin to Negroes to draw an absolute color line. Antar, one of the great pre-Islamic poets of Arabia, was the son of a black woman, and one of the great poets at the court of Haroun al Raschid was black. In the twelfth century a learned Negro poet resided at Seville, and Sidjilmessa, the last town in Lower Morocco toward the desert, was founded in 757 by a Negro who ruled over the Berber inhabitants. Indeed, many towns in the Sudan and the desert were thus ruled, and felt no incongruity in this arrangement. They say, to be sure, that the Moors destroyed Audhoghast because it paid tribute to the black town of Ghana, but this was because the town was heathen and not because it was black. On the other hand, there is a story that a Berber king overthrew one of the cities of the Sudan and all the black women committed suicide, being too proud to allow themselves to fall into the hands of white men.

In the west the Moslems first came into touch with the Negro kingdom of Ghana. Here large quantities of gold were gathered in early days, and we have names of seventy-four rulers before 300 A.D. running through twenty-one generations. This would take us back approximately a thousand years to 700 B.C., or about the time that Pharaoh Necho of Egypt sent out the Phœnician expedition which circumnavigated Africa, and possibly before the time when Hanno, the Carthaginian, explored the west coast of Africa.

By the middle of the eleventh century Ghana was the principal kingdom in the western Sudan. Already the town had a native and a Mussulman quarter, and was built of wood and stone with surrounding gardens. The king had an army of two hundred thousand and the wealth of the country was great. A century later the king had become Mohammedan in faith and had a palace with sculptures and glass windows. The great reason for this development was the desert trade. Gold, skins, ivory, kola nuts, gums, honey, wheat, and cotton were exported, and the whole Mediterranean coast traded in the Sudan. Other and lesser black kingdoms like Tekrou, Silla, and Masina surrounded Ghana.

In the early part of the thirteenth century the prestige of Ghana began to fall before the rising Mandingan kingdom to the west. Melle, as it was called, was founded in 1235 and formed an open door for Moslem and Moorish traders. The new kingdom, helped by its expanding trade, began to grow, and Islam slowly surrounded the older Negro culture west, north, and east. However, a great mass of the older heathen culture, pushing itself upward from the Guinea coast, stood firmly against Islam down to the nineteenth century.

Steadily Mohammedanism triumphed in the growing states which almost encircled the protagonists of ancient Atlantic culture. Mandingan Melle eventually supplanted Ghana in prestige and power, after Ghana had been overthrown by the heathen Su Su from the south.

The territory of Melle lay southeast of Ghana and some five hundred miles north of the Gulf of Guinea. Its kings were known by the title of Mansa, and from the middle of the thirteenth century to the middle of the fourteenth the Mellestine, as its dominion was called, was the leading power in the land of the blacks. Its greatest king, Mari Jalak (Mansa Musa), made his pilgrimage to Mecca in 1324, with a caravan of sixty thousand persons, including twelve thousand young slaves gowned in figured cotton and Persian silk. He took eighty camel loads of gold dust (worth about five million dollars) to defray his expenses, and greatly impressed the people of the East with his magnificence.

On his return he found that Timbuktu had been sacked by the Mossi, but he rebuilt the town and filled the new mosque with learned blacks from the University of Fez. Mansa Musa reigned twenty-five years and "was distinguished by his ability and by the holiness of his life. The justice of his administration was such that the memory of it still lives."[2] The Mellestine preserved its preëminence until the beginning of the sixteenth century, when the rod of Sudanese empire passed to Songhay, the largest and most famous of the black empires.

The known history of Songhay covers a thousand years and three dynasties and centers in the great bend of the Niger. There were thirty kings of the First Dynasty, reigning from 700 to 1335. During the reign of one of these the Songhay kingdom became the vassal kingdom of Melle, then at the height of its glory. In addition to this the Mossi crossed the valley, plundered Timbuktu in 1339, and separated Jenne, the original seat of the Songhay, from the main empire. The six-teenth king was converted to Mohammedanism in 1009, and after that all the Songhay princes were Mohammedans. Mansa Musa took two young Songhay princes to the court of Melle to be educated in 1326. These boys when grown ran away and founded a new dynasty in Songhay, that of the Sonnis, in 1355. Seventeen of these kings reigned, the last and greatest being Sonni Ali, who ascended the throne in 1464. Melle was at this time declining, other cities like Jenne, with its seven thousand villages, were rising, and the Tuaregs (Berbers with Negro blood) had captured Timbuktu.

Sonni Ali was a soldier and began his career with the conquest of Timbuktu in 1469. He also succeeded in capturing Jenne and attacked the Mossi and other enemies on all sides. Finally he concentrated his forces for the destruction of Melle and subdued nearly the whole empire on the west bend of the Niger. In summing up Sonni Ali's military career the chronicle says of him, "He sur-passed all his predecessors in the numbers and valor of his soldiery. His con-quests were many and his renown extended from the rising to the setting of the sun. If it is the will of God, he will be long spoken of."[3]

Sonni Ali was a Songhay Negro whose father was a Berber. He was succeeded by a full-blooded black, Mohammed Abou Bekr, who had been his prime minister. Mohammed was hailed as "Askia" (usurper) and is best known as Mohammed Askia. He was strictly orthodox where Ali was rather a scoffer, and an organizer where Ali was a warrior. On his pilgrimage to Mecca in 1495 there was nothing of the barbaric splendor of Mansa Musa, but a brilliant group of scholars and holy men with a small escort of fifteen hundred soldiers and nine hundred thousand dollars in gold. He stopped and consulted with scholars and politicians and studied matters of taxation, weights and measures, trade, religious tolerance, and manners. In Cairo, where he was invested by the reigning caliph of Egypt, he may have heard of the struggle of Europe for the trade of the Indies, and perhaps of the parceling of the new world between Portugal and Spain. He returned to the Sudan in 1497, instituted a standing army of slaves, undertook a holy war against the indomitable Mossi, and finally marched against the Hausa. He subdued these cities and even imposed the rule of black men on the Berber town of Agades, a rich city of merchants and artificers with stately mansions. In fine Askia, during his reign, conquered and consolidated an empire two thou-sand miles long by one thousand wide at its greatest diameters; a territory as large as all Europe. The territory was divided into four vice royalties, and the system of Melle, with its semi-independent native dynasties, was carried out. His empire extended from the Atlantic to Lake Chad and from the salt mines of Tegazza and the town of Augila in the north to the 10th degree of north latitude toward the south.

It was a six months' journey across the empire and, it is said, "he was obeyed with as much docility on the farthest limits of the empire as he was in his own palace, and there reigned everywhere great plenty and absolute peace."[4] The University of Sankore became a center of learning in correspondence with Egypt and North Africa and had a swarm of black Sudanese students. Law, lit-erature, grammar, geography and surgery were studied. Askia the Great reigned thirty-six years, and his dynasty continued on the throne until after the Moorish conquest in 1591.

Meanwhile, to the eastward, two powerful states appeared. They never disputed the military supremacy of Songhay, but their industrial development was marvelous. The Hausa states were formed by seven original cities, of which Kano was the oldest and Katsena the most famous. Their greatest leaders, Mohammed Rimpa and Ahmadu Kesoke, arose in the fifteenth and early sixteenth centuries. The land was subject to the Songhay, but the cities became industrious centers of smelting, weaving, and dyeing. Katsena especially, in the middle of the sixteenth century, is described as a place thirteen or fourteen miles in circumference, divided into quarters for strangers, for visitors from various other states, and for the different trades and industries, as saddlers, shoemakers, dyers, etc.

Beyond the Hausa states and bordering on Lake Chad was Bornu. The people of Bornu had a large infiltration of Berber blood, but were predominantly Negro. Berber mulattoes had been kings in early days, but they were soon replaced by black men. Under the early kings, who can be traced back to the third century, these people had ruled nearly all the territory between the Nile and Lake Chad. The country was known as Kanem, and the pagan dynasty of Dugu reigned there from the middle of the ninth to the end of the eleventh century. Mohammedanism was introduced from Egypt at the end of the eleventh century, and under the Mohammedan kings Kanem became one of the first powers of the Sudan. By the end of the twelfth century the armies of Kanem were very powerful and its rulers were known as "Kings of Kanem and Lords of Bornu." In the thirteenth century the kings even dared to invade the southern country down toward the valley of the Congo.

Meantime great things were happening in the world beyond the desert, the ocean, and the Nile. Arabian Mohammedanism had succumbed to the wild fanaticism of the Seljukian Turks. These new conquerors were not only firmly planted at the gates of Vienna, but had swept the shores of the Mediterranean and sent all Europe scouring the seas for their lost trade connections with the riches of India. Religious zeal, fear of conquest, and commercial greed inflamed Europe against the Mohammedan and led to the discovery of a new world, the riches of which poured first on Spain. Oppression of the Moors followed, and in 1502 they were driven back into Africa, despoiled and humbled. Here the Spaniards followed and harassed them and here the Turks, fighting the Christians, captured the Mediterranean ports and cut the Moors off permanently from Europe. In the slow years that followed, huddled in Northwest Africa, they became a decadent people and finally cast their eyes toward Negroland.

The Moors in Morocco had come to look upon the Sudan as a gold mine, and knew that the Sudan was especially dependent upon salt. In 1545 Morocco claimed the principal salt mines at Tegazza, but the reigning Askia refused to recognize the claim.

When the Sultan Elmansour came to the throne of Morocco, he increased the efficiency of his army by supplying it with fire arms and cannon. Elmansour determined to attack the Sudan and sent four hundred men under Pasha Djouder, who left Morocco in 1590. The Songhay, with their bows and arrows, were helpless against powder and shot, and they were defeated at Tenkadibou April 12, 1591. Askia Ishak, the king, offered terms, and Djouder Pasha referred them to Morocco. The sultan, angry with his general's delay, deposed him and sent another, who crushed and treacherously murdered the king and set up a puppet. Thereafter there were two Askias, one under the Moors at Timbuktu and one who maintained himself in the Hausa states, which the Moors could not subdue. Anarchy reigned in Songhay. The Moors tried to put down disorder with a high hand, drove out and murdered the distinguished men of Timbuktu, and as a result let loose a riot of robbery and decadence throughout the Sudan. Pasha now succeeded pasha with revolt and misrule until in 1612 the soldiers elected their own pasha and deliberately shut themselves up in the Sudan by cutting off approach from the north.

Hausaland and Bornu were still open to Turkish and Mohammedan influence from the east, and the Gulf of Guinea to the slave trade from the south, but the face of the finest Negro civilization the modern world had ever produced was veiled from Europe and given to the defilement of wild Moorish soldiers. In 1623 it is written "excesses of every kind are now committed unchecked by the soldiery," and "the country is profoundly convulsed and oppressed."[5] The Tuaregs marched down from the desert and deprived the Moors of many of the principal towns. The rest of the empire of the Songhay was by the end of the eighteenth century divided among separate Moorish chiefs, who bought supplies from the Negro peasantry and were "at once the vainest, proudest, and perhaps the most bigoted, ferocious, and intolerant of all the nations of the south."[6] They lived a nomadic life, plundering the Negroes. To such depths did the mighty Songhay fall.

As the Songhay declined a new power arose in the nineteenth century, the Fula. The Fula, who vary in race from Berber mulattoes to full-blooded Negroes, may be the result of a westward migration of some people like the "Leukoæthiopi" of Pliny, or they may have arisen from the migration of Berber mulattoes in the western oases, driven south by Romans and Arabs.

These wandering herdsmen lived on the Senegal River and the ocean in very early times and were not heard of until the nineteenth century. By this time they had changed to a Negro or dark mulatto people and lived scattered in small communities between the Atlantic and Darfur. They were without political union or national sentiment, but were all Mohammedans. Then came a sudden change, and led by a religious fanatic, these despised and persecuted people became masters of the central Sudan. They were the ones who at last broke down that great wedge of resisting Atlantic culture, after it had been undermined and disintegrated by the American slave trade.

Thus Islam finally triumphed in the Sudan and the ancient culture combined with the new. In the Sudan to-day one may find evidences of the union of two classes of people. The representatives of the older civilization dwell as peasants in small communities, carrying on industries and speaking a large number of different languages. With them or above them is the ruling Mohammedan caste, speaking four main languages: Mandingo, Hausa, Fula, and Arabic. These latter form the state builders. Negro blood predominates among both classes, but naturally there is more Berber blood among the Mohammedan invaders.

Europe during the middle ages had some knowledge of these movements in the Sudan and Africa. Melle and Songhay appear on medieval maps. In literature we have many allusions: the mulatto king, Feirifis, was one of Wolfram von Eschenbach's heroes; Prester John furnished endless lore; Othello, the warrior, and the black king represented by medieval art as among the three wise men, and the various black Virgin Marys' all show legendary knowledge of what African civilization was at that time doing.

It is a curious commentary on modern prejudice that most of this splendid history of civilization and uplift is unknown to-day, and men confidently assert that Negroes have no history.

NOTES

1. Frobenius: *Voice of Africa*, II, 359–360.
2. Ibn Khaldun, quoted in Lugard, p. 128.
3. Quoted in Lugard, p. 180.
4. Es-Sa'di, quoted by Lugard, p. 199.
5. Lugard, p. 373.
6. Mungo Park, quoted in Lugard, p. 374.

CHAPTER V

◆

Guinea and Congo

One of the great cities of the Sudan was Jenne. The chronicle says "that its markets are held every day of the week and its populations are very enormous. Its seven thousand villages are so near to one another that the chief of Jenne has no need of messengers. If he wishes to send a note to Lake Dibo, for instance, it is cried from the gate of the town and repeated from village to village, by which means it reaches its destination almost instantly."[1]

From the name of this city we get the modern name Guinea, which is used to-day to designate the country contiguous to the great gulf of that name—a territory often referred to in general as West Africa. Here, reaching from the mouth of the Gambia to the mouth of the Niger, is a coast of six hundred miles, where a marvelous drama of world history has been enacted. The coast and its hinterland comprehends many well-known names. First comes ancient Guinea, then, modern Sierra Leone and Liberia; then follow the various "coasts" of ancient traffic—the grain, ivory, gold, and slave coasts—with the adjoining territories of Ashanti, Dahomey, Lagos, and Benin, and farther back such tribal and territorial names as those of the Mandingoes, Yorubas, the Mossi, Nupe, Borgu, and others.

Recent investigation makes it certain that an ancient civilization existed on this coast which may have gone back as far as three thousand years before Christ. Frobenius, perhaps fancifully, identified this African coast with the Atlantis of the Greeks and as part of that great western movement in human culture, "beyond the pillars of Hercules," which thirteen centuries before Christ strove with Egypt and the East. It is, at any rate, clear that ancient commerce reached down the west coast. The Phœnicians, 600 B.C., and the Carthaginians, a century or more later, record voyages, and these may have been attempted revivals of still more ancient intercourse.

These coasts at some unknown prehistoric period were peopled from the Niger plateau toward the north and west by the black West African type of Negro, while along the west end of the desert these Negroes mingled with the Berbers, forming various Negroid races.

Movement and migration is evident along this coast in ancient and modern times. The Yoruba-Benin-Dahomey peoples were among the earliest arrivals, with their remarkable art and industry, which places them in some lines of technique abreast with the modern world. Behind them came the Mossi from the north, and many other peoples in recent days have filtered through, like the Limba and Temni of Sierra Leone and the Agni-Ashanti, who moved from Borgu some two thousand years ago to the Gold and Ivory coasts.

We have already noted in the main the history of black men along the wonderful Niger and seen how, pushing up from the Gulf of Guinea, a powerful wedge of ancient culture held back Islam for a thousand years, now victorious, now stubbornly disputing every inch of retreat. The center of this culture lay probably, in oldest times, above the Bight of Benin, along the Slave Coast, and reached east, west, and north. We trace it to-day not only in the remarkable tradition of the natives, but in stone monuments, architecture, industrial and social organization, and works of art in bronze, glass, and terra cotta.

Benin art has been practiced without interruption for centuries, and Von Luschan says that it is "of extraordinary significance that by the sixteenth and seventeenth centuries a local and monumental art had been learned in Benin which in many respects equaled European art and developed a technique of the very highest accomplishment."[2]

Summing up Yoruban civilization, Frobenius concluded that "the technical summit of that civilization was reached in the terra-cotta industry, and that the most important achievements in art were not expressed in stone, but in fine clay baked in the furnace; that hollow casting was thoroughly known, too, and practiced by these people; that iron was mainly used for decoration; that, whatever their purpose, they kept their glass beads in stoneware urns within their own locality, and that they manufactured both earthen and glass ware; that the art of weaving was highly developed among them; that the stone monuments, it is true, show some dexterity in handling and are so far instructive, but in other respects evidence a cultural condition insufficiently matured to grasp the utility of stone monumental material; and, above all, that the then great and significant idea of the universe as imaged in the Templum was current in those days."[3]

Effort has naturally been made to ascribe this civilization to white people. First it was ascribed to Portuguese influence, but much of it is evidently older than the Portuguese discovery. Egypt and India have been evoked and Greece and Carthage. But all these explanations are far-fetched. If ever a people exhibited unanswerable evidence of indigenous civilization, it is the west-coast Africans. Undoubtedly they adapted much that came to them, utilized new ideas, and grew from contact. But their art and culture is Negro through and through.

Yoruba forms one of the three city groups of West Africa; another is around Timbuktu, and a third in the Hausa states. The Timbuktu cities have from five to fifteen hundred towns, while the Yoruba cities have one hundred and fifty thousand inhabitants and more. The Hausa cities are many of them important, but few are as large as the Yoruba cities and they lie farther apart. All three centers, however, are connected with the Niger, and the group nearest the coast—that is, the Yoruba cities—has the greatest numbers of towns, the most developed architectural styles, and the oldest institutions.

The Yoruba cities are not only different from the Sudanese in population, but in their social relations. The Sudanese cities were influenced from the desert and the Mediterranean, and form nuclei of larger surrounding monarchial states. The Yoruba cities, on the other hand, remained comparatively autonomous organizations down to modern times, and their relative importance changed from time to time without developing an imperialistic idea or subordinating the group to one overpowering city.

This social and industrial state of the Yorubas formerly spread and wielded great influence. We find Yoruba reaching out and subduing states like Nupe toward the northward. But the industrial democracy and city autonomy of Yoruba lent itself indifferently to conquest, and the state fell eventually a victim to the fanatical Fula Mohammedans and was made a part of the modern sultanate of Gando.

West of Yoruba on the lower courses of the Niger is Benin, an ancient state which in 1897 traced its twenty-three kings back one thousand years; some legends even named a line of sixty kings. It seems probable that Benin developed the imperial idea and once extended its rule into the Congo valley. Later and also to the west of the Yoruba come two states showing a fiercer and ruder culture, Dahomey and Ashanti. The state of Dahomey was founded by Tacondomi early in the seventeenth century, and developed into a fierce and bloody tyranny with wholesale murder. The king had a body of two thousand to five thousand Amazons renowned for their bravery and armed with rifles. The kingdom was overthrown by the French in 1892–93. Under Sai Tutu, Ashanti arose to power in the seventeenth century. A military aristocracy with cruel blood sacrifices was formed. By 1816 the king had at his disposal two hundred thousand soldiers. The Ashanti power was crushed by the English in the war of 1873–74.

In these states and in later years in Benin the whole character of west-coast culture seems to change. In place of the Yoruban culture, with its city democracy, its elevated religious ideas, its finely organized industry, and its noble art, came Ashanti and Dahomey. What was it that changed the character of the west coast from this to the orgies of war and blood sacrifice which we read of later in these lands?

There can be but one answer: the slave trade. Not simply the sale of men, but an organized traffic of such proportions and widely organized ramifications as to turn the attention and energies of men from nearly all other industries, encourage war and all the cruelest passions of war, and concentrate this traffic in precisely that part of Africa farthest from the ancient Mediterranean lines of trade.

We need not assume that the cultural change was sudden or absolute. Ancient Yoruba had the cruelty of a semi-civilized land, but it was not dominant or tyrannical. Modern Benin and Dahomey showed traces of skill, culture, and industry along with inexplicable cruelty and bloodthirstiness. But it was the slave trade that turned the balance and set these lands backward. Dahomey was the last word in a series of human disasters which began with the defeat of the Askias at Tenkadibou.[4]

From the middle of the fifteenth to the last half of the nineteenth centuries the American slave trade centered in Guinea and devastated the coast morally, socially, and physically. European rum and fire arms were traded for human beings, and it was not until 1787 that any measures were taken to counteract this terrible scourge. In that year the idea arose of repatriating stolen Negroes on that coast and establishing civilized centers to supplant the slave trade. About four hundred Negroes from England were sent to Sierra Leone, to whom the promoters considerately added sixty white prostitutes as wives. The climate on the low coast, however, was so deadly that new recruits were soon needed. An American Negro, Thomas Peters, who had served as sergeant under Sir Henry Clinton in the British army in America, went to England seeking an allotment of land for his fellows. The Sierra Leone Company welcomed him and offered free passage and land in Sierra Leone to the Negroes of Nova Scotia. As a result fifteen vessels sailed with eleven hundred and ninety Negroes in 1792. Arriving in Africa, they found the chief white man in control there so drunk that he soon died of delirium tremens. John Clarkson, however, brother of Thomas Clarkson, the abolitionist, eventually took the lead, founded Freetown, and the colony began its checkered career. In 1896 the colony was saved from insurrection by the exiled Maroon Negroes from Jamaica. After 1833, when emancipation in English colonies took place, severer measures against the slave trade was possible and the colony began to grow. To-day its imports and exports amount to fifteen million dollars a year.

Liberia was a similar American experiment. In 1816 American philanthropists decided that slavery was bound to die out, but that the problem lay in getting rid of the freed Negroes, of which there were then two hundred thousand in the United States. Accordingly the American Colonization Society was proposed this year and founded January 1, 1817, with Bushrod Washington as President. It was first thought to encourage migration to Sierra Leone, and eighty-eight Negroes were sent, but they were not welcomed. As a result territory was bought in the present confines of Liberia, December 15, 1821, and colonists began to arrive. A little later an African depot for recaptured slaves taken in the contraband slave trade, provided for in the Act of 1819, was established and an agent was sent to Africa to form a settlement. Gradually this settlement was merged with the settlement of the Colonization Society, and from this union Liberia was finally evolved.

The last white governor of Liberia died in 1841 and was succeeded by the first colored governor, Joseph J. Roberts, a Virginian. The total population in 1843 was about twenty-seven hundred and ninety, and with this as a beginning in 1847 Governor Roberts declared the independence of the state. The recognition of Liberian independence by all countries except the United States followed in 1849. The United States, not wishing to receive a Negro minister, did not recognize Liberia until 1862.

No sooner was the independence of Liberia announced than England and France began a long series of aggressions to limit her territory and sovereignty. Considerable territory was lost by treaty, and in the effort to get capital to develop the rest, Liberia was saddled with a debt of four hundred thousand dollars, of which she received less than one hundred thousand dollars in actual cash. Finally the Liberians turned to the United States for capital and protection. As a result the Liberian customs have been put under international control and Major Charles Young, the ranking Negro officer in the United States army, with several colored assistants, has been put in charge of the making of roads and drilling a constabulary to keep order in the interior.

To-day Liberia has an area of forty thousand square miles, about three hundred and fifty miles of coast line, and an estimated total population of two million of which fifty thousand are civilized. The revenue amounted in 1913 to $531,500. The imports in 1912 were $1,667,857 and the exports $1,199,152. The latter consisted chiefly of rubber, palm oil and kernels, coffee, piassava fiber, ivory, ginger, camwood, and arnotto.

Perhaps Liberia's greatest citizen was the late Edward Wilmot Blyden, who migrated in early life from the Danish West Indies and became a prophet of the renaissance of the Negro race.

Turning now from Guinea we pass down the west coast. In 1482 Diego Cam of Portugal, sailing this coast, set a stone at the mouth of a great river which he called "The Mighty," but which eventually came to be known by the name of the powerful Negro kingdom through which it flowed—the Congo.

We must think of the valley of the Congo with its intricate interlacing of water routes and jungle of forests as a vast caldron shut away at first from the African world by known and unknown physical hindrances. Then it was penetrated by the tiny red dwarfs and afterward horde after horde of tall black men swirled into the valley like a maelstrom, moving usually from north to east and from south to west.

The Congo valley became, therefore, the center of the making of what we know to-day as the Bantu nations. They are not a unified people, but a congeries of tribes of considerable physical diversity, united by the compelling bond of language and other customs imposed on the conquered by invading conquerors.

The history or these invasions we must to-day largely imagine. Between two and three thousand years ago the wilder tribes of Negroes began to move out of the region south or southeast of Lake Chad. This was always a land of shadows and legends, where fearful cannibals dwelt and where no Egyptian or Ethiopian or Sudanese armies dared to go. It is possible, however, that pressure from civilization in the Nile valley and rising culture around Lake Chad was at this time reënforced by expansion of the Yoruba-Benin culture on the west coast. Perhaps, too, developing culture around the Great Lakes in the east beckoned or the riotous fertility of the Congo valleys became known. At any rate the movement commenced, now by slow stages, now in wild forays. There may have been a preliminary movement from east to west to the Gulf of Guinea. The main movement, however, was eastward, skirting the Congo forests and passing down by the Victoria Nyanza and Lake Tanganyika. Here two paths beckoned: the lakes and the sea to the east, the Congo to the west. A great stream of men swept toward the ocean and, dividing, turned northward and fought its way down the Nile valley and into the Abyssinian highlands; another branch turned south and approached the Zambesi, where we shall meet it again.

Another horde of invaders turned westward and entered the valley of the Congo in three columns. The northern column moved along the Lualaba and Congo rivers to the Cameroons; the second column became the industrial and state-building Luba and Lunda peoples in the southern Congo valley and Angola; while the third column moved into Damaraland and mingled with Bushman and Hottentot.

In the Congo valley the invaders settled in village and plain, absorbed such indigenous inhabitants as they found or drove them deeper into the forest, and immediately began to develop industry and political organization. They became skilled agriculturists, raising in some localities a profusion of cereals, fruit, and vegetables such as manioc, maize, yams, sweet potatoes, ground nuts, sorghum, gourds, beans, peas, bananas, and plantains. Everywhere they showed skill in mining and the welding of iron, copper, and other metals. They made weapons, wire and ingots, cloth, and pottery, and a widespread system of trade arose. Some tribes extracted rubber from the talamba root; others had remarkable breeds of fowl and cattle, and still others divided their people by crafts into farmers, smiths, boat builders, warriors, cabinet makers, armorers, and speakers. Women here and there took part in public assemblies and were rulers in some cases. Large towns were built, some of which required hours to traverse from end to end.

Many tribes developed intelligence of a high order. Wissmann called the Ba Luba "a nation of thinkers." Bateman found them "thoroughly and unimpeachably honest, brave to foolhardiness, and faithful to each other and to their superiors." One of their kings, Calemba, "a really princely prince," Bateman says would "amongst any people be a remarkable and indeed in many respects a magnificent man."[5]

These beginnings of human culture were, however, peculiarly vulnerable to invading hosts of later comers. There were no natural protecting barriers like the narrow Nile valley or the Kong mountains or the forests below Lake Chad. Once the pathways to the valley were open and for hundreds of years the newcomers kept arriving, especially from the welter of tribes south of the Sudan and west of the Nile, which rising culture beyond kept in unrest and turmoil.

Against these intruders there was but one defense, the State. State building was thus forced on the Congo valley. How early it started we cannot say, but when the Portuguese arrived in the fifteenth century, there had existed for centuries a large state among the Ba-Congo, with its capital at the city now known as San Salvador.

The Negro Mfumu, or emperor, was eventually induced to accept Christianity. His sons and many young Negroes of high birth were taken to Portugal to be educated. There several were raised to the Catholic priesthood and one became bishop; others distinguished themselves at the universities. Thus suddenly there arose a Catholic kingdom south of the valley of the Congo, which lasted three centuries, but was partially overthrown by invading barbarians from the interior in the seventeenth century. A king of Congo still reigns as pensioner of Portugal, and on the coast to-day are the remains of the kingdom in the civilized blacks and mulattoes, who are intelligent traders and boat builders.

Meantime the Luba-Lunda people to the eastward founded Kantanga and other states, and in the sixteenth century the larger and more ambitious realm of the Mwata Yamvo. The last of the fourteen rulers of this line was feudal lord of about three hundred chiefs, who paid him tribute in ivory, skins, corn, cloth, and salt. His territory included about one hundred thousand square miles and two million or more inhabitants. Eventually this state became torn by internal strife and revolt, especially by attacks from the south across the Congo-Zambesi divide.

Farther north, among the Ba-Lolo and the Ba-Songo, the village policy persisted and the cannibals of the northeast pressed down on the more settled tribes. The result was a curious blending of war and industry, artistic tastes and savage customs.

The organized slave trade of the Arabs penetrated the Congo valley in the sixteenth century and soon was aiding all the forces of unrest and turmoil. Industry was deranged and many tribes forced to take refuge in caves and other hiding places.

Here, as on the west coast, disintegration and retrogression followed, for as the American traffic lessened, the Arabian traffic increased. When, therefore, Stanley opened the Congo valley to modern knowledge, Leopold II of Belgium conceived the idea of founding here a free international state which was to bring civilization to the heart of Africa. Consequently there was formed in 1878 an international committee to study the region. Stanley was finally commissioned to inquire as to the best way of introducing European trade and culture. "I am charged," he said, "to open and keep open, if possible, all such districts and countries as I may explore, for the benefit of the commercial world. The mission is supported by a philanthropic society, which numbers nobleminded men of several nations. It is not a religious society, but my instructions are entirely of that spirit. No violence must be used, and wherever rejected, the mission must withdraw to seek another field."[6]

The Bula Matadi or Stone Breaker, as the natives called Stanley, threw himself energetically into the work and had by 1881 built a road past the falls to the plateau, where thousands of miles of river navigation were thus opened. Stations were established, and by 1884 Stanley returned armed with four hundred and fifty "treaties" with the native chiefs, and the new "State" appealed to the world for recognition.

The United States first recognized the "Congo Free State," which was at last made a sovereign power under international guarantees by the Congress of Berlin in the year 1885, and Leopold II was chosen its king. The state had an area of about nine hundred thousand square miles, with a population of about thirty million.

One of the first tasks before the new state was to check the Arab slave traders. The Arabs had hitherto acted as traders and middlemen along the upper Congo, and when the English and Congo state overthrew Mzidi, the reigning king in the Kantanga country, a general revolt of the Arabs and mulattoes took place. For a time, 1892–93, the whites were driven out, but in a year or two the Arabs and their allies were subdued.

Humanity and commerce, however, did not replace the Arab slave traders. Rather European greed and serfdom were substituted. The land was confiscated by the state and farmed out to private Belgian corporations. The wilder cannibal tribes were formed into a militia to prey on the industrious, who were taxed with specific amounts of ivory and rubber, and scourged and mutilated if they failed to pay. Harris declares that King Leopold's regime meant the death of twelve million natives.

"Europe was staggered at the Leopoldian atrocities, and they were terrible indeed; but what we, who were behind the scenes, felt most keenly was the fact that the real catastrophe in the Congo was the desolation and murder in the larger sense. The invasion of family life, the ruthless destruction of every social barrier, the shattering of every tribal law, the introduction of criminal practices which struck the chiefs of the people dumb with horror—in a word, a veritable avalanche of filth and immorality overwhelmed the Congo tribes."[7]

So notorious did the exploitation and misrule become that Leopold was forced to take measures toward reform, and finally in 1909 the Free State became a Belgian colony. Some reforms have been inaugurated and others may follow, but the valley of the Congo will long stand as a monument of shame to Christianity and European civilization.

NOTES

1. Quoted in Du Bois: *Timbuktu*.
2. Von Luschan: *Verhandlungen der berliner Gesellschaft für Anthropologie,* etc., 1898.
3. Frobenius: *Voice of Africa*, Vol. I.
4. Cf. p. 58.
5. Keane: *Africa*, II, 117–118.
6. *The Congo*, I, Chap. III.
7. Harris: *Dawn in Africa*.

CHAPTER VI

◆

The Great Lakes and Zymbabwe

We have already seen how a branch of the conquering Bantus turned eastward by the Great Lakes and thus reached the sea and eventually both the Nile and South Africa.

This brought them into the ancient and mysterious land far up the Nile, south of Ethiopia. Here lay the ancient Punt of the Egyptians (whether we place it in Somaliland or, as seems far more likely, around the Great Lakes) and here, as the Egyptians thought, their civilization began. The earliest inhabitants of the land were apparently of the Bushman or Hottentot type of Negro. These were gradually pushed southward and westward by the intrusion of the Nilotic Negroes. Five thousand years before Christ the mulatto Egyptians were in the Nile valley below the First Cataract. The Negroes were in the Nile valley down as far as the Second Cataract and between the First and Second Cataracts were Negroes into whose veins Semitic blood had penetrated more or less. These mixed elements became the ancestors of the modern Somali, Gala, Bishari, and Beja and spread Negro blood into Arabia beyond the Red Sea. The Nilotic Negroes to the south early became great traders in ivory, gold, leopard skins, gums, beasts, birds, and slaves, and they opened up systematic trade between Egypt and the Great Lakes.

The result was endless movement and migration both in ancient and modern days, which makes the cultural history of the Great Lakes region very difficult to understand. Three great elements are, however, clear: first, the Egyptian element, by the northward migration of the Negro ancestors of predynastic Egypt and the southern conquests and trade of dynastic Egypt; second, the Semitic influence from Arabia and Persia; third, the Negro influences from western and central Africa.

The migration of the Bantu is the first clearly defined movement of modern times. As we have shown, they began to move southward at least a thousand years before Christ, skirting the Congo forests and wandering along the Great Lakes and down to the Zambesi. What did they find in this land?

We do not know certainly, but from what we do know we may reconstruct the situation in this way: the primitive culture of the Hottentots of Punt had been further developed by them and by other stronger Negro stocks until it reached a highly developed culture. Widespread agriculture, and mining of gold, silver, and precious stones started a trade that penetrated to Asia and North Africa. This may have been the source of the gold of the Ophir.

The state that thus arose became in time strongly organized; it employed slave labor in crushing the hard quartz, sinking pits, and carrying underground galleries; it carried out a system of irrigation and built stone buildings and fortifications. There exists to-day many remains of these building operations in the Kalahari desert and in northern Rhodesia. Five hundred groups, covering over an area of one hundred and fifty thousand square miles, lie between the Limpopo and Zambesi rivers. Mining operations have been carried on in these plains for generations, and one estimate is that at least three hundred and seventy-five million dollars' worth of gold had been extracted. Some have thought that the older workings must date back to one or even three thousand years before the Christian era.

"There are other mines," writes De Barros in the seventeenth century,[1] "in a district called Toroa, which is otherwise known as the kingdom of Butua, whose ruler is a prince, by name Burrow, a vassal of Benomotapa. This land is near the other which we said consisted of extensive plains, and those ruins are the oldest that are known in that region. They are all in a plain, in the middle of which stands a square fortress, all of dressed stones within and without, well wrought and of marvelous size, without any lime showing the joinings, the walls of which are over twenty-five hands thick, but the height is not so great compared to the thickness. And above the gateway of that edifice is an inscription which some Moorish [Arab] traders who were there could not read, nor say what writing it was. All these structures the people of this country call Symbaoe [Zymbabwe], which with them means a court, for every place where Benomotapa stays is so called."

Later investigation has shown that these buildings were in many cases carefully planned and built fortifications. At Niekerk, for instance, nine or ten hills are fortified on concentric walls thirty to fifty feet in number, with a place for the village at the top. The buildings are forts, miniature citadels, and also workshops and cattle kraals. Iron implements and handsome pottery were found here, and close to the Zambesi there are extraordinary fortifications. Farther south at Inyanga there is less strong defense, and at Umtali there are no fortifications, showing that builders feared invasion from the north.

These people worked in gold, silver, tin, copper, and bronze and made beautiful pottery. There is evidence of religious significance in the buildings, and what is called the temple was the royal residence and served as a sort of acropolis. The surrounding residences in the valley were evidently occupied by wealthy traders and were not fortified. Here the gold was received from surrounding districts and bartered with traders.

As usual there have been repeated attempts to find an external and especially an Asiatic origin for this culture. So far, however, archeological research seems to confirm its African origin. The implements, weapons, and art are characteristically African and there is no evident connection with outside sources. How far back this civilization dates it is difficult to say, a great deal depending upon the dating of the iron age in South Africa. If it was the same as in the Mediterranean regions, the earliest limit was 1000 B.C.; it might, however, have been much earlier, especially if, as seems probable, the use of iron originated in Africa. On the other hand the culmination of this culture has been placed by some as late as the modern middle ages.

What was it that overthrew this civilization? Undoubtedly the same sort of raids of barbarous warriors that we have known in our day. For instance, in 1570 there came upon the country of Mozambique, farther up the coast, "such an inundation of pagans that they could not be numbered. They came from that part of Monomotapa where is the great lake from which spring these great rivers. They left no other signs of the towns they passed but the heaps of ruins and the bones of inhabitants." So, too, it is told how the Zimbas came, "a strange people never before seen there, who, leaving their own country, traversed a great part of this Ethiopia like a scourge of God, destroying every living thing they came across. They were twenty thousand strong and marched without children or women," just as four hundred years later the Zulu impi marched. Again in 1602 a horde of people came from the interior called the Cabires, or cannibals. They entered the kingdom of Monomotapa, and the reigning king, being weak, was in great terror. Thus gradually the Monomotapa fell, and its power was scattered until the Kaffir-Zulu raids of our day.[2]

The Arab writer, Macoudi, in the tenth century visited the East African coast somewhere north of the equator. He found the Indian Sea at that time frequented by Arab and Persian vessels, but there were no Asiatic settlements on the African shore. The Bantu, or as he calls them, Zenji, inhabited the country as far south as Sofala, where they bordered upon the Bushmen. These Bantus were under a ruler with the dynastic title of Waklimi. He was paramount over all the other tribes of the north and could put three hundred thousand men in the field. They used oxen as beasts of burden and the country produced gold in abundance, while panther skin was largely used for clothing. Ivory was sold to Asia and the Bantu used iron for personal adornment instead of gold or silver. They rode on their oxen, which ran with great speed, and they ate millet and honey and the flesh of animals.

Inland among the Bantu arose later the line of rulers called the Monomotapa among the gifted Makalanga. Their state was very extensive, ranging from the coast far into the interior and from Mozambique down to the Limpopo. It was strongly organized, with feudatory allied states, and carried on an extensive commerce by means of the traders on the coast. The kings were converted to nominal Christianity by the Portuguese.

There are indications of trade between Nupe in West Africa and Sofala on the east coast, and certainly trade between Asia and East Africa is earlier than the beginning of the Christian era. The Asiatic traders settled on the coast and by means of mulatto and Negro merchants brought Central Africa into contact with Arabia, India, China, and Malaysia.

The coming of the Asiatics was in this wise: Zaide, great-grandson of Ali, nephew and son-in-law of Mohammed, was banished from Arabia as a heretic. He passed over to Africa and formed temporary settlements. His people mingled with the blacks, and the resulting mulatto traders, known as the Emoxaidi, seem to have wandered as far south as the equator. Soon other Arabian families came over on account of oppression and founded the towns of Magadosho and Brava, both not far north of the equator. The first town became a place of importance and other settlements were made. The Emoxaidi, whom the later immigrants regarded as heretics, were driven inland and became the interpreting traders between the coast and the Bantu. Some wanderers from Magadosho came into the Port of Sofala and there learned that gold could be obtained. This led to a small Arab settlement at that place.

Seventy years later, and about fifty years before the Norman conquest of England, certain Persians settled at Kilwa in East Africa, led by Ali, who had been despised in his land because he was the son of a black Abyssinian slave mother. Kilwa, because of this, eventually became the most important commercial station on the East African coast, and in this and all these settlements a very large mulatto population grew up, so that very soon the whole settlement was indistinguishable in color from the Bantu.

In 1330 Ibn Batuta visited Kilwa. He found an abundance of ivory and some gold and heard that the inhabitants of Kilwa had gained victories over the Zenji or Bantu. Kilwa had at that time three hundred mosques and was "built of handsome houses of stone and lime, and very lofty, with their windows like those of the Christians; in the same way it has streets, and these houses have got terraces, and the wood-work is with the masonry, with plenty of gardens, in which there are many fruit trees and much water."[3] Kilwa after a time captured Sofala, seizing it from Magadosho. Eventually Kilwa became mistress of the island of Zanzibar, of Mozambique, and of much other territory. The forty-third ruler of Kilwa after Ali was named Abraham, and he was ruling when the Portuguese arrived. The latter reported that these people cultivated rice and cocoa, built ships, and had considerable commerce with Asia. All the people, of whatever color, were Mohammedans, and the richer were clothed in gorgeous robes of silk and velvet. They traded with the inland Bantus and met numerous tribes, receiving gold, ivory, millet, rice, cattle, poultry, and honey.

On the islands the Asiatics were independent, but on the main lands south of Kilwa the sheiks ruled only their own people, under the overlordship of the Bantus, to whom they were compelled to pay large tribute each year.

Vasco da Gama doubled the Cape of Good Hope in 1497 and went north on the east coast as far as India. In the next ten years the Portuguese had occupied more than six different points on that coast, including Sofala.[4]

Thus civilization waxed and waned in East Africa among prehistoric Negroes, Arab and Persian mulattoes on the coast, in the Zend or Zeng empire of Bantu Negroes, and later in the Bantu rule of the Monomotapa. And thus, too, among later throngs of the fiercer, warlike Bantu, the ancient culture of the land largely died. Yet something survived, and in the modern Bantu state, language, and industry can be found clear links that establish the essential identity of the absorbed peoples with the builders of Zymbabwe.

So far we have traced the history of the lands into which the southward stream of invading Bantus turned, and have followed them to the Limpopo River. We turn now to the lands north from Lake Nyassa.

The aboriginal Negroes sustained in prehistoric time invasions from the northeast by Negroids of a type like the ancient Egyptians and like the modern Gallas, Masai, and Somalis. To these migrations were added attacks from the Nile Negroes to the north and the Bantu invaders from the south. This has led to great differences among the groups of the population and in their customs. Some are fierce mountaineers, occupying hilly plateaus six thousand feet above the sea level; others, like the Wa Swahili, are traders on the coast. There are the Masai, chocolate-colored and frizzly-haired, organized for war and cattle lifting; and Negroids like the Gallas, who, blending with the Bantus, have produced the race of modern Uganda.

It was in this region that the kingdom of Kitwara was founded by the Galla chief, Kintu. About the beginning of the nineteenth century the empire was dismembered, the largest share falling to Uganda. The ensuing history of Uganda is of great interest. When King Mutesa came to the throne in 1862, he found Mohammedan influences in his land and was induced to admit English Protestants and French Catholics. Uganda thereupon became an extraordinary religious battlefield between these three beliefs. Mutesa's successor, Mwanga, caused an English bishop to be killed in 1885, believing (as has since proven quite true) that the religion he offered would be used as a cloak for conquest. The final result was that, after open war between the religions, Uganda was made an English protectorate in 1894.

The Negroes of Uganda are an intelligent people who had organized a complex feudal state. At the head stood the king, and under him twelve feudal lords. The present king, Daudi Chua, is the young grandson of Mutesa and rules under the overlordship of England.

Many things show the connection between Egypt and this part of Africa. The same glass beads are found in Uganda and Upper Egypt, and similar canoes are built. Harps and other instruments bear great resemblance. Finally the Bahima, as the Galla invaders are called, are startlingly Egyptian in type; at the same time they are undoubtedly Negro in hair and color. Perhaps we have here the best racial picture of what ancient Egyptian and upper Nile regions were in predynastic times and later.

Thus in outline was seen the mission of The People—La Bantu as they called themselves. They migrated, they settled, they tore down, and they learned, and they in turn were often overthrown by succeeding tribes of their own folk. They rule with their tongue and their power all Africa south of the equator, save where the Europeans have entered. They have never been conquered, although the gold and diamond traders have sought to debauch them, and the ivory and rubber capitalists have cruelly wronged their weaker groups. They are the Africans with whom the world of to-morrow must reckon, just as the world of yesterday knew them to its cost.

NOTES

1. Quoted in Bent: *Ruined Cities of Mashonaland*, pp. 203 ff.
2. Cf. "Ethiopia Oriental," by J. Dos Santos, in Theal's *Records of South Africa*, Vol. VII.
3. Barbosa, quoted in Keane, II, 482.
4. It was called Sofala, from an Arabic word, and may be associated with the Ophir of Solomon. So, too, the river Sabi, a little off Sofala, may be associated with the name of the Queen of Sheba, whose lineage was supposed to be perpetuated in the powerful Monomotapa as well as the Abyssinians.

CHAPTER VII

◆

The War of Races at Land's End

Primitive man in Africa is found in the interior jungles and down at Land's End in South Africa. The Pygmy people in the jungles represent to-day a small survival from the past, but a survival of curious interest, pushed aside by the torrent of conquest. Also pushed on by these waves of Bantu conquest, moved the ancient Abatwa or Bushmen. They are small in stature, yellow in color, with crisp-curled hair. The traditions of the Bushmen say that they came southward from the regions of the Great Lakes, and indeed the king and queen of Punt, as depicted by the Egyptians, were Bushmen or Hottentots.

Their tribes may be divided, in accordance with their noticeable artistic talents, into the painters and the sculptors. The sculptors entered South Africa by moving southward through the more central portions of the country, crossing the Zambesi, and coming down to the Cape. The painters, on the other hand, came through Damaraland on the west coast; when they came to the great mountain regions, they turned eastward and can be traced as far as the mountains opposite Delagoa Bay. The mass of them settled down in the lower part of the Cape and in the Kalahari desert. The painters were true cave dwellers, but the sculptors lived in large communities on the stony hills, which they marked with their carvings.

These Bushmen believed in an ancient race of people who preceded them in South Africa. They attributed magic power to these unknown folk, and said that some of them had been translated as stars to the sky. Before their groups were dispersed the Bushmen had regular government. Tribes with their chiefs occupied well-defined tracts of country and were subdivided into branch tribes under subsidiary chiefs. The great cave represented the dignity and glory of the entire tribe.

The Bushmen suffered most cruelly in the succeeding migrations and conquests of South Africa. They fought desperately in self-defense; they saw their women and children carried into bondage and they themselves hunted like wild beasts. Both savage and civilized men appropriated their land. Still they were brave people. "In this struggle for existence their bitterest enemies, of whatever shade of color they might be, were forced to make an unqualified acknowledgement of the courage and daring they so invariably exhibited."[1]

Here, to a remote corner of the world, where, as one of their number said, they had supposed that the only beings in the world were Bushmen and lions, came a series of invaders. It was the outer ripples of civilization starting far away, the indigenous and external civilizations of Africa beating with great impulse among the Ethiopians and the Egyptian mulattoes and Sudanese Negroes and Yorubans, and driving the Bantu race southward. The Bantus crowded more and more upon the primitive Bushmen, and probably a mingling of the Bushmen and the Bantus gave rise to the Hottentots.

The Hottentots, or as they called themselves, Khoi Khoin (Men of Men), were physically a stronger race than the Abatwa and gave many evidences of degeneration from a high culture, especially in the "phenomenal perfection" of a language which "is so highly developed, both in its rich phonetic system, as represented by a very delicately graduated series of vowels and diphthongs, and in its varied grammatical structure, that Lepsius sought for its affinities in the Egyptian at the other end of the continent."

When South Africa was first discovered there were two distinct types of Hottentot. The more savage Hottentots were simply large, strong Bushmen, using weapons superior to the Bushmen, without domestic cattle or sheep. Other tribes nearer the center of South Africa were handsomer in appearance and raised an Egyptian breed of cattle which they rode.

In general the Hottentots were yellow, with close-curled hair, high cheek bones, and somewhat oblique eyes. Their migration commenced about the end of the fourteenth century and was, as is usual in such cases, a scattered, straggling movement. The traditions of the Hottentots point to the lake country of Central Africa as their place of origin, whence they were driven by the Bechuana tribes of the Bantu. They fled westward to the ocean and then turned south and came upon the Bushmen, whom they had only partially subdued when the Dutch arrived as settlers in 1652.

The Dutch "Boers" began by purchasing land from the Hottentots and then, as they grew more powerful, they dispossessed the dark men and tried to enslave them. There grew up a large Dutch-Hottentot class. Indeed the filtration of Negro blood noticeable in modern Boers accounts for much curious history. Soon after the advent of the Dutch some of the Hottentots, of whom there were not more than thirty or forty thousand, led by the Korana clans, began slowly to retreat northward, followed by the invading Dutch and fighting the Dutch, each other, and the wretched Bushmen. In the latter part of the eighteenth century the Hottentots had reached the great interior plain and met the on-coming outposts of the Bantu nations.

The Bechuana, whom the Hottentots first met, were the most advanced of the Negro tribes of Central Africa. They had crossed the Zambesi in the fourteenth or fifteenth century; their government was a sort of feudal system with hereditary chiefs and vassals; they were careful agriculturists, laid out large towns with great regularity, and were the most skilled of smiths. They used stone in building, carved on wood, and many of them, too, were keen traders. These tribes, coming southward, occupied the east-central part of South Africa comprising modern Bechuanaland. Apparently they had started from the central lake country somewhere late in the fifteenth century, and by the middle of the eighteenth century one of their great chiefs, Tao, met the on-coming Hottentots.

The Hottentots compelled Tao to retreat, but the mulatto Gricquas arrived from the south, and, allying themselves with the Bechuana, stopped the rout. The Gricquas sprang from and took their name from an old Hottentot tribe. They were led by Kok and Barends, and by adding other elements they became, partly through their own efforts and partly through the efforts of the missionaries, a community of fairly well civilized people. In Gricqualand West the mulatto Gricquas, under their chiefs Kok and Waterboer, lived until the discovery of diamonds.

The Griquas and Bechuana tribes were thus gradually checking the Hottentots when, in the nineteenth century, there came two new developments: first, the English took possession of Cape Colony, and the Dutch began to move in larger numbers toward the interior; secondly, a newer and fiercer element of the Bantu tribes, the Zulu-Kaffirs, appeared. The Kaffirs, or as they called themselves, the Amazosas, claimed descent from Zuide, a great chief of the fifteenth century in the lake country. They are among the tallest people in the world, averaging five feet ten inches, and are slim, well-proportioned, and muscular. The more warlike tribes were usually clothed in leopard or ox skins. Cattle formed their chief wealth, stock breeding and hunting and fighting their main pursuits. Mentally they were men of tact and intelligence, with a national religion based upon ancestor worship, while their government was a patriarchal monarchy limited by an aristocracy and almost feudal in character. The common law which had grown up from the decisions of the chiefs made the head of the family responsible for the conduct of its branches, a village for all its residents, and the clan for all its villages. Finally there was a paramount chief, who was the civil and military father of his people. These people laid waste to the coast regions and in 1779 came in contact with the Dutch. A series of Dutch-Kaffir wars ensued between 1779 and 1795 in which the Dutch were hard pressed.

In 1806 the English took final possession of Cape Colony. At that time there were twenty-five thousand Boers, twenty-five thousand pure and mixed Hottentots, and twenty-five thousand slaves secured from the east coast. Between 1811 and 1877 there were six Kaffir-English wars. One of these in 1818 grew out of the ignorant interference of the English with the Kaffir tribal system; then there came a terrible war between 1834 and 1835, followed by the annexation of all the country as far as the Kei River. The war of the Axe (1846–48) led to further annexation by the British.

Hostilities broke out again in 1856 and 1863. In the former year, despairing of resistance to invading England, a prophet arose who advised the wholesale destruction of all Kaffir property except weapons, in order that this faith might bring back their dead heroes. The result was that almost a third of the nation perished from hunger. Fresh troubles occurred in 1877, when the Ama-Xosa confederacy was finally broken up, and to-day gradually these tribes are passing from independence to a state of mild vassalage to the British.

Meantime the more formidable part of the Zulu-Kaffirs had been united under the terrible Chief Chaka. He had organized a military system, not a new one by any means, but one of which we hear rumors back in the lake regions in the fourteenth and fifteenth centuries. McDonald says, "There has probably never been a more perfect system of discipline than that by which Chaka ruled his army and kingdom. At a review an order might be given in the most unexpected manner, which meant death to hundreds. If the regiment hesitated or dared to remonstrate, so perfect was the discipline and so great the jealousy that another was ready to cut them down. A warrior returning from battle without his arms was put to death without trial. A general returning unsuccessful in the main purpose of his expedition shared the same fate. Whoever displeased the king was immediately executed. The traditional courts practically ceased to exist so far as the will and action of the tyrant was concerned." With this army Chaka fell on tribe after tribe. The Bechuana fled before him and some tribes of them were entirely destroyed. The Hottentots suffered severely and one of his rival Zulu tribes under Umsilikatsi fled into Matabililand, pushing back the Bechuana. By the time the English came to Port Natal, Chaka was ruling over the whole southeastern seaboard, from the Limpopo River to Cape Colony, including the Orange and Transvaal states and the whole of Natal. Chaka was killed in 1828 and was eventually succeeded by his brother Dingan, who reigned twelve years. It was during Dingan's reign that England tried to abolish slavery in Cape Colony, but did not pay promptly for the slaves, as she had promised; the result was the so-called "Great Trek," about 1834, when thousands of Boers went into the interior across the Orange and Vaal rivers.

Dingan and these Boers were soon engaged in a death struggle in which the Zulus were repulsed and Dingan replaced by Panda. Under this chief there was something like repose for sixteen years, but in 1856 civil war broke out between his sons, one of whom, Cetewayo, succeeded his father in 1882. He fell into border disputes with the English, and the result was one of the fiercest clashes of Europe and Africa in modern days. The Zulus fought desperately, annihilating at one time a whole detachment and killing the young prince Napoleon. But after all it was assagais against machine guns, and the Zulus were finally defeated at Ulundi, July 4, 1879. Thereupon Zululand was divided among thirteen semi-independent chiefs and became a British protectorate.

Since then the best lands have been gradually reoccupied by a large number of tribes—Kaffirs from the south and Zulus from the north. The tribal organization, without being actually broken up, has been deprived of its dangerous features by appointing paid village headmen and transforming the hereditary chief into a British government official. In Natal there are about one hundred and seventy tribal chiefs, and nearly half of these have been appointed by the governor.

Umsilikatsi, who had been driven into Matabililand by the terrible Chaka in 1828 and defeated by the Dutch in 1837, had finally reestablished his headquarters in Rhodesia in 1838. Here he introduced the Zulu military system and terrorized the peaceful and industrious Bechuana populations. Lobengula succeeded Umsilikatsi in 1870 and, realizing that his power was waning, began to retreat northward toward the Zambesi. He was finally defeated by the British and native forces in 1893 and the land was incorporated into South Central Africa.

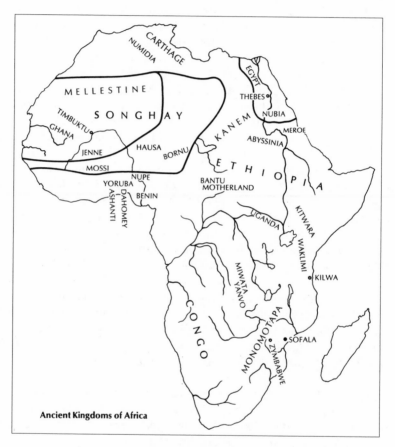

Ancient Kingdoms of Africa

The result of all these movements was to break the inhabitants of Bechuanaland into numerous fragments. There were small numbers of mulatto Gricquas in the southwest and similar Bastaards in the northwest. The Hottentots and Bushmen were dispersed into groups and seem doomed to extinction, the last Hottentot chief being deposed in 1810 and replaced by an English magistrate. Partially civilized Hottentots still live grouped together in their kraals and are members of Christian churches. The Bechuana hold their own in several centers; one is in Basutoland, west of Natal, where a number of tribes were welded together under the far-sighted Moshesh into a modern and fairly well civilized nation. In the north part of Bechuanaland are the self-governing Bamangwato and the Batwana, the former ruled by Khama, one of the canniest of modern rulers in Africa.

Meantime, in Portuguese territory south of the Zambesi, there arose Gaza, a contemporary and rival of Chaka. His son, Manikus, was deputed by Dingan, Chaka's successor, to drive out the Portuguese. This Manikus failed to do, and to escape vengeance he migrated north of the Limpopo. Here he established his military kraal in a district thirty-six hundred and fifty feet above the sea and one hundred and twenty miles inland from Sofala. From this place his soldiery nearly succeeded in driving the Portuguese out of East Africa. He was succeeded by his son, Umzila, and Umzila's brother, Guzana (better known as Gungunyana), who exercised for a time joint authority. Gungunyana was finally overthrown in November, 1895, captured, and removed to the Azores.

North of the Zambesi, in British territory, the chief role in recent times has been played by the Bechuana, the first of the Bantu to return northward after the South African migration. Livingstone found there the Makolo, who with other tribes had moved northward on account of the pressure of the Dutch and Zulus below, and by conquering various tribes in the Zambesi region had established a strong power. This kingdom was nearly overthrown by the rebellion of the Barotse, and in 1875 the Barotse kingdom comprised a large territory. To-day their king, Lewanika, rules directly and indirectly fifty thousand square miles, with a population between one and two and a half million. They are under a protectorate of the British.

In Southwest Africa, Hottentot mulattoes crossing from the Cape caused widespread change. They were strong men and daring fighters and soon became dominant in what is now German Southwest Africa, where they fought fiercely with the Bantu Ova-Hereros. Armed with fire arms, these Namakwa Hottentots threatened Portuguese West Africa, but Germany intervened, ostensibly to protect missionaries. By spending millions of dollars and thousands of soldiers Germany has nearly exterminated these brave men.

Thus we have between the years 1400 and 1900 a great period of migration up to 1750, when Bushmen, Hottentot, Bantu, and Dutch appeared in succession at Land's End. In the latter part of the eighteenth century we have the clash of the Hottentots and Bechuana, followed in the nineteenth century by the terrible wars of Chaka, the Kaffirs, and Matabili. Finally, in the latter half of the nineteenth century, we see the gradual subjection of the Kaffir-Zulus and the Bechuana under the English and the final conquest of the Dutch. The resulting racial problem in South Africa is one of great intricacy.

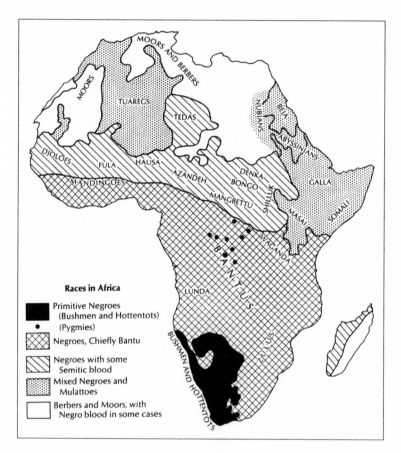

Races in Africa

■ Primitive Negroes
   (Bushmen and Hottentots)
● (Pygmies)
▨ Negroes, Chiefly Bantu
▧ Negroes with some
   Semitic blood
▦ Mixed Negroes and
   Mulattoes
□ Berbers and Moors, with
   Negro blood in some cases

Races in Africa

To the racial problem has been added the tremendous problem of modern capital brought by the discovery of gold and diamond mines, so that the future of the Negro race is peculiarly bound up in developments here at Land's End, where the ship of the Flying Dutchman beats back and forth on its endless quest.

NOTES

1. Stowe: *Native Races of South Africa*, pp. 215–216.

CHAPTER VIII

---◆---

African Culture

We have followed the history of mankind in Africa down the valley of the Nile, past Ethiopia to Egypt; we have seen kingdoms arise along the great bend of the Niger and strive with the ancient culture at its mouth. We have seen the remnants of mankind at Land's End, the ancient culture at Punt and Zymbabwe, and followed the invading Bantu east, south, and west to their greatest center in the vast jungle of the Congo valleys.

We must now gather these threads together and ask what manner of men these were and how far and in what way they progressed on the road of human culture.

That Negro peoples were the beginners of civilization along the Ganges, the Euphrates, and the Nile seems proven. Early Babylon was founded by a Negroid race. Hammurabi's code, the most ancient known, says "Anna and Bel called me, Hammurabi the exalted prince, the worshiper of the gods; to cause justice to prevail in the land, to destroy the wicked, to prevent the strong from oppressing the weak, to go forth like the sun over the black-head race, to enlighten the land, and to further the welfare of the people." The Assyrians show a distinct Negroid strain and early Egypt was predominantly Negro. These earliest of cultures were crude and primitive, but they represented the highest attainment of mankind after tens of thousands of years in unawakened savagery.

It has often been assumed that the Negro is physically inferior to other races and markedly distinguishable from them; modern science gives no authority for such an assumption. The supposed inferiority cannot rest on color,[1] for that is "due to the combined influences of a great number of factors of environment working through physiological processes," and "however marked the contrasts may be, there is no corresponding difference in anatomical structure discoverable."[2] So, too, difference in texture of hair is a matter of degree, not kind, and is caused by heat, moisture, exposure, and the like.

The bony skeleton presents no distinctly racial lines of variation. Prognathism "presents too many individual varieties to be taken as a distinctive character of race."[3] Difference in physical measurements does not show the Negro to be a more primitive evolutionary form. Comparative ethnology to-day affords "no support to the view which sees in the so-called lower races of mankind a transition stage from beast to man."[4]

Much has been made of the supposed smaller brain of the Negro race; but this is as yet an unproved assumption, based on the uncritical measurement of less than a thousand Negro brains as compared with eleven thousand or more European brains. Even if future measurement prove the average Negro brain lighter, the vast majority of Negro brain weights fall within the same limits as the whites; and finally, "neither size nor weight of the brain seems to be of importance" as an index of mental capacity. We may, therefore, say with Ratzel, "There is only one species of man. The variations are numerous, but do not go deep."[5]

To this we may add the word of the Secretary of the First Races Congress: "We are, then, under the necessity of concluding that an impartial investigator would be inclined to look upon the various important peoples of the world as to all intents and purposes essentially equal in intellect, enterprise, morality, and physique."[6]

If these conclusions are true, we should expect to see in Africa the human drama play itself out much as in other lands, and such has actually been the fact. At the same time we must expect peculiarities arising from the physiography of the land—its climate, its rainfall, its deserts, and the peculiar inaccessibility of the coast.

Three principal zones of habitation appear: first, the steppes and deserts around the Sahara in the north and the Kalahari desert in the south; secondly, the grassy highlands bordering the Great Lakes and connecting these two regions; thirdly, the forests and rivers of Central and West Africa. In the deserts are the nomads, and the Pygmies are in the forest fastnesses. Herdsmen and their cattle cover the steppes and highlands, save where the tsetse fly prevents. In the open forests and grassy highlands are the agriculturists.

Among the forest farmers the village is the center of life, while in the open steppes political life tends to spread into larger political units. Political integration is, however, hindered by an ease of internal communication almost as great as the difficulty of reaching outer worlds beyond the continent. The narrow Nile valley alone presented physical barriers formidable enough to keep back the invading barbarians of the south, and even then with difficulty. Elsewhere communication was all too easy. For a while the Congo forests fended away the restless, but this only temporarily.

On the whole Africa from the Sahara to the Cape offered no great physical barrier to the invader, and we continually have whirlwinds of invading hosts rushing now southward, now northward, from the interior to the coast and from the coast inland, and hurling their force against states, kingdoms, and cities. Some resisted for generations, some for centuries, some but a few years. It is, then, this sudden change and the fear of it that marks African culture, particularly in its political aspects, and which makes it so difficult to trace this changing past. Nevertheless beneath all change rests the strong substructure of custom, religion, industry, and art well worth the attention of students.

Starting with agriculture, we learn that "among all the great groups of the 'natural' races, the Negroes are the best and keenest tillers of the ground. A minority despise agriculture and breed cattle; many combine both occupations. Among the genuine tillers the whole life of the family is taken up in agriculture, and hence the months are by preference called after the operations which they demand. Constant clearings change forests to fields, and the ground is manured with the ashes of the burnt thicket. In the middle of the fields rise the light watch-towers, from which a watchman scares grain-eating birds and other thieves. An African cultivated landscape is incomplete without barns. The rapidity with which, when newly imported, the most various forms of cultivation spread in Africa says much for the attention which is devoted to this branch of economy. Industries, again, which may be called agricultural, like the preparation of meal from millet and other crops, also from cassava, the fabrication of fermented drinks from grain, or the manufacture of cotton, are widely known and sedulously fostered."[7]

Bücher reminds us of the deep impression made upon travelers when they sight suddenly the well-attended fields of the natives on emerging from the primeval forests. "In the more thickly populated parts of Africa these fields often stretch for many a mile, and the assiduous care of the Negro women shines in all the brighter light when we consider the insecurity of life, the constant feuds and pillages, in which no one knows whether he will in the end be able to harvest what he has sown. Livingstone gives somewhere a graphic description of the devastations wrought by slave hunts; the people were lying about slain, the dwellings were demolished; in the fields, however, the grain was ripening and there was none to harvest it."[8]

Sheep, goat, and chickens are domestic animals all over Africa, and Von Franzius considers Africa the home of the house cattle and the Negro as the original tamer. Northeastern Africa especially is noted for agriculture, cattle raising, and fruit culture. In the eastern Sudan, and among the great Bantu tribes extending from the Sudan down toward the south, cattle are evidences of wealth; one tribe, for instance, having so many oxen that each village had ten or twelve thousand head. Lenz (1884), Bouet-Williaumez (1848), Hecquard (1854), Bosman (1805), and Baker (1868) all bear witness to this, and Schweinfurth (1878) tells us of great cattle parks with two to three thousand head and of numerous agricultural and cattle-raising tribes. Von der Decken (1859–61) described the paradise of the dwellers about Kilimanjaro—the bananas, fruit, beans and peas, cattle raising with stall feed, the fertilizing of the fields, and irrigation. The Negroid Gallas have seven or eight cattle to each inhabitant. Livingstone bears witness to the busy cattle raising of the Bantus and Kaffirs. Hulub (1881) and Chapman (1868) tell of agriculture and fruit raising in South Africa. Shutt (1884) found the tribes in the southwestern basin of the Congo with sheep, swine, goats, and cattle. On this agricultural and cattle-raising economic foundation has arisen the organized industry of the artisan, the trader, and the manufacturer.

While the Pygmies, still living in the age of wood, make no iron or stone implements, they seem to know how to make bark cloth and fiber baskets and simple outfits for hunting and fishing. Among the Bushmen the art of making weapons and working in hides is quite common. The Hottentots are further advanced in the industrial arts, being well versed in the manufacture of clothing, weapons, and utensils. In the dressing of skins and furs, as well as in the plaiting of cords and the weaving of mats, we find evidences of their workmanship. In addition they are good workers in iron and copper, using the sheepskin bellows for this purpose. The Ashantis of the Gold Coast know how to make "cotton fabrics, turn and glaze earthenware, forge iron, fabricate instruments and arms, embroider rugs and carpets, and set gold and precious stones."[9] Among the people of the banana zone we find rough basket work, coarse pottery, grass cloth, and spoons made of wood and ivory. The people of the millet zone, because of uncertain agricultural resources, quite generally turn to manufacturing. Charcoal is prepared by the smiths, iron is smelted, and numerous implements are manufactured. Among them we find axes, hatchets, hoes, knives, nails, scythes, and other hardware. Cloaks, shoes, sandals, shields, and water and oil vessels are made from leather which the natives have dressed. Soap is manufactured in the Bautschi district, glass is made, formed, and colored by the people of Nupeland, and in almost every city cotton is spun and woven and dyed. Barth tells us that the weaving of cotton was known in the Sudan as early as the eleventh century. There is also extensive manufacture of wooden ware, tools, implements, and utensils.

In describing particular tribes, Baker and Felkin tell of smiths of wonderful adroitness, goatskins prepared better than a European tanner could do, drinking cups and kegs of remarkable symmetry, and polished clay floors. Schweinfurth says, "The arrow and the spear heads are of the finest and most artistic work; their bristlelike barbs and points are baffling when one knows how few tools these smiths have." Excellent wood carving is found among the Bongo, Ovambo, and Makololo. Pottery and basketry and careful hut building distinguish many tribes. Cameron (1877) tells of villages so clean, with huts so artistic, that, save in book knowledge, the people occupied no low plane of civilization. The Mangbettu work both iron and copper. "The masterpieces of the Monbutto [Mangbettu] smiths are the fine chains worn as ornaments, and which in perfection of form and fineness compare well with our best steel chains." Shubotz in 1911 called the Mangbettu "a highly cultivated people" in architecture and handicraft. Barth found copper exported from Central Africa in competition with European copper at Kano.

Nor is the iron industry confined to the Sudan. About the Great Lakes and other parts of Central Africa it is widely distributed. Thornton says, "This iron industry proves that the East Africans stand by no means on so low a plane of culture as many travelers would have us think. It is unnecessary to be reminded what a people without instruction, and with the rudest tools to do such skilled work, could do if furnished with steel tools." Arrows made east of Lake Nyanza were found to be nearly as good as the best Swedish iron in Birmingham. From Egypt to the Cape, Livingstone assures us that the mortar and pestle, the long-handled axe, the goatskin bellows, etc., have the same form, size, etc., pointing to a migration southwestward. Holub (1879), on the Zambesi, found fine workers in iron and bronze. The Bantu huts contain spoons, wooden dishes, milk pails, calabashes, handmills, and axes.

Kaffirs and Zulus, in the extreme south, are good smiths, and the latter melt copper and tin together and draw wire from it, according to Kranz (1880). West of the Great Lakes, Stanley (1878) found wonderful examples of smith work: figures worked out of brass and much work in copper. Cameron (1878) saw vases made near Lake Tanganyika which reminded him of the amphoræ in the Villa of Diomedes, Pompeii. Horn (1882) praises tribes here for iron and copper work. Livingstone (1871) passed thirty smelting houses in one journey, and Cameron came across bellows with valves, and tribes who used knives in eating. He found tribes which no Europeans had ever visited, who made ingots of copper in the form of the St. Andrew's cross, which circulated even to the coast. In the southern Congo basin iron and copper are worked; also wood and ivory carving and pottery making are pursued. In equatorial West Africa, Lenz and Du Chaillu (1861) found iron workers with charcoal, and also carvers of bone and ivory. Near Cape Lopez, Hübbe-Schleiden found tribes making ivory needles inlaid with ebony, while the arms and dishes of the Osaka are found among many tribes even as far as the Atlantic Ocean. Wilson (1856) found natives in West Africa who could repair American watches.

Gold Coast Negroes make gold rings and chains, forming the metal into all kinds of forms. Soyaux says, "The works in relief which natives of Lower Guinea carve with their own knives out of ivory and hippopotamus teeth are really entitled to be called works of art, and many wooden figures of fetishes in the Ethnographical Museum of Berlin show some understanding of the proportions of the human body." Great Bassam is called by Hecquard the "Fatherland of Smiths." The Mandingo in the northwest are remarkable workers in iron, silver, and gold, we are told by Mungo Park (1800), while there is a mass of testimony as to the work in the north-west of Africa in gold, tin, weaving, and dyeing. Caille found the Negroes in Bambana manufacturing gunpowder (1824–28), and the Hausa make soap; so, too, Negroes in Uganda and other parts have made guns after seeing European models.

So marked has been the work of Negro artisans and traders in the manufacture and exchange of iron implements that a growing number of archeologists are disposed to-day to consider the Negro as the originator of the art of smelting iron. Gabriel de Mortillet (1883) declared Negroes the only iron users among primitive people. Some would, therefore, argue that the Negro learned it from other folk, but Andree declares that the Negro developed his own "Iron Kingdom." Schweinfurth, Von Luschan, Boaz, and others incline to the belief that the Negroes invented the smelting of iron and passed it on to the Egyptians and to modern Europe.

Boaz says, "It seems likely that at a time when the European was still satisfied with rude stone tools, the African had invented or adopted the art of smelting iron. Consider for a moment what this invention has meant for the advance of the human race. As long as the hammer, knife, saw, drill, the spade, and the hoe had to be chipped out of stone, or had to be made of shell or hard wood, effective industrial work was not impossible, but difficult. A great progress was made when copper found in large nuggets was hammered out into tools and later on shaped by melting, and when bronze was introduced; but the true advancement of industrial life did not begin until the hard iron was discovered. It seems not unlikely that the people who made the marvelous discovery of reducing iron ores by smelting were the African Negroes. Neither ancient Europe, nor ancient western Asia, nor ancient China knew the iron, and everything points to its introduction from Africa. At the time of the great African discoveries toward the end of the past century, the trade of the blacksmith was found all over Africa, from north to south and from east to west. With his simple bellows and a charcoal fire he reduced the ore that is found in many parts of the continent and forged implements of great usefulness and beauty."[10]

Torday has argued recently, "I feel convinced by certain arguments that seem to prove to my satisfaction that we are indebted to the Negro for the very key-stone of our modern civilization and that we owe him the discovery of iron. That iron could be discovered by accident in Africa seems beyond doubt: if this is so in other parts of the world, I am not competent to say. I will only remind you that Schweinfurth and Petherick record the fact that in the northern part of East Africa smelting furnaces are worked without artificial air current and, on the other hand, Stuhlmann and Kollmann found near Victoria Nyanza that the natives simply mixed powdered ore with charcoal and by introduction of air currents obtained the metal. These simple processes make it simple that iron should have been discovered in East or Central Africa. No bronze implements have ever been found in black Africa; had the Africans received iron from the Egyptians, bronze would have preceded this metal and all traces of it would not have disappeared. Black Africa was for a long time an exporter of iron, and even in the twelfth century exports to India and Java are recorded by Idrisi.

"It is difficult to imagine that Egypt should have obtained it from Europe where the oldest find (in Hallstadt) cannot be of an earlier period than 800 B.C., or from Asia, where iron is not known before 1000 B.C., and where, in the times of Ashur Nazir Pal, it was still used concurrently with bronze, while iron beads have been only recently discovered by Messrs. G. A. Wainwright and Bushe Fox in a predynastic grave, and where a piece of this metal, possibly a tool, was found in the masonry of the great pyramid."[11]

The Negro is a born trader. Lenz says, "our sharpest European merchants, even Jews and Armenians, can learn much of the cunning and trade of the Negroes." We know that the trade between Central Africa and Egypt was in the hands of Negroes for thousands of years, and in early days the cities of the Sudan and North Africa grew rich through Negro trade.

Leo Africanus, writing of Timbuktu in the sixteenth century, said, "It is a wonder to see what plentie of Merchandize is daily brought hither and how costly and sumptuous all things be . . . . Here are many shops of artificers and mer-chants and especially of such as weave linnen and cloth."

Long before cotton weaving was a British industry, West Africa and the Sudan were supplying a large part of the world with cotton cloth. Even to-day cities like Kuka on the west shore of Lake Chad and Sokota are manufacturing centers where cotton is spun and woven, skins tanned, implements and iron ornaments made.

"Travelers," says Bücher, "have often observed this tribal or local development of industrial technique. 'The native villages,' relates a Belgian observer of the Lower Congo, 'are often situated in groups. Their activities are based upon reciprocality, and they are to a certain extent the complements of one another. Each group has its more or less strongly defined specialty. One carries on fishing; another produces palm wine; a third devotes itself to trade and is broker for the others, supplying the community with all products from outside; another has reserved to itself work in iron and copper, making weapons for war and hunting, various utensils, etc. None may, however, pass beyond the sphere of its own specialty without exposing itself to the risk of being universally proscribed.'"

From the Loango Coast, Bastian tells of a great number of centers for special products of domestic industry. "Loango excels in mats and fishing baskets, while the carving of elephants' tusks is specially followed in Chilungo. The so-called Mafooka hats with raised patterns are drawn chiefly from the bordering country of Kakongo and Mayyume. In Bakunya are made potter's wares, which are in great demand; in Basanza, excellent swords; in Basundi, especially beautiful ornamented copper rings; on the Congo, clever wood and tablet carvings; in Loango, ornamented clothes and intricately designed mats; in Mayumbe, clothing of finely woven mat-work; in Kakongo, embroidered hats and also burnt clay pitchers; and among the Bayakas and Mantetjes, stuffs of woven grass."[12]

A native Negro student tells of the development of trade among the Ashanti. "It was a part of the state system of Ashanti to encourage trade. The king once in every forty days, at the Adai custom, distributed among a number of chiefs various sums of gold dust with a charge to turn the same to good account. These chiefs then sent down to the coast caravans of tradesmen, some of whom would be their slaves, sometimes some two or three hundred strong, to barter ivory for European goods, or buy such goods with gold dust, which the king obtained from the royal alluvial workings. Down to 1873 a constant stream of Ashanti traders might be seen daily wending their way to the merchants of the coast and back again, yielding more certain wealth and prosperity to the merchants of the Gold Coast and Great Britain than may be expected for some time yet to come from the mining industry and railway development put together. The trade chiefs would, in due time, render a faithful account to the king's stewards, being allowed to retain a fair portion of the profit. In the king's household, too, he would have special men who directly traded for him. Important chiefs carried on the same system of trading with the coast as did the king. Thus every member of the state, from the king downward, took an active interest in the promotion of trade and in the keeping open of trade routes into the interior."[13]

The trade thus encouraged and carried on in various parts of West Africa reached wide areas. From the Fish River to Kuka, and from Lagos to Zanzibar, the markets have become great centers of trade, the leading implement to civilization. Permanent markets are found in places like Ujiji and Nyangwe, where everything can be bought and sold from earthenware to wives; from the one to three thousand traders flocked here.

"How like is the market traffic, with all its uproar and sound of human voices, to one of our own markets! There is the same rivalry in praising the goods, the violent, brisk movements, the expressive gesture, the inquiring, searching glance, the changing looks of depreciation or triumph, of apprehension, delight, approbation. So says Stanley. Trade customs are not everywhere alike. If when negotiating with the Bangalas of Angola you do not quickly give them what they want, they go away and do not come back. Then perhaps they try to get possession of the coveted object by means of theft. It is otherwise with the Songos and Kiokos, who let you deal with them in the usual way. To buy even a small article you must go to the market; people avoid trading anywhere else. If a man says to another; 'Sell me this hen' or 'that fruit,' the answer as a rule will be, 'Come to the market place.' The crowd gives confidence to individuals, and the inviolability of the visitor to the market, and of the market itself, looks like an idea of justice consecrated by long practice. Does not this remind us of the old Germanic 'market place'?"[14]

Turning now to Negro family and social life we find, as among all primitive peoples, polygamy and marriage by actual or simulated purchase. Out of the family develops the typical African village organization, which is thus described in Ashanti by a native Gold Coast writer: "The headman, as his name implies, is the head of a village community, a ward in a township, or of a family. His position is important, inasmuch as he has directly to deal with the composite elements of the general bulk of the people.

"It is the duty of the head of a family to bring up the members thereof in the way they should go; and by 'family' you must understand the entire lineal descendants of a materfamilias, if I may coin a convenient phrase. It is expected of him by the state to bring up his charge in the knowledge of matters political and traditional. It is his work to train up his wards in the ways of loyalty and obedience to the powers that be. He is held responsible for the freaks of recalcitrant members of his family, and he is looked to to keep them within bounds and to insist upon conformity of their party with the customs, laws, and traditional observances of the community. In early times he could send off to exile by sale a troublesome relative who would not observe the laws of the community.

"It is a difficult task that he is set to, but in this matter he has all-powerful helpers in the female members of the family, who will be either the aunts, or the sisters, or the cousins, or the nieces of the headman; and as their interests are identical with his in every particular, the good women spontaneously train up their children to implicit obedience to the headman, whose rule in the family thus becomes a simple and an easy matter. 'The hand that rocks the cradle rules the world.' What a power for good in the native state system would the mothers of the Gold Coast and Ashanti become by judicious training upon native lines!

"The headman is par excellence the judge of his family or ward. Not only is he called upon to settle domestic squabbles, but frequently he sits judge over more serious matters arising between one member of the ward and another; and where he is a man of ability and influence, men from other wards bring him their disputes to settle. When he so settles disputes, he is entitled to a hearing fee, which, however, is not so much as would be payable in the regular court of the king or chief.

"The headman is naturally an important member of his company and often is a captain thereof. When he combines the two offices of headman and captain, he renders to the community a very important service. For in times of war, where the members of the ward would not serve cordially under a stranger, they would in all cases face any danger with their own kinsman as their leader. The headman is always succeeded by his uterine brother, cousin, or nephew—the line of succession, that is to say, following the customary law."[15]

We may contrast this picture with the more warlike Bantus of Southeast Africa. Each tribe lived by itself in a town with from five to fifteen thousand inhabitants, surrounded by gardens of millet, beans, and watermelon. Beyond these roamed their cattle, sheep, and goats. Their religion was ancestor worship with sacrifice to spirits and the dead, and some of the tribes made mummies of the corpses and clothed them for burial. They wove cloth of cotton and bark, they carved wood and built walls of unhewn stone. They had a standing military organization, and the tribes had their various totems, so that they were known as the Men of Iron, the Men of the Sun, the Men of the Serpents, Sons of the Corn Cleaners, and the like. Their system of common law was well conceived and there were organized tribunals of justice. In difficult cases precedents were sought and learned antiquaries consulted. At the age of fifteen or sixteen the boys were circumcised and formed into guilds. The land was owned by the tribe and apportioned to the chief by each family, and the main wealth of the tribe was in its cattle.

In general, among the African clans the idea of private property was but imperfectly developed and never included land. The main mass of visible wealth belonged to the family and clan rather than to the individual; only in the matter of weapons and ornaments was exclusive private ownership generally recognized.

The government, vested in fathers and chiefs, varied in different tribes from absolute despotisms to limited monarchies, almost republican. Viewing the Basuto National Assembly in South Africa, Lord Bryce recently wrote, "The resemblance to the primary assemblies of the early peoples of Europe is close enough to add another to the arguments which discredit the theory that there is any such thing as an Aryan type of institutions."[16]

While women are sold into marriage throughout Africa, nevertheless their status is far removed from slavery. In the first place the tracing of relationships through the female line, which is all but universal in Africa, gives the mother great influence. Parental affection is very strong, and throughout Negro Africa the mother is the most influential councilor, even in cases of tyrants like Chaka or Mutesa.

"No mother can love more tenderly or be more deeply beloved than the Negro mother. Robin tells of a slave in Martinique who, with his savings, freed his mother instead of himself. 'Everywhere in Africa,' writes Mungo Park, 'I have noticed that no greater affront can be offered a Negro than insulting his mother. 'Strike me,' cried a Mandingo to his enemy, 'but revile not my mother!' . . . The Herero swears 'By my mother's tears!' . . . The Angola Negroes have a saying, 'As a mist lingers on the swamps, so lingers the love of father and mother.'"[17]

Black queens have often ruled African tribes. Among the Ba-Lolo, we are told, women take part in public assemblies where all-important questions are discussed. The system of educating children among such tribes as the Yoruba is worthy of emulation by many more civilized peoples.

Close knit with the family and social organization comes the religious life of the Negro. The religion of Africa is the universal animism or fetishism of primitive peoples, rising to polytheism and approaching monotheism chiefly, but not wholly, as a result of Christian and Islamic missions. Of fetishism there is much misapprehension. It is not mere senseless degradation. It is a philosophy of life. Among primitive Negroes there can be, as Miss Kingsley reminds us, no such divorce of religion from practical life as is common in civilized lands. Religion is life, and fetish an expression of the practical recognition of dominant forces in which the Negro lives. To him all the world is spirit. Miss Kingsley says, "If you want, for example, to understand the position of man in nature according to fetish, there is, as far as I know, no clearer statement of it made than is made by Goethe in his superb 'Prometheus.'"[18] Fetish is a severely logical way of accounting for the world in terms of good and malignant spirits.

"It is this power of being able logically to account for everything that is, I believe, at the back of the tremendous permanency of fetish in Africa, and the cause of many of the relapses into it by Africans converted to other religions; it is also the explanation of the fact that white men who live in the districts where death and danger are everyday affairs, under a grim pall of boredom, are liable to believe in fetish, though ashamed of so doing. For the African, whose mind has been soaked in fetish during his early and most impressionable years, the voice of fetish is almost irresistible when affliction comes to him."[19]

Ellis tells us of the spirit belief of the Ewe people, who believe that men and all nature have the indwelling "Kra," which is immortal; that the man himself after death may exist as a ghost, which is often conceived of as departed from the "Kra," a shadowy continuing of the man. Bryce, speaking of the Kaffirs of South Africa, says, "To the Kaffirs, as to the most savage races, the world was full of spirits—spirits of the rivers, the mountains, and the woods. Most important were the ghosts of the dead, who had power to injure or help the living, and who were, therefore, propitiated by offerings at stated periods, as well as on occasions when their aid was especially desired. This kind of worship, the worship once most generally diffused throughout the world, and which held its ground among the Greeks and Italians in the most flourishing period of ancient civilization, as it does in China and Japan to-day, was, and is, virtually the religion of the Kaffirs."[20]

African religion does not, however, stop with fetish, but, as in the case of other peoples, tends toward polytheism and monotheism. Among the Yoruba, for instance, Frobenius shows that religion and city-state go hand in hand.

"The first experienced glance will here detect the fact that this nation originally possessed a clear and definite organization so duly ordered and so logical that we but seldom meet with its like among all the peoples of the earth. And the basic idea of every clan's progeniture is a powerful God; the legitimate order in which the descendants of a particular clan unite in marriage to found new families, the essential origin of every new-born babe's descent in the founder of its race and its consideration as a part of the God in Chief; the security with which the newly wedded wife not only may, but should, minister to her own God in an unfamiliar home."[21]

The Yoruba have a legend of a dying divinity. "This people . . . give evidence of a generalized system; a theocratic scheme, a well-conceived perceptible organization, reared in rhythmically proportioned manner."

Miss Kingsley says, "The African has a great Over God."[22] Nassau, the missionary, declares, "After more than forty years' residence among these tribes, fluently using their language, conversant with their customs, dwelling intimately in their huts, associating with them in the various relations of teacher, pastor, friend, master, fellow-traveler, and guest, and in my special office as missionary, searching after their religious thought (and therefore being allowed a deeper entrance into the arcana of their soul than would be accorded to a passing explorer), I am able unhesitatingly to say that among all the multitude of degraded ones with whom I have met, I have seen or heard of none whose religious thought was only a superstition.

"Standing in the village street, surrounded by a company whom their chief has courteously summoned at my request, when I say to him, 'I have come to speak to your people,' I do not need to begin by telling them that there is a God. Looking on that motley assemblage of villagers,—the bold, gaunt cannibal with his armament of gun, spear, and dagger; the artisan with rude adze in hand, or hands soiled at the antique bellows of the village smithy; women who have hasted from their kitchen fire with hands white with the manioc dough or still grasping the partly scaled fish; and children checked in their play with tiny bow and arrow or startled from their dusty street pursuit of dog or goat,—I have yet to be asked, 'Who is God?'"[23]

The basis of Egyptian religion was "of a purely Nigritian character,"[24] and in its developed form Sudanese tribal gods were invoked and venerated by the priests. In Upper Egypt, near the confines of Ethiopia, paintings repeatedly represent black priests conferring on red Egyptian priests the instruments and symbols of priesthood. In the Sudan to-day Frobenius distinguishes four principal religions: first, earthly ancestor worship; next, the social cosmogony of the Atlantic races; third, the religion of the Bori, and fourth, Islam. The Bori religion spreads from Nubia as far as the Hausa, and from Lake Chad in the Niger as far as the Yoruba. It is the religion of possession and has been connected by some with Asiatic influences.

From without have come two great religious influences, Islam and Christianity. Islam came by conquest, trade, and proselytism. As a conqueror it reached Egypt in the seventh century and had by the end of the fourteenth century firm footing in the Egyptian Sudan. It overran the central Sudan by the close of the seventeenth century, and at the beginning of the nineteenth century had swept over Senegambia and the whole valley of the Niger down to the Gulf of Guinea. On the east Islam approached as a trader in the eighth century; it spread into Somaliland and overran Nubia in the fourteenth century. To-day Islam dominates Africa north of ten degrees north latitude and is strong between five and ten degrees north latitude. In the east it reaches below the Victoria Nyanza.

Christianity early entered Africa; indeed, as Mommsen says, "It was through Africa that Christianity became the religion of the world. Tertullian and Cyprian were from Carthage, Arnobius from Sicca Veneria, Lactantius, and probably in like manner Minucius Felix, in spite of their Latin names, were natives of Africa, and not less so Augustine. In Africa the Church found its most zealous confessors of the faith and its most gifted defenders."[25]

The Africa referred to here, however, was not Negroland, but Africa above the desert, where Negro blood was represented in the ancient Mediterranean race and by intercourse across the desert. On the other hand Christianity was early represented in the valley of the Nile under "the most holy pope and patriarch of the great city of Alexandria and of all of the land of Egypt, of Jerusalem, the holy city, of Nubia, Abyssinia, and Pentapolis, and all the preaching of St. Mark." This patriarchate had a hundred bishoprics in the fourth century and included thousands of black Christians. Through it the Cross preceded the Crescent in some of the remotest parts of black Africa.

All these beginnings were gradually overthrown by Islam except among the Copts in Egypt, and in Abyssinia. The Portuguese in the sixteenth century began to replant the Christian religion and for a while had great success, both on the east and west coasts. Roman Catholic enterprise halted in the eighteenth century and the Protestants began. To-day the west coast is studded with English and German missions, South Africa is largely Christian through French and English influence, and the region about the Great Lakes is becoming christianized. The Roman Catholics have lately increased their activities, and above all the Negroes of America have entered with their own churches and with the curiously significant "Ethiopian" movement.

Coming now to other spiritual aspects of African culture, we can speak at present only in a fragmentary way. Roughly speaking, Africa can be divided into two language zones: north of the fifth degree of north latitude is the zone of diversity, with at least a hundred groups of widely divergent languages; south of the line there is one minor language (Bushman-Hottentot), spoken by less than fifty thousand people, and elsewhere the predominant Bantu tongue with its various dialects, spoken by at least fifty million. The Bantu tongue, which thus rules all Central, West, and South Africa, is an agglutinative tongue which makes especial use of prefixes. The hundreds of Negro tongues or dialects in the north represent most probably the result of war and migration and the breaking up of ancient centers of culture. In Abyssinia and the great horn of East Africa the influence of Semitic tongues is noted. Despite much effort on the part of students, it has been impossible to show any Asiatic origin for the Egyptian language. As Sergi maintains, "everything favors an African origin."[26] The most brilliant suggestion of modern days links together the Egyptian of North Africa and the Hottentot and Bushmen tongues of South Africa.

Language was reduced to writing among the Egyptians and Ethiopians and to some extent elsewhere in Africa. Over 100 manuscripts of Ethiopian and Ethiopic-Arabian literature are extant, including a version of the Bible and historical chronicles. The Arabic was used as the written tongue of the Sudan, and Negroland has given us in this tongue many chronicles and other works of black authors. The greatest of these, the Epic of the Sudan (Tarikh-es-Soudan), deserves to be placed among the classics of all literature. In other parts of Africa there was no written language, but there was, on the other hand, an unusual perfection of oral tradition through bards, and extraordinary efficiency in telegraphy by drum and horn.

The folklore and proverbs of the African tribes are exceedingly rich. Some of these have been made familiar to English writers through the work of "Uncle Remus." Others have been collected by Johnston, Ellis, and Theal.

A black bard of our own day has described the onslaught of the Matabili in poetry of singular force and beauty:

> They saw the clouds ascend from the plains:
> It was the smoke of burning towns.
>   The confusion of the whirlwind
> Was in the heart of the great chief of the blue-colored cattle.
>   The shout was raised,
>   "They are friends!"
>   But they shouted again,
>   "They are foes!"
> Till their near approach proclaimed them Matabili.
>   The men seized their arms,
> And rushed out as if to chase the antelope.
>   The onset was as the voice of lightning,
> And their javelins as the shaking of the forest in the autumn storm.[27]

There can be no doubt of the Negro's deep and delicate sense of beauty in form, color, and sound. Soyaux says of African industry, "Whoever denies to them independent invention and individual taste in their work either shuts his eyes intentionally before perfectly evident facts, or lack of knowledge renders him an incompetent judge."[28] M. Rutot had lately told us how the Negro race brought art and sculpture to pre-historic Europe. The bones of the European Negroids are almost without exception found in company with drawings and sculpture in high and low relief; some of their sculptures, like the Wellendorff "Venus," are unusually well finished for primitive man. So, too, the painting and carving of the Bushmen and their forerunners in South Africa has drawn the admiration of students. The Negro has been prolific in the invention of musical instruments and has given a new and original music to the western world.

Schweinfurth, who has preserved for us much of the industrial art of the Negroes, speaks of their delight in the production of works of art for the embellishment and convenience of life. Frobenius expressed his astonishment at the originality of the African in the Yoruba temple which he visited. "The lofty veranda was divided from the passageway by fantastically carved and colored pillars. On the pillars were sculptured knights, men climbing trees, women, gods, and mythical beings. The dark chamber lying beyond showed a splendid red room with stone hatchets, wooden figures, cowry beads, and jars. The whole picture, the columns carved in colors in front of the colored altar, the old man sitting in the circle of those who reverenced him, the open scaffolding of ninety rafters, made a magnificent impression."[29]

The Germans have found, in Kamarun, towns built, castellated, and fortified in a manner that reminds one of the prehistoric cities of Crete. The buildings and fortifications of Zymbabwe have already been described and something has been said of the art of Benin, with its brass and bronze and ivory. All the work of Benin in bronze and brass was executed by casting, and by methods so complicated that it would be no easy task for a modern European craftsman to imitate them.

Perhaps no race has shown in its earlier development a more magnificent art impulse than the Negro, and the student must not forget how far Negro genius entered into the art in the valley of the Nile from Meroe and Nepata down to the great temples of Egypt.

Frobenius has recently directed the world's attention to art in West Africa. Quartz and granite he found treated with great dexterity. But more magnificent than the stone monument is the proof that at some remote era glass was made and molded in Yorubaland and that the people here were brilliant in the production of terra-cotta images. The great mass of potsherds, lumps of glass, heaps of slag, etc., "proves, at all events, that the glass industry flourished in this locality in ages past. It is plain that the glass beads found to have been so very common in Africa were not only not imported, but were actually manufactured in great quantities at home."

The terra-cotta pieces are "remains of another ancient and fine type of art" and were "eloquent of a symmetry, a vitality, a delicacy of form, and practically a reminiscence of the ancient Greeks." The antique bronze head Frobenius describes as "a head of marvelous beauty, wonderfully cast," and "almost equal in beauty and, at least, no less noble in form, and as ancient as the terra-cotta heads."[30]

In a park of monuments Frobenius saw the celebrated forge and hammer: a mighty mass of iron, like a falling drop in shape, and a block of quartz fashioned like a drum. Frobenius thinks these were relics dating from past ages of culture, when the manipulation of quartz and granite was thoroughly understood and when iron manipulation gave evidence of a skill not met with to-day.

Even when we contemplate such revolting survivals of savagery as cannibalism we cannot jump too quickly at conclusions. Cannibalism is spread over many parts of Negro Africa, yet the very tribes who practice cannibalism show often other traits of industry and power. "These cannibal Bassonga were, according to the types we met with, one of those rare nations of the African interior which can be classed with the most esthetic and skilled, most discreet and intelligent of all those generally known to us as the so-called natural races. Before the Arabic and European invasion they did not dwell in 'hamlets,' but in towns with twenty or thirty thousand inhabitants, in towns whose highways were shaded by avenues of splendid palms planted at regular intervals and laid out with the symmetry of colonnades. Their pottery would be fertile in suggestion to every art craftsman in Europe. Their weapons of iron were so perfectly fashioned that no industrial art from abroad could improve upon their workmanship. The iron blades were cunningly ornamented with damascened copper, and the hilts artistically inlaid with the same metal. Moreover, they were most industrious and capable husbandmen, whose careful tillage of the suburbs made them able competitors of any gardener in Europe. Their sexual and parental relations evidenced an amount of tact and delicacy of feelings unsurpassed among ourselves, either in the simplicity of the country or the refinements of the town. Originally their political and municipal system was organized on the lines of a representative republic. True, it is on record that these well-governed towns often waged an internecine warfare; but in spite of this it had been their invariable custom from time immemorial, even in times of strife, to keep the trade routes open and to allow their own and foreign merchants to go their ways unharmed. And the commerce of these nations ebbed and flowed along a road of unknown age, running from Itimbiri to Batubenge, about six hundred miles in length. This highway was destroyed by the 'missionaries of civilization' from Arabia only toward the close of the eighteenth century. But even in my own time there were still smiths who knew the names of places along that wonderful trade route driven through the heart of the 'impenetrable forests of the Congo.' For every scrap of imported iron was carried over it."[31]

In disposition the Negro is among the most lovable of men. Practically all the great travelers who have spent any considerable time in Africa testify to this and pay deep tribute to the kindness with which they were received. One has but to remember the classic story of Mungo Park, the strong expressions of Livingstone, the words of Stanley and hundreds of others to realize this.

Ceremony and courtesy mark Negro life. Livingstone again and again reminds us of "true African dignity." "When Ilifian men or women salute each other, be it with a plain and easy curtsey (which is here the simplest form adopted), or kneeling down, or throwing oneself upon the ground, or kissing the dust with one's forehead, no matter which, there is yet a deliberateness, a majesty, a dignity, a devoted earnestness in the manner of its doing, which brings to light with every gesture, with every fold of clothing, the deep significance and essential import of every single action. Everyone may, without too greatly straining his attention, notice the very striking precision and weight with which the upper and lower native classes observe these niceties of intercourse."[32]

All this does not mean that the African Negro is not human with the all-too-well-known foibles of humanity. Primitive life among them is, after all, as bare and cruel as among primitive Germans or Chinese, but it is not more so, and the more we study the Negro the more we realize that we are dealing with a normal human stock which under reasonable conditions has developed and will develop in the same lines as other men. Why is it, then, that so much of misinformation and contempt is widespread concerning Africa and its people, not simply among the unthinking mass, but among men of education and knowledge?

One reason lies undoubtedly in the connotation of the term "Negro." In North America a Negro may be seven-eights white, since the term refers to any person of Negro descent. If we use the term in the same sense concerning the inhabitants of the rest of world, we may say truthfully that Negroes have been among the leaders of civilization in every age of the world's history from ancient Babylon to modern America; that they have contributed wonderful gifts in art, industry, political organization, and religion, and that they are doing the same to-day in all parts of the world.

In sharp contrast to this usage the term "Negro" in Africa has been more and more restricted until some scientists, late in the last century, declared that the great mass of the black and brown people of Africa were not Negroes at all, and that the "real" Negro dwells in a small space between the Niger and the Senegal. Ratzel says, "If we ask what justifies so narrow a limitation, we find that the hideous Negro type, which the fancy of observers once saw all over Africa, but which, as Livingstone says, is really to be seen only as a sign in front of tobacco shops, has on closer inspection evaporated from all parts of Africa, to settle no one knows how in just this region. If we understand that an extreme case may have been taken for the genuine and pure form, even so we do not comprehend the ground of its geographical limitation and location; for wherever dark, woolly-haired men dwell, this ugly type also crops up. We are here in the presence of a refinement of science which to an unprejudiced eye will hardly hold water."[33]

In this restricted sense the Negro has no history, culture, or ability, for the simple fact that such human beings as have history and evidence culture and ability are not Negroes! Between these two extreme definitions, with unconscious adroitness, the most extraordinary and contradictory conclusions have been reached.

Let it therefore be said, once for all, that racial inferiority is not the cause of anti-Negro prejudice. Boaz, the anthropologist, says, "An unbiased estimate of the anthropological evidence so far brought forward does not permit us to countenance the belief in a racial inferiority which would unfit an individual of the Negro race to take his part in modern civilization. We do not know of any demand made on the human body or mind in modern life that anatomical or ethnological evidence would prove to be beyond the powers of the Negro."[34]

"We have every reason to suppose that all races are capable, under proper guidance, of being fitted into the complex scheme of our modern civilization, and the policy of artificially excluding them from its benefits is as unjustifiable scientifically as it is ethically abhorrent."[35] What is, then, this so-called "instinctive" modern prejudice against black folk?

Lord Bryce says of the intermingling of blacks and whites in South America, "The ease with which the Spaniards have intermingled by marriage with the Indian tribes—and the Portuguese have done the like, not only with the Indians, but with the more physically dissimilar Negroes—shows that race repugnance is no such constant and permanent factor in human affairs as members of the Teutonic peoples are apt to assume. Instead of being, as we Teutons suppose, the rule in the matter, we are rather the exception, for in the ancient world there seems to have been little race repulsion."

In nearly every age and land men of Negro descent have distinguished themselves. In literature there is Terence in Rome, Nosseyeb and Antar in Arabia, Es-Sa'di in the Sudan, Pushkin in Russia, Dumas in France, Al Kanemi in Spain, Heredia in the West Indies, and Dunbar in the United States, not to mention the alleged Negro strain in Æsop and Robert Browning. As rulers and warriors we remember such Negroes as Queen Nefertari and Amenhotep III among many others in Egypt; Candace and Ergamenes in Ethiopia; Mansa Musa, Sonni Ali, and Mohammed Askai in the Sudan; Diaz in Brazil, Toussaint L'Ouverture in Hayti, Hannivalov in Russia, Sakanouye Tamuramaro in Japan, the elder Dumas in France, Cazembe and Chaka among the Bantu, and Menelik, of Abyssinia; the numberless black leaders of India, and the mulatto strain of Alexander Hamilton. In music and art we recall Bridgewater, the friend of Beethoven, and the unexplained complexion of Beethoven's own father; Coleridge-Taylor in England, Tanner in America, Gomez in Spain; Ira Aldridge, the actor, and Johnson, Cook, and Burleigh, who are making the new American syncopated music. In the Church we know that Negro blood coursed in the veins of many of the Catholic African fathers, if not in certain of the popes; and there were in modern days Benoit of Palermo, St. Benedict, Bishop Crowther, the Mahdi who drove England from the Sudan, and Americans like Allen, Lot Carey, and Alexander Crummell. In science, discovery, and invention the Negroes claim Lislet Geoffroy of the French Academy, Latino and Amo, well known in European university circles; and in America the explorers Dorantes and Henson; Banneker, the almanac maker; Wood, the telephone improver; McCoy, inventor of modern lubrication; Matseliger, who revolutionized shoemaking. Here are names representing all degrees of genius and talent from the mediocre to the highest, but they are strong human testimony to the ability of this race.

We must, then, look for the origin of modern color prejudice not to physical or cultural causes, but to historic facts. And we shall find the answer in modern Negro slavery and the slave trade.

NOTES

1. "Some authors write that the Ethiopians paint the devil white, in disdain of our complexions." —Ludolf: *History of Ethiopia*, p. 72.
2. Ripley: *Races of Europe*, pp. 58, 62.
3. Denniker: *Races of Men*, p. 63.
4. G. Finot: *Race Prejudice*. F. Herz: *Moderne Rassentheorien*.
5. Ratzel: quoted in Spiller: *Inter-Racial Problems*, p. 31.
6. Spiller: *Inter-Racial Problems*, p. 35.
7. Ratzel: *History of Mankind*, II, 380 ff.
8. *Industrial Evolution*, p. 47.
9. These and other references in this chapter are from Schneider: *Culturfähigkeit des Negers*.
10. Atlanta University Leaflet, No. 19.
11. *Journal of the Royal Anthropological Institute*, XLIII, 414, 415. Cf. also *The Crisis*, Vol. IX, p. 234.
12. Bücher: *Industrial Revolution* (tr. by Wickett), pp. 57–58.
13. Hayford: *Native Institutions*, pp. 95–96.
14. Ratzel, II, 376.
15. Hayford: *Native Institutions*, pp. 76 ff.
16. *Impressions of South Africa*, 3d ed., p. 352.
17. William Schneider.
18. *West African Studies*, Chap. V.
19. *Op. cit.*
20. *Impressions of South Africa*.
21. Frobenius: *Voice of Africa*, Vol. I.
22. *West African Studies*, p. 107.
23. Nassau: *Fetishism in West Africa*, p. 36.
24. *Encyclopædia Britannica*, 9th ed., XX, 362.
25. *The African Provinces*, II, 345.
26. *Mediterranean Race*, p. 10.
27. Stowe: *Native Races*, etc., pp. 553–554.
28. Quoted in Schneider.

29. Frobenius: *Voice of Africa*, Vol. I, Chap. XIV.
30. Frobenius: *Voice of Africa*, Vol. I.
31. Frobenius: *Voice of Africa*, I, 14–15.
32. Frobenius: *Voice of Africa*, I, 272.
33. Ratzel: *History of Mankind*, II, 313.
34. Atlanta University Publications, No. 11.
35. Robert Lowie in the *New Review*, Sept., 1914.

CHAPTER IX

◆

The Trade in Men

Color was never a badge of slavery in the ancient or medieval world, nor has it been in the modern world outside of Christian states. Homer sings of a black man, a "reverend herald"

> Of visage solemn, sad, but sable hue,
> Short, woolly curls, o'erfleeced his bending head, . . .
> Eurybiates, in whose large soul alone,
> Ulysses viewed an image of his own.

Greece and Rome had their chief supplies of slaves from Europe and Asia. Egypt enslaved races of all colors, and if there were more blacks than others among her slaves, there were also more blacks among her nobles and Pharaohs, and both facts are explained by her racial origin and geographical position. The fall of Rome led to a cessation of the slave trade, but after a long interval came the white slave trade of the Saracens and Moors, and finally the modern trade in Negroes.

Slavery as it exists universally among primitive people is a system whereby captives in war are put to tasks about the homes and in the fields, thus releasing the warriors for systematic fighting and the women for leisure. Such slavery has been common among all peoples and was wide-spread in Africa. The relative number of African slaves under these conditions was small and the labor not hard; they were members of the family and might and did often rise to high position in the tribe.

Remembering that in the fifteenth century there was no great disparity between the civilization of Negroland and that of Europe, what made the striking difference in subsequent development? European civilization, cut off by physical barriers from further incursions of barbaric races, settled more and more to systematic industry and to the domination of one religion; African culture and industries were threatened by powerful barbarians from the west and central regions of the continent and by the Moors in the north, and Islam had only partially converted the leading peoples.

When, therefore, a demand for workmen arose in America, European exportation was limited by religious ties and economic stability. African exportation was encouraged not simply by the Christian attitude toward heathen, but also by the Moslem enmity toward the unconverted Negroes. Two great modern religions, therefore, agreed at least in the policy of enslaving heathen blacks, while the overthrow of black Askias by the Moors at Tenkadibou brought that economic chaos among the advanced Negro peoples and movement among the more barbarous tribes which proved of prime advantage to the development of a systematic trade in men.

The modern slave trade began with the Mohammedan conquests in Africa, when heathen Negroes were seized to supply the harems, and as soldiers and servants. They were bought from the masters and seized in war, until the growing wealth and luxury of the conquerors demanded larger numbers. Then Negroes from the Egyptian Sudan, Abyssinia, and Zanzibar began to pass into Arabia, Persia, and India in increased numbers. As Negro kingdoms and tribes rose to power they found the slave trade lucrative and natural, since the raids in which slaves were captured were ordinary inter-tribal wars. It was not until the eighteenth and nineteenth centuries that the demand for slaves in Christian lands made slaves the object, and not the incident, of African wars.

In Mohammedan countries there were gleams of hope in slavery. In fiction and in truth the black slave had a chance. Once converted to Islam, he became a brother to the best, and the brotherhood of the faith was not the sort of idle lie that Christian slave masters made it. In Arabia black leaders arose like Antar; in India black slaves carved out principalities where their descendants still rule.

Some Negro slaves were brought to Europe by the Spaniards in the fourteenth century, and a small trade was continued by the Portuguese, who conquered territory from the "tawny" Moors of North Africa in the early fifteenth century. Later, after their severe repulse at Al-Kasr-Al-Kabu, the Portuguese began to creep down the west coast in quest of trade. They reached the River of Gold in 1441, and their story is that their leader seized certain free Moors and the next year exchanged them for ten black slaves, a target of hide, ostrich eggs, and some gold dust. The trade was easily justified on the ground that the Moors were Mohammedans and refused to be converted to Christianity, while heathen Negroes would be better subjects for conversion and stronger laborers. In the next few years a small number of Negroes continued to be imported into Spain and Portugal as servants. We find, for instance, in 1474, that Negro slaves were common in Seville. There is a letter from Ferdinand and Isabella in the year 1474 to a celebrated Negro, Juan de Valladolid, commonly called the "Negro Count" (El Conde Negro), nominating him to the office of "mayoral of the Negroes" in Seville. The slaves were apparently treated kindly, allowed to keep their own dances and festivals, and to have their own chief, who represented them in the courts, as against their own masters, and settled their private quarrels.

Between 1455 and 1492 little mention is made of slaves in the trade with Africa. Columbus is said to have suggested Negroes for America, but Ferdinand and Isabella refused. Nevertheless, by 1501, we have the first incidental mention of Negroes going to America in a declaration that Negro slaves "born in the power of Christians were to be allowed to pass to the Indies, and the officers of the royal revenue were to receive the money to be paid for their permits."

About 1501 Ovando, Governor of Spanish America, was objecting to Negro slaves and "solicited that no Negro slaves should be sent to Hispaniola, for they fled amongst the Indians and taught them bad customs, and never could be captured." Nevertheless a letter from the king to Ovando, dated Segovia, the fifteenth of September, 1505, says, "I will send more Negro slaves as you request; I think there may be a hundred. At each time a trustworthy person will go with them who may have some share in the gold they may collect and may promise them ease if they work well."[1] There is a record of a hundred slaves being sent out this very year, and Diego Columbus was notified of fifty to be sent from Seville for the mines in 1510.

After this time frequent notices show that Negroes were common in the new world.[2] When Pizarro, for instance, had been slain in Peru, his body was dragged to the cathedral by two Negroes. After the battle of Anaquito the head of the viceroy was cut off by a Negro, and during the great earthquake in Guatemala a most remarkable figure was a gigantic Negro seen in various parts of the city. Nunez had thirty Negroes with him on the top of the Sierras, and there was rumor of an aboriginal tribe of Negroes in South America. One of the last acts of King Ferdinand was to urge that no more Negroes be sent to the West Indies, but under Charles V, Bishop Las Casas drew up a plan of assisted migration to America and asked in 1517 the right for immigrants to import twelve Negro slaves, in return for which the Indians were to be freed.

Las Casas, writing in his old age, owns his error: "This advice that license should be given to bring Negro slaves to these lands, the Clerigo Casas first gave, not considering the injustice with which the Portuguese take them and make them slaves; which advice, after he had apprehended the nature of the thing, he would not have given for all he had in the world. For he always held that they had been made slaves unjustly and tyrannically; for the same reason holds good of them as of the Indians."[3]

As soon as the plan was broached a Savoyard, Lorens de Gomenot, Governor of Bresa, obtained a monopoly of this proposed trade and shrewdly sold it to the Genoese for twenty-five thousand ducats. Other monopolies were granted in 1523, 1527, and 1528.[4] Thus the American trade became established and gradually grew, passing successively into the hands of the Portuguese, the Dutch, the French, and the English.

At first the trade was of the same kind and volume as that already passing northward over the desert routes. Soon, however, the American trade developed. A strong, unchecked demand for brute labor in the West Indies and on the continent of America grew until it culminated in the eighteenth century, when Negro slaves were crossing the Atlantic at the rate of fifty to one hundred thousand a year. This called for slave raiding on a scale that drew upon every part of Africa—upon the west coast, the western and Egyptian Sudan, the valley of the Congo, Abyssinia, the lake regions, the east coast, and Madagascar. Not simply the degraded and weaker types of Negroes were seized, but the strong Bantu, the Mandingo and Songhay, the Nubian and Nile Negroes, the Fula, and even the Asiatic Malay, were represented in the raids.

There was thus begun in modern days a new slavery and slave trade. It was different from that of the past, because more and more it came in time to be founded on racial caste, and this caste was made the foundation of a new industrial system. For four hundred years, from 1450 to 1850, European civilization carried on a systematic trade in human beings of such tremendous proportions that the physical, economic, and moral effects are still plainly to be remarked throughout the world. To this must be added the large slave trade of Mussulman lands, which began with the seventh century and raged almost unchecked until the end of the nineteenth century.

These were not days of decadence, but a period that gave the world Shakespeare, Martin Luther, and Raphael, Haroun-al-Raschid and Abraham Lincoln. It was the day of the greatest expansion of two of the world's most pretentious religions and of the beginnings of the modern organization of industry. In the midst of this advance and uplift this slave trade and slavery spread more human misery, inculcated more disrespect for and neglect of humanity, a greater callousness to suffering, and more petty, cruel, human hatred than can well be calculated. We may excuse and palliate it, and write history so as to let men forget it; it remains the most inexcusable and despicable blot on modern human history.

The Portuguese built the first slave-trading fort at Elmina, on the Gold Coast, in 1482, and extended their trade down the west coast and up the east coast. Under them the abominable traffic grew larger and larger, until it became far the most important in money value of all the commerce of the Zambesi basin. There could be no extension of agriculture, no mining, no progress of any kind where it was so extensively carried on.[5]

It was the Dutch, however, who launched the oversea slave trade as a regular institution. They began their fight for freedom from Spain in 1579; in 1595, as a war measure against Spain, who at that time was dominating Portugal, they made their first voyage to Guinea. By 1621 they had captured Portugal's various slave forts on the west coast and they proceeded to open sixteen forts along the coast of the Gulf of Guinea. Ships sailed from Holland to Africa, got slaves in exchange for their goods, carried the slaves to the West Indies or Brazil, and returned home laden with sugar. In 1621 the private companies trading in the west were all merged into the Dutch West India Company, which sent in four years fifteen thousand four hundred and thirty Negroes to Brazil, carried on war with Spain, supplied even the English plantations, and gradually became the great slave carrier of the day.

The commercial supremacy of the Dutch early excited the envy and emulation of the English. The Navigation Ordinance of 1651 was aimed at them, and two wars were necessary to wrest the slave trade from them and place it in the hands of the English. The final terms of peace, among other things, surrendered New Netherlands to England and opened the way for England to become henceforth the world's greatest slave trader.

The English trade began with Sir John Hawkins' voyages in 1562 and later, in which "the Jesus, our chiefe shippe" played a leading part. Desultory trade was kept up by the English until the middle of the seventeenth century, when English chartered slave-trading companies began to appear. In 1662 the "Royal Adventurers," including the king, the queen dowager, and the Duke of York, invested in the trade, and finally the Royal African Company, which became the world's chief slave trader, was formed in 1672 and carried on a growing trade for a quarter of a century. Jamaica had finally been captured and held by Oliver Cromwell in 1655 and formed a West Indian base for the trade in men.

The chief contract for trade in Negroes was the celebrated "Asiento" or agreement of the King of Spain to the importation of slaves into Spanish domains. The Pope's Bull or Demarkation, 1493, debarred Spain from African possessions, and compelled her to contract with other nations for slaves. This contract was in the hands of the Portuguese in 1600; in 1640 the Dutch received it, and in 1701 the French. The War of the Spanish Succession brought this monopoly to England.

This Asiento of 1713 was an agreement between England and Spain by which the latter granted the former a monopoly of the Spanish colonial slave trade for thirty years, and England engaged to supply the colonies within that time with at least one hundred and forty-four thousand slaves at the rate of forty-eight hundred per year. The English counted this prize as the greatest result of the Treaty of Utrecht (1713), which ended the mighty struggle against the power of Louis XIV. The English held the monopoly until the Treaty of Aix-la-Chapelle (1748), although they had to go to war over it in 1739.

From this agreement the slave traders reaped a harvest. The trade centered at Liverpool, and that city's commercial greatness was built largely on this foundation. In 1709 it sent out one slaver of thirty tons' burden; encouraged by Parliamentary subsidies which amounted to nearly half a million dollars between 1729 and 1750, the trade amounted to fifty-three ships in 1751; eighty-six in 1765, and at the beginning of the nineteenth century one hundred and eighty-five, which carried forty-nine thousand two hundred and thirteen slaves in one year.

The slave trade thus begun by the Portuguese, enlarged by the Dutch, and carried to its culmination by the English centered on the west coast near the seat of perhaps the oldest and most interesting culture of Africa. It came at a critical time. The culture of Yoruba, Benin, Mossiland, and Nupe had exhausted itself in a desperate attempt to stem the on-coming flood of Mohammedan culture. It has succeeded in maintaining its small, loosely federated city-states suited to trade, industry, and art. It had developed strong resistance toward the Sudan state builders toward the north, as in the case of the fighting Mossi; but behind this warlike resistance lay the peaceful city life which gave industrial ideas to Byzantium and shared something of Ethiopian and Mediterranean culture.

The first advent of the slave traders increased and encouraged native industry, as is evidenced by the bronze work of Benin; but soon this was pushed into the background, for it was not bronze metal but bronze flesh that Europe wanted. A new tyranny, blood-thirsty, cruel, and built on war, forced itself forward in the Niger delta. The powerful state of Dahomey arose early in the eighteenth century and became a devastating tyranny, reaching its highest power early in the nineteenth century. Ashanti, a similar kingdom, began its conquests in 1719 and grew with the slave trade. Thus state building in West Africa began to replace the city economy, but it was a state built on war and on war supported and encouraged largely for the sake of trade in human flesh. The native industries were changed and disorganized. Family ties and government were weakened. Far into the heart of Africa this devilish disintegration, coupled with Christian rum and Mohammedan raiding, penetrated. The face of Africa was turned south on these slave traders instead of northward toward the Mediterranean, where for two thousand years and more Europe and Africa had met in legitimate trade and mutual respect. The full significance of the battle of Tenkadibou, which overthrew the Askias, was now clear. Hereafter Africa for centuries was to appear before the world, not as the land of gold and ivory, of Mansa Musa and Meroe, but as a bound and captive slave, dumb and degraded.

The natural desire to avoid a painful subject has led historians to gloss over the details of the slave trade and leave the impression that it was a local west-coast phenomenon and confined to a few years. It was, on the contrary, continent wide and centuries long and an economic, social, and political catastrophe probably unparalleled in human history.

The exact proportions of the slave trade can be estimated only approximately. From 1680 to 1688 we know that the English African Company alone sent 249 ships to Africa, shipped there 60,783 Negro slaves, and after losing 14,387 on the middle passage, delivered 46,396 in America.

It seems probable that 25,000 Negroes a year arrived in America between 1698 and 1707. After the Asiento of 1713 this number rose to 30,000 annually, and before the Revolutionary War it had reached at least 40,000 and perhaps 100,000 slaves a year.

The total number of slaves imported is not known. Dunbar estimates that nearly 900,000 came to America in the sixteenth century, 2,750,000 in the seventeenth, 7,000,000 in the eighteenth, and over 4,000,000 in the nineteenth, perhaps 15,000,000 in all. Certainly it seems that at least 10,000,000 Negroes were expatriated. Probably every slave imported represented on the average five corpses in Africa or on the high seas. The American slave trade, therefore, meant the elimination of at least 60,000,000 Negroes from their fatherland. The Mohammedan slave trade meant the expatriation or forcible migration in Africa of nearly as many more. It would be conservative, then, to say that the slave trade cost Negro Africa 100,000,000 souls. And yet people ask to-day the cause of the stagnation of culture in that land since 1600!

Such a large number of slaves could be supplied only by organized slave raiding in every corner of Africa. The African continent gradually became revolutionized. Whole regions were depopulated, whole tribes disappeared; villages were built in caves and on hills or in forest fastnesses; the character of peoples like those of Benin developed their worst excesses of cruelty instead of the already flourishing arts of peace. The dark, irresistible grasp of fetish took firmer hold on men's minds.

Further advances toward civilization became impossible. Not only was there the immense demand for slaves which had its outlet on the west coast, but the slave caravans were streaming up through the desert to the Mediterranean coast and down the valley of the Nile to the centers of Mohammedanism. It was a rape of a continent to an extent never paralleled in ancient or modern times.

In the American trade there was not only the horrors of the slave raid, which lined the winding paths of the African jungles with bleached bones, but there was also the horrors of what was called the "middle passage," that is, the voyage across the Atlantic. As Sir William Dolben said, "The Negroes were chained to each other hand and foot, and stowed so close that they were not allowed above a foot and a half for each in breadth. Thus crammed together like herrings in a barrel, they contracted putrid and fatal disorders; so that they who came to inspect them in a morning had occasionally to pick dead slaves out of their rows, and to unchain their carcases from the bodies of their wretched fellow-sufferers to whom they had been fastened."[6]

It was estimated that out of every one hundred lot shipped from Africa only about fifty lived to be effective laborers across the sea, and among the whites more seamen died in that trade in one year than in the whole remaining trade of England in two. The full realization of the horrors of the slave trade was slow in reaching the ears and conscience of the modern world, just as to-day the treatment of dark natives in European colonies is brought to publicity with the greatest difficulty. The first move against the slave trade in England came in Parliament in 1776, but it was not until thirty-one years later, in 1807, that the trade was banned through the arduous labors of Clarkson, Wilberforce, Sharpe, and others.

Denmark had already abolished the trade, and the United States attempted to do so the following year. Portugal and Spain were induced to abolish the trade between 1815 and 1830. Notwithstanding these laws, the contraband trade went on until the beginning of the Civil War in America. The reasons for this were the enormous profit of the trade and the continued demand of the American slave barons, who had no sympathy with the efforts to stop their source of cheap labor supply.

However, philanthropy was not working alone to overthrow Negro slavery and the slave trade. It was seen, first in England and later in other countries, that slavery as an industrial system could not be made to work satisfactorily in modern times. Its cost was too great, and one of the causes of this cost was the slave insurrections from the very beginning, when the slaves rose on the plantation of Diego Columbus down to the Civil War in America. Actual and potential slave insurrection in the West Indies, in North and South America, kept the slave owners in apprehension and turmoil, or called for a police system difficult to maintain. In North America revolt finally took the form of organized running away to the North, and this, with the growing scarcity of suitable land and the moral revolt, led to the Civil War and the disappearance of the American slave trade.

There was still, however, the Mohammedan slave trade to deal with, and this has been the work of the nineteenth and early twentieth centuries. In the last quarter of the nineteenth century ten thousand slaves annually were being distributed on the southern and eastern coast of the Mediterranean and at the great slave market in Bornu.

On the east coast of Africa in 1862 nineteen thousand slaves were passed into Zanzibar and thence into Arabia and Persia. As late as 1880, three thousand annually were being thus transplanted, but now the trade is about stopped. To-day the only centers of actual slave trading may be said to be the cocoa plantations of the Portuguese Islands on the west coast of Africa, and the Congo Free State.

Such is the story of the Rape of Ethiopia—a sordid, pitiful, cruel tale. Raphael painted, Luther preached, Corneille wrote, and Milton sung; and through it all, for four hundred years, the dark captives wound to the sea amid the bleaching bones of the dead; for four hundred years the sharks followed the scurrying ships; for four hundred years America was strewn with the living and dying millions of a transplanted race; for four hundred years Ethiopia stretched forth her hands unto God.

NOTES

1. Cf. Helps: *Spanish Conquest*, IV, 401.
2. Helps, *op. cit.*, I, 219–220.
3. Helps, *op. cit.*, II, 18–19.
4. Helps, *op. cit.*, III, 211–212.
5. Theal: *History and Ethnography of South Africa before 1795*, I, 476.
6. Ingram: *History of Slavery*, p. 152.

CHAPTER X

◆

The West Indies and
Latin America

That was a wonderful century, the fifteenth, when men realized that beyond the scowling waste of western waters were dreams come true. Curious and yet crassly human it is that, with all this poetry and romance, arose at once the filthiest institution of the modern world and the costliest. For on Negro slavery in America was built, not simply the abortive cotton kingdom, but the foundations of that modern imperialism which is based on the despising of backward men.

According to some accounts Alonzo, "the Negro," piloted one of the ships of Columbus, and certainly there was Negro blood among his sailors. As early as 1528 there were nearly ten thousand Negroes in the new world. We hear of them in all parts. In Honduras, for instance, a Negro is sent to burn a native village; in 1555 the town council of Santiago de Chile voted to allow an enfranchised Negro possession of land in the town, and evidently treated him just as white applicants were treated. D'Allyon, who explored the coast of Virginia in the first quarter of the sixteenth century, used Negro slaves (who afterward revolted) to build his ships and help in exploration; Balboa had with him thirty Negroes, who, in 1513, helped to build the first ships on the Pacific coast; Cortez had three hundred Negro porters in 1522.

Before 1530 there were enough Negroes in Mexico to lead to an insurrection, where the Negroes fought desperately, but were overcome and their ringleaders executed. Later the followers of another Negro insurgent, Bayano, were captured and sent back to Spain. Negroes founded the town of Santiago del Principe in 1570, and in 1540 a Negro slave of Hernandez de Alarcon was the only one of the party to carry a message across the country to the Zunis of New Mexico. A Negro, Stephen Dorantes, discovered New Mexico. This Stephen or "Estevanico" was sent ahead by certain Spanish friars to the "Seven Cities of Cibola." "As soon as Stephen had left said friars, he determined to earn all the reputation and honor for himself, and that the boldness and daring of having alone discovered those villages of high stories so much spoken of throughout that country should be attributed to him; and carrying along with him the people who followed him, he endeavored to cross the wilderness which is between

Cibola and the country he had gone through, and he was so far ahead of the friars that when they arrived at Chichilticalli, which is on the edge of the wilderness, he was already at Cibola, which is eighty leagues of wilderness beyond." But the Indians of the new and strange country took alarm and concluded that Stephen "must be a spy or guide for some nations who intended to come and conquer them, because it seemed to them unreasonable for him to say that the people were white in the country from which he came, being black himself and being sent by them."[1]

Slaves imported under the Asiento treaties went to all parts of the Americas. Spanish America had by the close of the eighteenth century ten thousand in Santo Domingo, eighty-four thousand in Cuba, fifty thousand in Porto Rico, sixty thousand in Louisiana and Florida, and sixty thousand in Central and South America.

The history of the Negro in Spanish America centered in Cuba, Venezuela, and Central America. In the sixteenth century slaves began to arrive in Cuba and Negroes joined many of the exploring expeditions from there to various parts of America. The slave trade greatly increased in the latter part of the eighteenth century, and after the revolution in Hayti large numbers of French emigrants from that island settled in Cuba. This and Spanish greed increased the harshness of slavery and eventually led to revolt among the Negroes. In 1844 Governor O'Donnell began a cruel persecution of the blacks on account of a plot discovered among them. Finally in 1866 the Ten Years' War broke out in which Negro and white rebels joined. They demanded the abolition of slavery and equal political rights for natives and foreigners, whites and blacks. The war was cruel and bloody but ended in 1878 with the abolition of slavery, while a further uprising the following year secured civil rights for Negroes. Spanish economic oppression continued, however, and the leading chiefs of the Ten Years' War including such leaders as the mulatto, Antonio Maceo, with large numbers of Negro soldiers, took the field again in 1895. The result was the freeing of Cuba by the intervention of the United States. Negro regiments from the United States played here a leading role. A number of leaders in Cuba in political, industrial, and literary lines have been men of Negro descent.

Slavery was abolished by Guatemala in 1824 and by Mexico in 1829. Argentine, Peru, Bolivia, Chile, and Paraguay ceased to recognize it about 1825. Between 1840 and 1845 it came to an end in Colombia, Venezuela, and Ecquador. Bolivar, Paez, Sucre, and other South American leaders used Negro soldiers in fighting for freedom (1814–16), and Hayti twice at critical times rendered assistance and received Bolivar twice as a refugee.

Brazil was the center of Portuguese slavery, but slaves were not introduced in large numbers until about 1720, when diamonds were discovered in the territory above Rio Janeiro. Gradually the seaboard from Pernambuco to Rio Janeiro and beyond became filled with Negroes, and although the slave trade north of the equator was theoretically abolished by Portugal in 1815 and south of the equator in 1830, and by Brazil in these regions in 1826 and 1830, nevertheless between 1825 and 1850 over a million and a quarter of Negroes were introduced. Not until Brazil abolished slavery in 1888 did the importation wholly cease. Brazilian slavery allowed the slave to purchase his freedom, and the color line was not strict. Even in the eighteenth century there were black clergy and bishops; indeed the Negro clergy seem to have been on a higher moral level than the whites.

Insurrection was often attempted, especially among the Mohammedan Negroes around Bahia. In 1695 a tribe of revolted slaves held out for a long time. In 1719 a widespread conspiracy failed, but many of the leaders fled to the forest. In 1828 a thousand rose in revolt at Bahia, and again in 1830. From 1831 to 1837 revolt was in the air, and in 1835 came the great revolt of the Mohammedans, who attempted to enthrone a queen. The Negroes fought with furious bravery, but were finally defeated.

By 1872 the number of free Negroes had very greatly increased, so that emancipation did not come as a shock. While Mohammedan Negroes still gave trouble and were in some cases sent back to Africa, yet on the whole emancipation was peaceful, and whites, Negroes, and Indians are to-day amalgamating into a new race. "At the present moment there is scarcely a lowly or a highly placed federal or provincial official at the head of or within any of the great departments of state that has not more or less Negro or Amer-Indian blood in his veins."[2]

Lord Bryce says, "It is hardly too much to say that along the coast from Rio to Bahia and Pernambuco, as well as in parts of the interior behind these two cities, the black population predominates. . . . The Brazilian lower class intermarries freely with the black people; the Brazilian middle class intermarries with mulattoes and Quadroons. Brazil is the one country in the world, besides the Portuguese colonies on the east and west coasts of Africa, in which a fusion of the European and African races is proceeding unchecked by law or custom. The doctrines of human equality and human solidarity have here their perfect work. The result is so far satisfactory that there is little or no class friction. The white man does not lynch or maltreat the Negro; indeed I have never heard of a lynching anywhere in South America except occasionally as part of a political convulsion. The Negro is not accused of insolence and does not seem to develop any more criminality than naturally belongs to any ignorant population with loose notions of morality and property.

"What ultimate effect the intermixture of blood will have on the European element in Brazil I will not venture to predict. If one may judge from a few remarkable cases, it will not necessarily reduce the intellectual standard. One of the ablest and most refined Brazilians I have known had some color; and other such cases have been mentioned to me. Assumptions and preconceptions must be eschewed, however plausible they may seem."[3]

A Brazilian writer said at the First Races Congress: "The coöperation of the metis[4] in the advance of Brazil is notorious and far from inconsiderable. They played the chief part during many years in Brazil in the campaign for the abolition of slavery. I could quote celebrated names of more than one of these metis who put themselves at the head of the literary movement. They fought with firmness and intrepidity in the press and on the platform. They faced with courage the gravest perils to which they were exposed in their struggle against the powerful slave owners, who had the protection of a conservative government. They gave evidence of sentiments of patriotism, self-denial, and appreciation during the long campaign in Paraguay, fighting heroically at the boarding of the ships in the naval battle of Riachuelo and in the attacks on the Brazilian army, on numerous occasions in the course of this long South American war. It was owing to their support that the republic was erected on the ruins of the empire."[5]

The Dutch brought the first slaves to the North American continent. John Rolfe relates that the last of August, 1619, there came to Virginia "a Dutch man of warre that sold us twenty Negars."[6] This was probably one of the ships of the numerous private Dutch trading companies which early entered into the developed and the lucrative African slave trade. Although the Dutch thus commenced the continental slave trade they did not actually furnish a very large number of slaves to the English colonies outside the West Indies. A small trade had by 1698 brought a few thousand to New York and still fewer to New Jersey.

The Dutch found better scope for slaves in Guiana, which they settled in 1616. Sugar cane became the staple crop, but the Negroes early began to revolt and the Dutch brought in East Indian coolies. The slaves were badly treated and the runaways joined the revolted Bush Negroes in the interior. From 1715 to 1775 there was continuous fighting with the Bush Negroes or insurrections, until at last in 1749 a formal treaty between sixteen hundred Negroes and the Dutch was made. Immediately a new group revolted under a Mohammedan, Arabi, and they obtained land and liberty. In 1763 the coast Negroes revolted. They were checked, but made terms and settled in the interior. The Bush Negroes fought against both French and English to save Guiana to the Dutch, but Guiana was eventually divided between the three. The Bush Negroes still maintain their independence and vigor.

The French encouraged settlements in the West Indies in the seventeenth century, but at last, finding that French immigrants would not come, they began about 1642 to import Negroes. Owing to wars with England, slaves were supplied by the Dutch and Portuguese, although the Royal Senegal Company held the coveted Asiento from 1701 to 1713.

It was in the island of Hayti, however, that French slavery centered. Pirates from many nations, but chiefly French, began to frequent the island, and in 1663 the French annexed the eastern part, thus dividing the island between France and Spain. By 1680 there were so many slaves and mulattoes that Louis XIV issued his celebrated Code Noir, which was notable in compelling bachelor masters, fathers of slave children, to marry their concubines. Children followed the condition of the mother as to slavery or freedom; they could have no property; harsh punishments were provided for, but families could not be separated by sale except in the case of grown children; emancipation with full civil rights was made possible for any slave twenty years of age or more. When Louisiana was settled and the Alabama coast, slaves were introduced there. Louisiana was transferred to Spain in 1762, against the resistance of both settlers and slaves, but Spain took possession in 1769 and introduced more Negroes.

Later, in Hayti, a more liberal policy encouraged trade; war was over and capital and slaves poured in. Sugar, coffee, chocolate, indigo, dyes, and spices were raised. There were large numbers of mulattoes, many of whom were educated in France, and many masters married Negro women who had inherited large properties, just as in the United States to-day white men are marrying eagerly the landed Indian women in the West. When white immigration increased in 1749, however, prejudice arose against these mulattoes and severe laws were passed depriving them of civil rights, entrance into the professions, and the right to hold office; severe edicts were enforced as to clothing, names, and social intercourse. Finally, after 1777, mulattoes were forbidden to come to France.

When the French Revolution broke out, the Haytians managed to send two delegates to Paris. Nevertheless the planters maintained the upper hand, and one of the colored delegates, Oge, on returning, started a small rebellion. He and his companions were killed with great brutality. This led the French government to grant full civil rights to free Negroes. Immediately planters and free Negroes flew to arms against each other and then, suddenly, August 22, 1791, the black slaves, of whom there were four hundred and fifty-two thousand, arose in revolt to help the free Negroes.

For many years runaway slaves had hidden in the mountains under their own chiefs. One of the earliest of these chiefs was Polydor, in 1724, who was succeeded by Macandal. The great chief of these runaways or "Maroons" at the time of the slave revolt was Jean François, who was soon succeeded by Biassou.

Pierre Dominic Toussaint, known as Toussaint L'Ouverture, joined these Maroon bands, where he was called "the doctor of the armies of the king," and soon became chief aid to Jean François and Biassou. Upon their deaths Toussaint rose to the chief command. He acquired complete control over the blacks, not only in military matters, but in politics and social organization; "the soldiers regarded him as a superior being, and the farmers prostrated themselves before him. All his generals trembled before him (Dessalines did not dare to look in his face), and all the world trembled before his generals."[7]

The revolt once started, blacks and mulattoes murdered whites without mercy and the whites retaliated. Commissioners were sent from France, who asked simply civil rights for freedmen, and not emancipation. Indeed that was all that Toussaint himself had as yet demanded. The planters intrigued with the British and this, together with the beheading of the king (an impious act in the eyes of Negroes), induced Toussaint to join the Spaniards. In 1793 British troops were landed and the French commissioners in desperation declared the slaves emancipated. This at once won back Toussaint from the Spaniards. He became supreme in the north, while Rigaud, leader of the mulattoes, held the south and the west. By 1798 the British, having lost most of their forces by yellow fever, surrendered Mole St. Nicholas to Toussaint and departed. Rigaud finally left for France, and Toussaint in 1800 was master of Hayti. He promulgated a constitution under which Hayti was to be a self-governing colony; all men were equal before the law, and trade was practically free. Toussaint was to be president for life, with the power to name his successor.

Napoleon Bonaparte, master of France, had at this time dreams of a great American empire, and replied to Toussaint's new government by sending twenty-five thousand men under his brother-in-law to subdue the presumptuous Negroes, as a preliminary step to his occupation and development of the

Mississippi valley. Fierce fighting and yellow fever decimated the French, but matters went hard with the Negroes too, and Toussaint finally offered to yield. He was courteously received with military honors and then, as soon as possible, treacherously seized, bound, and sent to France. He was imprisoned at Fort Joux and died, perhaps of poison, after studied humiliations, April 7, 1803.

Thus perished the greatest of American Negroes and one of the great men of all time, at the age of fifty-six. A French planter said, "God in his terrestrial globe did not commune with a purer spirit."[8] Wendell Phillips said, "Some doubt the courage of the Negro. Go to Hayti and stand on those fifty thousand graves of the best soldiers France ever had and ask them what they think of the Negro's sword. I would call him Napoleon, but Napoleon made his way to empire over broken oaths and through a sea of blood. This man never broke his word. I would call him Cromwell, but Cromwell was only a soldier, and the state he founded went down with him into his grave. I would call him Washington, but the great Virginian held slaves. This man risked his empire rather than permit the slave trade in the humblest village of his dominions. You think me a fanatic, for you read history, not with your eyes, but with your prejudices. But fifty years hence, when Truth gets a hearing, the Muse of history will put Phocion for the Greek, Brutus for the Roman, Hampden for the English, La Fayette for France, choose Washington as the bright, consummate flower of our earlier civilization, then, dipping her pen in the sunlight, will write in the clear blue, above them all, the name of the soldier, the statesman, the martyr, Toussaint L'Ouverture."

The treacherous killing of Toussaint did not conquer Hayti. In 1802 and 1803 some forty thousand French soldiers died of war and fever. A new colored leader, Dessalines, arose and all the eight thousand remaining French surrendered to the blockading British fleet.

The effect of all this was far-reaching. Napoleon gave up his dream of American empire and sold Louisiana for a song. "Thus, all of Indian Territory, all of Kansas and Nebraska and Iowa and Wyoming and Montana and the Dakotas, and most of Colorado and Minnesota, and all of Washington and Oregon states, came to us as the indirect work of a despised Negro. Praise, if you will, the work of a Robert Livingstone or a Jefferson, but to-day let us not forget our debt to Toussaint L'Ouverture, who was indirectly the means of America's expansion by the Louisiana Purchase of 1803."[9]

With the freedom of Hayti in 1801 came a century of struggle to fit the people for the freedom they had won. They were yet slaves, crushed by a cruel servitude, without education or religious instruction. The Haytian leaders united upon Dessalines to maintain the independence of the republic. Dessalines, like Toussaint and his lieutenant Christophe, was noted in slavery days for his severity toward his fellows and the discipline which he insisted on. He had other characteristics of African chieftains. "There were seasons when he broke through his natural sullenness and showed himself open, affable, and even generous. His vanity was excessive and manifested itself in singular perversities."[10] He was a man of great personal bravery and succeeded in maintaining the independence of Hayti, which had already cost the Frenchmen fifty thousand lives.

On January 1, 1804, at the place whence Toussaint had been treacherously seized and sent to France, the independence of Hayti was declared by the military leaders. Dessalines was made governor-general for life and afterward proclaimed himself emperor. This was not an act of grandiloquence and mimicry. "It is truer to say that in it both Dessalines and later Christophe were actuated by a clear insight into the social history and peculiarities of their people. There was nothing in the constitution which did not have its companion in Africa, where the organization of society was despotic, with elective hereditary chiefs, royal families, polygamic marriages, councils, and regencies."[11]

The population was divided into soldiers and laborers. The territory was parceled out to chiefs, and the laborers were bound to the soil and worked under rigorous inspection; part of the products were reserved for their support, and the rest went to the chiefs, the king, the general government, and the army. The army was under stern discipline and military service was compulsory. Women did much of the agricultural labor. Under Toussaint the administration of this system was committed to Dessalines, who carried it out with rigor; it was afterward followed by Christophe. The latter even imported four thousand Negroes from Africa, from whom he formed a national guard for patrolling the land. These regulations brought back for a time a large part of the former prosperity of the island.

The severity with which Dessalines enforced the laws soon began to turn many against him. The educated mulattoes especially objected to submission to the savage African *mores*. Dessalines started to suppress their revolt, but was killed in ambush in October, 1806.

Great Britain now began to intrigue for a protectorate over the island and the Spanish end of the island threatened attack. These difficulties were overcome, but at a cost of great internal strain. After the death of Dessalines it seemed that Hayti was about to dissolve into a number of petty subdivisions. At one time Christophe was ruling as king in the north, Petion as president at Port au Prince, Rigaud in the south, and a semi-brigand, Goman, in the extreme southwest. Very soon, however, the rivalry narrowed down to Petion and Christophe. Petion was a man of considerable ability and did much, not simply for Hayti, but for South America. Already as early as 1779, before the revolution in Hayti, the Haytian Negroes had helped the United States. The British had captured Savannah in 1778. The French fleet appeared on the coast of Georgia late that year and was ordered to recruit men in Hayti. Eight hundred young freedmen, blacks and mulattoes, offered to take part in the expedition, and they fought valiantly in the siege and covered themselves with glory. It was this legion that made the charge on the British and saved the retreating American army. Among the men who fought there was Christophe.

When Simon Bolivar, Commodore Aury, and many Venezuelan families were driven from their country in 1815, they and their ships took temporary refuge in Hayti. Notwithstanding the embarrassed condition of the republic, Petion received them and gave them four thousand rifles with ammunition, provisions, and last and best a printing press. He also settled some international quarrels among members of the groups, and Bolivar expressed himself afterward as being "overwhelmed with magnanimous favors."[12]

Petion died in 1818 and was succeeded by his friend Boyer. Christophe committed suicide the following year and Boyer became not simply ruler of western Hayti, but also, by arrangement with the eastern end of the island, gained the mastery there, where they were afraid of Spanish aggression. Thus from 1822 to 1843 Boyer, a man of much ability, ruled the whole of the island and gained the recognition of Haytian independence from France and other nations.

France, under Charles X, demanded an indemnity of thirty million dollars to reimburse the planters for confiscated lands and property. This Hayti tried to pay, but the annual installment was a tremendous burden to the impoverished country. Further negotiations were entered into. Finally in 1838 France recognized the independence of the republic and the indemnity was reduced to twelve million dollars. Even this was a large burden for Hayti, and the payment of it for years crippled the island.

The United States and Great Britain in 1825–26 recognized the independence of Hayti. A concordat was arranged with the Pope for governing the church in Hayti, and finally in 1860 the church placed under the French hierarchy. Thus Boyer did unusually well; but his necessary concessions to France weakened his influence at home, and finally an earthquake, which destroyed several towns in 1842, raised the superstitious of the populace against him. He resigned in 1843, leaving the treasury well filled; but with his withdrawal the Spanish portion of the island was lost to Hayti.

The subsequent history of Hayti since 1843 has been the struggle of a small divided country to maintain political independence. The rich resources of the country called for foreign capital, but outside capital meant political influence from abroad, which the little nation rightly feared. Within, the old antagonism between the freedman and the slave settled into a color line between the mulatto and the black, which for a time meant the difference between educated liberalism and reactionary ignorance. This difference has largely disappeared, but some vestiges of the color line remain. The result has been reaction and savagery under Soulouque, Dominique, and Nord Alexis, and decided advance under presidents like Nissage-Saget, Solomon, Legitime, and Hyppolite.

In political life Hayti is still in the sixteenth century; but in economic life she has succeeded in placing on their own little farms the happiest and most contented peasantry in the world, after raising them from a veritable hell of slavery. If modern capitalistic greed can be restrained from interference until the best elements of Hayti secure permanent political leadership the triumph of the revolution will be complete.

In other parts of the French-American dominion the slaves achieved freedom also by insurrection. In Guadeloupe they helped the French drive out the British, and thus gained emancipation. In Martinique it took three revolts and a civil war to bring freedom.

The English slave empire in America centered in the Bermudas, Barbadoes, Jamaica and the lesser islands, and in the United States. Barbadoes developed a savage slave code, and the result was attempted slave insurrections in 1674, 1692, and 1702. These were not successful, but a rising in 1816 destroyed much property under the leadership of a mulatto, Washington Franklin, and the repeal of bad laws and eventual enfranchisement of the colored people followed. One Barbadian mulatto, Sir Conrad Reeves, has held the position of chief justice in the island and was knighted. A Negro insurrection in Dominica under Farcel greatly exercised England in 1791 and 1794 and delayed slave trade abolition; in 1844 and 1847 further uprisings took place, and these continued from 1853 to 1893.

The chief island domain of English slavery was Jamaica. It was Oliver Cromwell who, in his zeal for God and the slave trade, sent an expedition to seize Hayti. His fleet, driven off there, took Jamaica in 1655. The English found the mountains already infested with runaway slaves known as "Maroons," and more Negroes joined them when the English arrived. In 1663 the freedom of the Maroons was acknowledged, land was given them, and their leader, Juan de Bolas, was made a colonel in the militia. He was killed, however, in the following year, and from 1664 to 1738 the three thousand or more black Maroons fought the British Empire in guerrilla warfare. Soldiers, Indians, and dogs were sent against them, and finally in 1738 Captain Cudjo and other chiefs made a formal treaty of peace with Governor Trelawney. They were granted twenty-five hundred acres and their freedom was recognized.

The peace lasted until 1795, when they rebelled again and gave the British a severe drubbing, besides murdering planters. Bloodhounds again were imported. The Maroons offered to surrender on the express condition that none of their number should be deported from the island, as the legislature wished. General Walpole hesitated, but could get peace on no other terms and gave his word. The Maroons surrendered their arms, and immediately the whites seized six hundred of the ringleaders and transported them to the snows of Nova Scotia! The legislature then voted a sword worth twenty-five hundred dollars to General Walpole, which he indignantly refused to accept. Eventually these exiled Maroons found their way to Sierra Leone, West Africa, in time to save that colony to the British crown.[13]

The pressing desire for peace with the Maroons on the part of the white planters arose from the new sugar culture introduced in 1673. A greatly increased demand for slaves followed, and between 1700 and 1786 six hundred and ten thousand slaves were imported; nevertheless, so severely were they driven, that there were only three hundred thousand Negroes in Jamaica in the latter year.

Despite the Moravian missions and other efforts late in the eighteenth century, unrest among the Jamaica slaves and freedmen grew and was increased by the anti-slavery agitation in England and the revolt in Hayti. There was an insurrection in 1796; and in 1831 again the Negroes of northwest Jamaica, impatient because of the slow progress of the emancipation, arose in revolt and destroyed nearly three and a half million dollars' worth of property, well-nigh ruining the planters there. The next year two hundred and fifty-five thousand slaves were set free, for which the planters were paid nearly thirty million dollars. There ensued a discouraging condition of industry. The white officials sent out in these days were arbitrary and corrupt. Little was done for the mass of the people and there was outrageous over-taxation. Nevertheless the backwardness of the colony was attributed to the Negro. Governor Eyre complained in 1865 that the young and strong were good for nothing and were filling the jails; but a simultaneous report by a missionary told the truth concerning the officials. This aroused the colored people, and a mulatto, George William Gordon, called a meeting. Other meetings were afterward held, and finally the Negro peasantry began a riot in 1861, in which eighteen people were killed, only a few of whom were white.

The result was that Governor Eyre tried and executed by court-martial 354 persons, and in addition to this killed without trial 85, a total of 439. One thousand Negro homes were burned to the ground and thousands of Negroes flogged or mutilated. Children had their brains dashed out, pregnant women were murdered, and Gordon was tried by court-martial and hanged. In fact the punishment was, as the royal commissioners said, "reckless and positively barbarous."[14]

This high-handed act aroused England. Eyre was not punished, but the island was made a crown colony in 1866, and given representation in the legislature in 1886.

In the island of St. Vincent, Indians first sought to enslave the fugitive Negroes wrecked there, but the Negroes took the Carib women and then drove the Indian men away. These "black Caribs" fought with Indians, English, and others for three quarters of a century, until the Indians were exterminated. The British took possession in 1763. The black Caribs resisted, and after hard fighting signed a treaty in 1773, receiving one-third of the island as their property. They afterward helped the French against the British, and were finally deported to the island of Ruatan, off Honduras. In Trinidad and British Guiana there have been mutinies and rioting of slaves and a curious mingling of races.

Other parts of South America must be dismissed briefly, because of insufficient data. Colombia and Venezuela, with perhaps eight million people, have at least one-third of their population of Negro and Indian descent. Here Simon Bolivar with his Negro, mulatto, and Indian forces began the war that liberated South America. Central America has a smaller proportion of Negroids, perhaps one hundred thousand in all. Bolivia and Peru have small amounts of Negro blood, while Argentine and Uruguay have very little. The Negro population in these lands is everywhere in process of rapid amalgamation with whites and Indians.

NOTES

1. H.O. Flipper's translation of Castaneda de Nafera's narrative.
2. Johnston: *Negro in the New World*, p. 109.
3. Bryce: *South America*, pp. 479–480.
4. I.e., mulattoes.
5. *Inter-Racial Problems*, p. 381.
6. Smith: *General History of Virginia*.
7. La Croix: *Mémoires sur la Révolution*, I, 253, 408.
8. Marquis d'Hermonas. Cf. Johnston: *Negro in the New World*, p. 158.
9. DeWitt Talmage, in *Christian Herald*, November 28, 1906.
10. Aimes: *African Institutions in America* (reprinted from *Journal of American Folk Lore*), p. 25.
11. Brown: *History of San Domingo*, II, 158–159.
12. See Leger: *Hayti*, Chap. XI.
13. Cf. Chapter V, p. 69.
14. Johnston: *Negro in the New World*.

CHAPTER XI

◆

The Negro in the United States

There were half a million slaves in the confines of the United States when the Declaration of Independence declared "that all men are created equal; that they are endowed by their Creator with certain unalienable rights; that among these are life, liberty, and the pursuit of happiness." The land that thus magniloquently heralded its advent into the family of nations had supported the institution of human slavery for one hundred and fifty-seven years and was destined to cling to it eighty-seven years longer.

The greatest experiment in Negro slavery as a modern industrial system was made on the mainland of North America and in the confines of the present United States. And this experiment was on such a scale and so long-continued that it is profitable for study and reflection. There were in the United States in its dependencies, in 1910, 9,828,294 persons of acknowledged Negro descent, not including the considerable infiltration of Negro blood which is not acknowledged and often not known. To-day the number of persons called Negroes is probably about ten and a quarter million. These persons are almost entirely descendants of African slaves, brought to America in the sixteenth, seventeenth, eighteenth, and nineteenth centuries.

The importation of Negroes to the mainland of North America was small until the British got the coveted privilege of the Asiento in 1713. Before that Northern States like New York had received some slaves from the Dutch, and New England had early developed a trade by which she imported a number of house servants. Ships went out to the African coast with rum, sold the rum, and brought the slaves to the West Indies; there they exchanged the slaves for sugar and molasses and brought the molasses back to New England, to be made into rum for further exploits. After the Asiento treaty the Negro population increased in the eighteenth century from about 50,000 in 1710 to 220,000 in 1750 and to 462,000 in 1770. When the colonies became independent, the foreign slave trade was soon made illegal; but illicit trade, annexation of territory and natural increase enlarged the Negro population from a little over a million at the beginning of the nineteenth century to four and a half millions at the outbreak of the Civil War and to about ten and a quarter millions in 1914.

The present so-called Negro population of the United States is:

1. A mixture of the various African populations, Bantu, Sudanese, west-coast Negroes, some dwarfs, and some traces of Arab, Berber, and Semitic blood.
2. A mixture of these strains with the blood of white Americans through a system of concubinage of colored women in slavery days, together with some legal intermarriage.

The figures as to mulattoes[1] have been from time to time officially acknowledged to be understatements. Probably one-third of the Negroes of the United States have distinct traces of white blood. This blending of the races has led to interesting human types, but racial prejudice has hitherto prevented any scientific study of the matter. In general the Negro population in the United States is brown in color, darkening to almost black and shading off in the other direction to yellow and white, and is indistinguishable in some cases from the white population.

Much has been written of the black man in America, but most of this has been from the point of view of the whites, so that we know of the effect of Negro slavery on the whites, the strife among the whites for and against abolition, and the consequent problem of the Negro so far as the white population is concerned.

This chapter, however, is dealing with the matter more from the point of view of the Negro group itself, and seeking to show what slavery meant to them, how they reacted against it, what they did to secure their freedom, and what they are doing with their partial freedom to-day.

The slaves landing from 1619 onward were received by the colonies at first as laborers, on the same plane as other laborers. For a long time there was in law no distinction between the indented white servant from England and the black servant from Africa, except in the term of their service. Even here the distinction was not always observed, some of the whites being kept beyond term of their service and Negroes now and then securing their freedom. Gradually the planters realized the advantage of laborers held for life, but they were met by certain moral difficulties. The opposition to slavery had from the first been largely stilled when it was stated that this was a method of converting the heathen to Christianity. The corollary was that when a slave was converted he became free. Up to 1660 or thereabouts it seemed accepted in most colonies and in the English West Indies that baptism into a Christian church would free a Negro slave. Masters therefore, were reluctant in the seventeenth century to have their slaves receive Christian instruction. Massachusetts first apparently legislated on this matter by enacting in 1641 that slavery should be confined to captives in just wars "and such strangers as willingly sell themselves or are sold to us,"[2] meaning by "strangers" apparently heathen, but saying nothing as to the effect of conversion. Connecticut adopted similar legislation in 1650, and Virginia declared in 1661 that Negroes "are incapable of making satisfaction" for time lost in running away by lengthening their time of services, thus implying that they were slaves for life. Maryland declared in 1663 that Negro slaves should serve *durante vita*, but it was not until 1667 that Virginia finally plucked up courage to attack the issue squarely and declared by law: "Baptism doth not alter the condition of the person as to his bondage or freedom, in order that diverse masters freed from this doubt may more carefully endeavor the propagation of Christianity."[3]

The transplanting of the Negro from his African clan life to the West Indian plantation was a social revolution. Marriage became geographical and transient, while women and girls were without protection.

The private home as a self-protective, independent unit did not exist. That powerful institution, the polygamous African home, was almost completely destroyed, and in its place in America arose sexual promiscuity, a weak community life, with common dwelling, meals, and child nurseries. The internal slave trade tended further to weaken natural ties. A small number of favored house servants and artisans were raised above this—had their private homes, came in contact with the culture of the master class, and assimilated much of American civilization. This was, however, exceptional; broadly speaking, the greatest social effect of American slavery was to substitute for the polygamous Negro home a new polygamy less guarded, less effective, and less civilized.

At first sight it would seem that slavery completely destroyed every vestige of spontaneous movement among the Negroes. This is not strictly true. The vast power of the priest in the African state is well known; his realm alone—the province of religion and medicine—remained largely unaffected by the plantation system. The Negro priest, therefore, early became an important figure on the plantation and found his function as the interpreter of the supernatural, the comforter of the sorrowing, and as the one who expressed, rudely but picturesquely, the longing and disappointment and resentment of a stolen people. From such beginnings arose and spread with marvelous rapidity the Negro church, the first distinctively Negro American social institution. It was not at first by any means a Christian church, but a mere adaptation of those rites of fetish which in America is termed obe worship, or "voodooism."[4] Association and missionary effort soon gave these rites a veneer of Christianity and gradually, after two centuries, the church became Christian, with a simple Calvinistic creed, but with many of the old customs still clinging to the services. It is this historic fact, that the Negro church of to-day bases itself upon the sole surviving social institution of the African fatherland, that accounts for its extraordinary growth and vitality.

The slave codes at first were really labor codes based on an attempt to reëstablish in America the waning feudalism of Europe. The laborers were mainly black and were held for life. Above them came the artisans, free whites with a few blacks, and above them the master class. The feudalism called for the plantation system, and the plantation system as developed in America, and particularly in Virginia, was at first a feudal domain. On these plantations the master was practically supreme. The slave codes in early days were but moderately harsh, allowing punishment by the master, but restraining him in extreme cases and providing for care of the slaves and of the aged. With the power, however, solely in the hands of the master class, and with the master supreme on his own plantation, his power over the slave was practically what he wished it to be. In some cases the cruelty was as great as on the worst West Indian plantations. In other cases the rule was mild and paternal.

Up through this American feudalism the Negro began to rise. He learned in the eighteenth century the English language, he began to be identified with the Christian church, he mingled his blood to a considerable extent with the master class. The house servants particularly were favored, in some cases receiving education, and the number of free Negroes gradually increased.

Present-day students are often puzzled at the apparent contradictions of Southern slavery. One hears, on the one hand, of the staid and gentle patriarchy, the wide and sleepy plantations with lord and retainers, ease and happiness; on the other hand one hears of barbarous cruelty and unbridled power and wide oppression of men. Which is the true picture? The answer is simple: both are true. They are not opposite sides of the same shield; they are different shields. They are pictures, on the one hand, of house service in the great country seats and in the towns, and on the other hand of the field laborers who raised the great tobacco, rice, and cotton crops. We have thus not only carelessly mixed pictures of what were really different kinds of slavery, but of that which represented different degrees in the development of the economic system. House service was the older feudal idea of personal retainership, developed in Virginia and Carolina in the seventeenth and eighteenth centuries. It had all the advantages and disadvantages of such a system; the advantage of the strong personal tie and disadvantage of unyielding caste distinctions, with the resultant immoralities. At its worst, however, it was a matter primarily of human relationships.

Out of this older type of slavery in the northern South there developed, during the eighteenth and nineteenth centuries, in the southern South the type of slavery which corresponds to the modern factory system in its worst conceivable form. It represented production of a staple product on a large scale; between the owner and laborer were interposed the overseer and the drivers. The slaves were whipped and driven to a mechanical task system. Wide territory was needed, so that at last absentee landlordship was common. It was this latter type of slavery that marked the cotton kingdom, and the extension of the area of this system southward and westward marked the aggressive world-conquering visions of the slave barons. On the other hand it was the milder and far different Virginia house service and the personal retainership of town life in which most white children grew up; it was this that impressed their imaginations and which they have so vividly portrayed. The Negroes, however, knew the other side, for it was under the harsher, heartless driving of the fields that fully nine-tenths of them lived.

There early began to be some internal development and growth of self-consciousness among the Negroes: for instance, in New England towns Negro "governors" were elected. This was partly an African custom transplanted and partly an endeavor to put the regulation of the slaves into their own hands. Negroes voted in those days: for instance, in North Carolina until 1835 the Constitution extended the franchise to every freeman, and when Negroes were disfranchised in 1835, several hundred colored men were deprived of the vote. In fact, as Albert Bushnell Hart says, "In the colonies freed Negroes, like freed indentured white servants, acquired property, founded families, and came into the political community if they had the energy, thrift, and fortune to get the necessary property."[5]

The humanitarian movement of the eighteenth century was active toward Negroes, because of the part which they played in the Revolutionary War. Negro regiments and companies were raised in Connecticut and Rhode Island, and a large number of Negroes were members of the continental armies elsewhere. Individual Negroes distinguished themselves. It is estimated that five thousand Negroes fought in the American armies.

The mass of the Americans considered at the time of the adoption of the Constitution that Negro slavery was doomed. There soon came a series of laws emancipating slaves in the North: Vermont began in 1779, followed by judicial decision in Massachusetts in 1780 and gradual emancipation in Pennsylvania beginning the same year; emancipation was accomplished in New Hampshire in 1783, and in Connecticut and Rhode Island in 1784. The momentous exclusion of slavery in the Northwest Territory took place in 1787, and gradual emancipation began in New York and New Jersey in 1799 and 1804.

Beneficial and insurance societies began to appear among colored people. Nearly every town of any size in Virginia in the early eighteenth century had Negro organizations for caring for the sick and burying the dead. As the number of free Negroes increased, particularly in the North, these financial societies began to be openly formed. One of the earliest was the Free African Society of Philadelphia. This eventually became the present African Methodist Church, which has to-day half a million members and over eleven million dollars' worth of property.

Negroes began to be received into the white church bodies in separate congregations, and before 1807 there is the record of the formation of eight such Negro churches. This brought forth leaders who were usually preachers in these churches. Richard Allen, the founder of the African Methodist Church, was one; Lot Carey, one of the founders of Liberia, was another. In the South there was John Chavis, who passed through a regular course of studies at what is now Washington and Lee University. He started a school for young white men in North Carolina and had among his pupils a United States senator, sons of a chief justice of North Carolina, a governor of the state, and many others. He was a full-blooded Negro, but a Southern writer says that "all accounts agree that John Chavis was a gentleman. He was received socially among the best whites and asked to table."[6]

In the war of 1812 thirty-three hundred Negroes helped Jackson win the battle of New Orleans, and numbers fought in New York State and in the navy under Perry, Channing, and others. Phyllis Wheatley, a Negro girl, wrote poetry, and the mulatto, Benjamin Banneker, published one of the first American series of almanacs.

In fine, it seemed in the early years of the nineteenth century that slavery in the United States would gradually disappear and that the Negro would have, in time, a man's chance. A change came, however, between 1820 and 1830, and it is directly traceable to the industrial revolution of the nineteenth century.

Between 1738 and 1830 there had come a remarkable series of inventions which revolutionized the methods of making cloth. This series included the invention of the fly shuttle, the carding machine, the steam engine, and the power loom. The world began to look about for a cheaper and larger supply of fiber for weaving. It was found in the cotton plant, and the southern United States was especially adapted to its culture. The invention of the cotton gin removed the last difficulties. The South now had a crop which could be attended to by unskilled labor and for which there was practically unlimited demand. There was land, and rich land, in plenty. The result was that the cotton crop in the United States increased from 8,000 bales in 1790 to 650,000 bales in 1820, to 2,500,000 bales in 1850, and to 4,000,000 bales in 1860.

In this growth one sees the economic foundation of the new slavery in the United States, which rose in the second decade of the nineteenth century. Manifestly the fatal procrastination in dealing with slavery in the eighteenth century received in the nineteenth century its terrible reward. The change in the attitude toward slavery was manifest in various ways. The South no longer excused slavery, but began to defend it as an economic system. The enforcement of the slave trade laws became notoriously lax and there was a tendency to make slave codes harsher.

This led to retaliation on the part of the Negroes. There had not been in the United States before this many attempts at insurrection. The slaves were distributed over a wide territory, and before they became intelligent enough to coöperate the chance of emancipation was held before them. Several small insurrections are alluded to in South Carolina early in the eighteenth century, and one by Cato at Stono in 1740 caused widespread alarm. The Negro plot in New York in 1712 put the city into hysterics. There was no further plotting on any scale until the Haytian revolt, when Gabriel in Virginia made an abortive attempt. In 1822 a free Negro, Denmark Vesey, in South Carolina, failed in a well-laid plot, and ten years after that, in 1831, Nat Turner led his insurrection in Virginia and killed fifty-one persons. The result of this insurrection was to crystallize tendencies toward harshness which the economic revolution was making advisable.

A wave of legislation passed over the South, prohibiting the slaves from learning to read and write, forbidding Negroes to preach, and interfering with Negro religious meetings. Virginia declared in 1831 that neither slaves nor free Negroes might preach, nor could they attend religious service at night without permission. In North Carolina slaves and free Negroes were forbidden to preach, exhort, or teach "in any prayer meeting or other association for worship where slaves of different families are collected together" on penalty of not more than thirty-nine lashes. Maryland and Georgia and other states had similar laws.

The real effective revolt of the Negro against slavery was not, however, by fighting, but by running away, usually to the North, which had been recently freed from slavery. From the beginning of the nineteenth century slaves began to escape in considerable numbers. Four geographical paths were chiefly followed: one, leading southward, was the line of swamps along the coast from Norfolk, Virginia, to the northern border of Florida. This gave rise to the Negro element among the Indians in Florida and led to the two Seminole wars of 1817 and 1835. These wars were really slave raids to make the Indians give up the Negro and half-breed slaves domiciled among them. The wars cost the United States ten million dollars and two thousand lives.

The great Appalachian range, with its abutting mountains, was the safest path northward. Through Tennessee and Kentucky and the heart of the Cumberland Mountains, using the limestone caverns, was the third route, and the valley of the Mississippi was the western tunnel.

These runaways and the freedmen of the North soon began to form a group of people who sought to consider the problem of slavery and the destiny of the Negro in America. They passed through many psychological changes of attitude in the years from 1700 to 1850. At first, in the early part of the eighteenth century, there was but one thought: revolt and revenge. The development of the latter half of the century brought an attitude of hope and adjustment and emphasized the differences between the slave and the free Negro. The first part of the nineteenth century brought two movements: among the free Negroes an effort at self-development and protection through organization; among slaves and recent fugitives a distinct reversion to the older idea of revolt.

As the new industrial slavery, following the rise of the cotton kingdom, began to press harder, a period of storm and stress ensued in the black world, and in 1829 came the first full-voiced, almost hysterical protest of a Negro against slavery and the color line in David Walker's Appeal, which aroused Southern legislatures to action.

The decade 1830–40 was a severe period of trial. Not only were the chains of slavery tighter in the South, but in the North the free Negro was beginning to feel the ostracism and competition of white workingmen, native and foreign. In Philadelphia, between 1829 and 1849, six mobs of hoodlums and foreigners murdered and maltreated Negroes. In the Middle West harsh black laws which had been enacted in earlier days were hauled from their hiding places and put into effect. No Negro was allowed to settle in Ohio unless he gave bond within twenty days to the amount of five thousand dollars to guarantee his good behavior and support. Harboring or concealing fugitives was heavily fined, and no Negro could give evidence in any case where a white man was party. These laws began to be enforced in 1829 and for three days riots went on in Cincinnati and Negroes were shot and killed. Aroused, the Negroes sent a deputation to Canada where they were offered asylum. Fully two thousand migrated from Ohio. Later large numbers from other parts of the United States joined them.

In 1830–31 the first Negro conventions were called in Philadelphia to consider the desperate condition of the Negro population, and in 1833 the convention met again and local societies were formed. The first Negro paper was issued in New York in 1827, while later emancipation in the British West Indies brought some cheer in the darkness.

A system of separate Negro schools was established and the little band of abolitionists led by Garrison and others appeared. In spite of all the untoward circumstances, therefore, the internal development of the free Negro in the North went on. The Negro population increased twenty-three per cent between 1830 and 1840; Philadelphia had, in 1838, one hundred small beneficial societies, while Ohio Negroes had ten thousand acres of land. The slave mutiny on the Creole, the establishment of the Negro Odd Fellows, and the growth of the Negro churches all indicated advancement.

Between 1830 and 1850 the concerted coöperation to assist fugitives came to be known as the Underground Railroad. It was an organization not simply of white philanthropists, but the coöperation of Negroes in the most difficult part of the work made it possible. Hundreds of Negroes visited the slave states to entice the slaves away, and the list of Underground Railroad operators given by Siebert contains one hundred and twenty-eight names of Negroes. In Canada and in the northern United States there was a secret society, known as the League of Freedom, which especially worked to help slaves run away. Harriet Tubman was one of the most energetic of these slave conductors and brought away several thousand slaves. William Lambert, a colored man, was reputed between 1829 and 1862 to have aided in the escape of thirty thousand.

The decade 1840–50 was a period of hope and uplift for the Negro group, with clear evidences of distinct self-assertion and advance. A few well-trained lawyers and physicians appeared, and colored men took their place among the abolition orators. The catering business in Philadelphia and other cities fell largely into their hands, and some small merchants arose here and there. Above all, Frederick Douglass made his first speech in 1841 and thereafter became one of the most prominent figures in the abolition crusade. A new series of national conventions began to assemble late in the forties, and the delegates were drawn from the artisans and higher servants, showing a great increase of efficiency in the rank and file of the free Negroes.

By 1850 the Negroes had increased to three and a half million. Those in Canada were being organized in settlements and were accumulating property. The escape of fugitive slaves was systematized and some of the most representative conventions met. One particularly, in 1854, grappled frankly with the problem of emigration. It looked as though it was going to be impossible for Negroes to remain in the United States and be free. As early as 1788 a Negro union of Newport, Rhode Island, had proposed a general exodus to Africa. John and Paul Cuffe, after petitioning for the right to vote in 1780, started in 1815 for Africa, organizing an expedition at their own expense which cost four thousand dollars. Lot Carey organized the African Mission Society in 1813, and the first Negro college graduate went to Liberia in 1829 and became superintendent of public schools. The Colonization Society encouraged this migration, and the Negroes themselves had organized the Canadian exodus.

The Rochester Negro convention in 1853 pronounced against migration, but nevertheless emissaries were sent in various directions to see what inducements could be offered. One went to the Niger valley, one to Central America, and one to Hayti. The Haytian trip was successful and about two thousand black emigrants eventually settled in Hayti.

Delaney, who went to Africa, concluded a treaty with eight kings offering inducements to Negroes, but nothing came of it. In 1853 Negroes like Purvis and Barbadoes helped in the formation of the American Anti-slavery society, and for a while colored men coöperated with John Brown and probably would have given him considerable help if they had thoroughly known his plans. As it was, six or seven of his twenty-two followers were Negroes.

Meantime the slave power was impelled by the high price of slaves and the exhaustion of cotton land to make increased demands. Slavery was forced north of Mason and Dixon's line in 1820; a new slave empire with thousands of slaves was annexed in 1850, and a fugitive slave law was passed which endangered the liberty of every free Negro; finally a determined attempt was made to force slavery into the Northwest in competition with free white labor, and less effective but powerful movements arose to annex more slave territory to the south and to reopen the African slave trade.

It looked like a triumphal march for the slave barons, but each step cost more than the last. Missouri gave rise to the early abolitionist movement. Mexico and the fugitive slave law aroused deep opposition in the North, and Kansas developed an attack upon the free labor system, not simply of the North, but of the civilized world. The result was war; but the war was not against slavery. It was fought to protect free white laborers against the competition of slaves, and it was thought possible to do this by segregating slavery.

The first thing that vexed the Northern armies on Southern soil during the war was the question of the disposition of the fugitive slaves, who immediately began to arrive in increasing numbers. Butler confiscated them, Fremont freed them, and Halleck caught and returned them; but their numbers swelled to such large proportions that the mere economic problem of their presence overshadowed everything else, especially after the Emancipation Proclamation. Lincoln was glad to have them come after once he realized their strength to the Confederacy.

The Emancipation Proclamation was forced, not simply by the necessity of paralyzing industry in the South, but also by the necessity of employing Negro soldiers. During the first two years of the war no one wanted Negro soldiers. It was declared to be a "white man's war." General Hunter tried to raise a regiment in South Carolina, but the War Department disavowed the act. In Louisiana the Negroes were anxious to enlist, but were held off. In the meantime the war did not go as well as the North had hoped, and on the twenty-sixth of January, 1863, the Secretary of War authorized the Governor of Massachusetts to raise two regiments of Negro troops. Frederick Douglass and others began the work with enthusiasm, and in the end one hundred and eighty-seven thousand Negroes enlisted in the Northern armies, of whom seventy thousand were killed and wounded. The conduct of these troops was exemplary. They were indispensable in camp duties and brave on the field, where they fought in two hundred and thirteen battles. General Banks wrote, "Their conduct was heroic. No troops could be more determined or more daring."[7]

The assault on Fort Wagner, led by a thousand black soldiers under the white Colonel Shaw, is one of the greatest deeds of desperate bravery on record. On the other hand the treatment of Negro soldiers when captured by the Confederates was barbarous. At Fort Pillow, after the surrender of the federal troops, the colored regiment was indiscriminately butchered and some of them were buried alive.

Abraham Lincoln said, "The slightest knowledge of arithmetic will prove to any man that the rebel armies cannot be destroyed with Democratic strategy.

It would sacrifice all the white men of the North to do it. There are now in the service of the United States near two hundred thousand able-bodied colored men, most of them under arms, defending and acquiring Union territory. . . . Abandon all the posts now garrisoned by black men; take two hundred thousand men from our side and put them in the battlefield or cornfield against us, and we would be compelled to abandon the war in three weeks."[8] Emancipation thus came as a war measure to break the power of the Confederacy, preserve the Union, and gain the sympathy of the civilized world.

However, two hundred and forty-four years of slavery could not be stopped by edict. There were legal difficulties, the whole slow problem of economic readjustment, and the subtle and far-reaching questions of future race relations.

The peculiar circumstances of emancipation forced the legal and political difficulties to the front, and these were so striking that they have since obscured the others in the eyes of students. Quite unexpectedly and without forethought the nation had emancipated four million slaves. Once the deed was done, the majority of the nation was glad and recognized that this was, after all, the only result of a fearful four years' war which in any degree justified it. But how was the result to be secured for all time? There were three possibilities: (1) to declare the slave free and leave him at the mercy of his former masters; (2) to establish a careful government guardianship designed to guide the slave from legal to real economic freedom; (3) to give the Negro the political power to guard himself as well as he could during this development. It is very easy to forget that the United States government tried each one of these in succession and was literally forced to adopt the third, because the first had utterly failed and the second was thought too "paternal" and especially too costly. To leave the Negroes helpless after a paper edict of emancipation was manifestly impossible. It would have meant that the war had been fought in vain.

Carl Schurz, who traversed the South just after the war, said, "A veritable reign of terror prevailed in many parts of the South. The Negro found scant justice in the local courts against the white man. He could look for protection only to the military forces of the United States still garrisoning the states lately in rebellion and to the Freedmen's Bureau."[9] This Freedmen's Bureau was proposed by Charles Sumner. If it had been presented to-day instead of fifty years ago, it would have been regarded as a proposal far less revolutionary than the state insurance of England and Germany. A half century ago, however, and in a country which gave the *laisser faire* economics their extremest trial, the Freedmen's Bureau struck the whole nation as unthinkable, save as a very temporary expedient and to relieve the more pointed forms of distress following war. Yet the proposals of the Bureau were both simple and sensible:

1. To oversee the making and enforcement of wage contracts for freedmen.
2. To appear in the courts as the freedmen's best friend.
3. To furnish the freedmen with a minimum of land and of capital.
4. To establish schools.
5. To furnish such institutions of relief as hospitals, outdoor relief stations, etc.

How a sensible people could expect really to conduct a slave into freedom with less than this it is hard to see. Even with such tutelage extending over a period of two or three decades, the ultimate end had to be enfranchisement and political and social freedom for those freedmen who attained a certain set standard. Otherwise the whole training had neither object nor guarantee. Precisely on this account the former masters opposed the Freedmen's Bureau with all their influence. They did not want the Negro trained or really freed, and they criticized mercilessly the many mistakes of the new Bureau.

The North at first thought to pay for the main cost of the Freedmen's Bureau by confiscating the property of former slave owners; but finding this not in accordance with law, they realized that they were embarking on an enterprise which bade fair to add many millions to the already staggering cost of the war. When, therefore, they saw that the abolition of slavery could not be left to the white South and could not be done by the North without time and money, they determined to put the responsibility on the Negro himself. This was without a doubt a tremendous experiment, but with all its manifest mistakes it succeeded to an astonishing degree. It made the immediate reëstablishment of the old slavery impossible, and it was probably the only quick method of doing this. It gave the freedmen's sons a chance to begin their education. It diverted the energy of the white South slavery to the recovery of political power, and in this interval, small as it was, the Negro took his first steps toward economic freedom.

The difficulties that stared reconstruction politicians in the face were these: (1) They must act quickly. (2) Emancipation had increased the political power of the South by one-sixth. Could this increased political power be put in the hands of those who, in defense of slavery, had disrupted the Union? (3) How was the abolition of slavery to be made effective? (4) What was to be the political position of the freedmen?

The Freedmen's Bureau in its short life accomplished a great task. Carl Schurz, in 1865, felt warranted in saying that "not half of the labor that has been done in the South this year, or will be done there next year, would have been or would be done but for the exertions of the Freedmen's Bureau. ... No other agency except one placed there by the national government could have wielded that moral power whose interposition was so necessary to prevent Southern society from falling at once into the chaos of a general collision between its different elements."[10] Notwithstanding this the Bureau was temporary, was regarded as a makeshift, and soon abandoned.

Meantime partial Negro suffrage seemed not only just, but almost inevitable. Lincoln, in 1864, "cautiously" suggested to Louisiana's private consideration "whether some of the colored people may not be let in as, for instance, the very intelligent, and especially those who fought gallantly in our ranks. They would probably help in some trying time to come, to keep the jewel of liberty in the family of freedom." Indeed, the "family of freedom" in Louisiana being somewhat small just then, who else was to be intrusted with the "jewel"? Later and for different reasons Johnson, in 1865, wrote to Mississippi, "If you could extend the elective franchise to all persons of color who can read the Constitution of the United States in English and write their name, and to all persons of color who own real estate valued at not less than two hundred and fifty dollars, and pay taxes thereon, you would completely disarm the adversary and set an example the other states will follow. This you can do with perfect safety, and you thus place the Southern States, in reference to free persons of color, upon the same basis with the free states. I hope and trust your convention will do this."

The Negroes themselves began to ask for the suffrage. The Georgia convention in Augusta (1866) advocated "a proposition to give those who could write and read well and possessed a certain property qualification the right of suffrage." The reply of the South to these suggestions was decisive. In Tennessee alone was any action attempted that even suggested possible Negro suffrage in the future, and that failed. In all other states the "Black Codes" adopted were certainly not reassuring to the friends of freedom. To be sure, it was not a time to look for calm, cool, thoughtful action on the part of the white South. Their economic condition was pitiable, their fear of Negro freedom genuine. Yet it was reasonable to expect from them something less than repression and utter reaction toward slavery. To some extent this expectation was fulfilled. The abolition of slavery was recognized on the statute book, and the civil rights of owning property and appearing as a witness in cases in which he was a party were generally granted the Negro; yet with these in many cases went harsh and unbearable regulations which largely neutralized the concessions and certainly gave ground for an assumption that, once free, the South would virtually reënslave the Negro. The colored people themselves naturally feared this, protesting, as in Mississippi, "against the reactionary policy prevailing and expressing the fear that the legislature will pass such prescriptive laws as will drive the freedmen from the state, or practically reënslave them."

The codes spoke for themselves. As Burgess says, "Almost every act, word, or gesture of the Negro, not consonant with good taste and good manners as well as good morals, was made a crime or misdemeanor for which he could first be fined by the magistrates and then be consigned to a condition of almost slavery for an indefinite time, if he could not pay the bill."[11]

All things considered, it seems probable that, if the South had been permitted to have its way in 1865, the harshness of Negro slavery would have been mitigated so as to make slave trading difficult, and so as to make it possible for a Negro to hold property and appear in some cases in court; but that in most other respects the blacks would have remained in slavery.

What could prevent this? A Freedmen's Bureau established for ten, twenty, or forty years, with a careful distribution of land and capital and a system of education for the children, might have prevented such an extension of slavery. But the country would not listen to such a comprehensive plan. A restricted grant of the suffrage voluntarily made by the states would have been a reassuring proof of a desire to treat the freedmen fairly and would have balanced in part, at least, the increased political power of the South. There was no such disposition evident.

In Louisiana, for instance, under the proposed reconstruction "not one Negro was allowed to vote, though at that very time the wealthy intelligent free colored people of the state paid taxes on property assessed at fifteen million dollars and many of them were well known for their patriotic zeal and love for the Union."[12]

Thus the arguments for universal Negro suffrage from the start were strong and are still strong, and no one would question their strength were it not for the assumption that the experiment failed. Frederick Douglass said to President Johnson, "Your noble and humane predecessor placed in our hands the sword to assist in saving the nation, and we do hope that you, his able successor, will favorably regard the placing in our hands the ballot with which to save ourselves."[13]

Carl Schurz wrote, "It is idle to say that it will be time to speak of Negro suffrage when the whole colored race will be educated, for the ballot may be necessary to him to secure his education."[14]

The granting of full Negro suffrage meant one of two alternatives to the South: (1) The uplift of the Negro for sheer self-preservation. This is what Schurz and the saner North expected. As one Southern school superintendent said, "The elevation of this class is a matter of prime importance, since a ballot in the hands of a black citizen is quite as potent as in the hands of a white one." Or (2) Negro suffrage meant a determined concentration of Southern effort by actual force to deprive the Negro of the ballot or nullify its use. This last is what really happened. But even in this case, so much energy was taken in keeping the Negro from voting that the plan for keeping him in virtual slavery and denying him education partially failed. It took ten years to nullify Negro suffrage in part and twenty years to escape the fear of federal intervention. In these twenty years a vast number of Negroes had arisen so far as to escape slavery forever. Debt peonage could be fastened on part of the rural South and was; but even here the new Negro landholder appeared. Thus despite everything the Fifteenth Amendment, and that alone, struck the death knell of slavery.

The steps toward the Fifteenth Amendment were taken slowly. First Negroes were allowed to take part in reconstructing the state governments. This was inevitable if loyal governments were to be obtained. Next the restored state governments were directed to enfranchise all citizens, black or white, or have their representation in Congress cut down proportionately. Finally the United States said the last word of simple justice: the states may regulate the suffrage, but no state may deprive a person of the right to vote simply because he is a Negro or has been a slave.

For such reasons the Negro was enfranchised. What was the result? No language has been spared to describe these results as the worst imaginable. This is not true. There were bad results, and bad results arising from Negro suffrage; but those results were not so bad as usually painted, nor was Negro suffrage the prime cause of many of them. Let us not forget that the white South believed it to be of vital interest to its welfare that the experiment of Negro suffrage should fail ignominiously and that almost to a man the whites were willing to insure this failure either by active force or passive acquiescence; that besides this there were, as might be expected, men, black and white, Northern and Southern, only too eager to take advantage of such a situation for feathering their own nests. Much evil must result in such case; but to charge the evil to Negro suffrage is unfair. It may be charged to anger, poverty, venality, and ignorance, but the anger and poverty were the almost inevitable aftermath of war; the venality was much greater among whites than Negroes both North and South, and while ignorance was the curse of Negroes, the fault was not theirs and they took the initiative to correct it.

The chief charges against the Negro governments are extravagance, theft, and incompetency of officials. There is no serious charge that these governments threatened civilization or the foundations of social order. The charge is that they threatened property and that they were inefficient. These charges are in part undoubtedly true, but they are often exaggerated. The South had been terribly impoverished and saddled with new social burdens. In other words, states with smaller resources were asked not only to do a work of restoration, but a larger social work. The property holders were aghast. They not only demurred, but, predicting ruin and revolution, they appealed to secret societies, to intimidation, force, and murder. They refused to believe that these novices in government and their friends were aught but scamps and fools. Under the circumstances occurring directly after the war, the wisest statesman would have been compelled to resort to increased taxation and would have, in turn, been execrated as extravagant, dishonest, and incompetent. It is easy, therefore, to see what flaming and incredible stories of Reconstruction governments could gain wide currency and belief. In fact the extravagance, although great, was not universal, and much of it was due to the extravagant spirit pervading the whole country in a day of inflated currency and speculation.

That the Negroes, led by the astute thieves, became at first tools and received some small share of the spoils is true. But two considerations must be added: much of the legislation which resulted in fraud was represented to the Negroes as good legislation, and thus their votes were secured by deliberate misrepresentation. Take, for instance, the land frauds of South Carolina. A wise Negro leader of that state, advocating the state purchase of farm lands, said, "One of the greatest of slavery bulwarks was the infernal plantation system, one man owning his thousand, another his twenty, another fifty thousand acres of land. This is the only way by which we will break up that system, and I maintain that our freedom will be of no effect if we allow it to continue. What is the main cause of the prosperity of the North? It is because every man has his own farm and is free and independent. Let the lands of the South be similarly divided."[15]

From such arguments the Negroes were induced to aid a scheme to buy land and distribute it. Yet a large part of eight hundred thousand dollars appropriated was wasted and went to the white landholders' pockets.

The most inexcusable cheating of the Negroes took place through the Freedmen's Bank. This bank was incorporated by Congress in 1865 and had in its list of incorporators some of the greatest names in America including Peter Cooper, William Cullen Bryan and John Jay. Yet the bank was allowed to fail in 1874 owing the freedmen their first savings of over three millions of dollars. They have never been reimbursed.

Many Negroes were undoubtedly venal, but more were ignorant and deceived. The question is: Did they show any signs of a disposition to learn to better things? The theory of democratic government is not that the will of the people is always right, but rather that normal human beings of average intelligence will, if given a chance, learn the right and best course by bitter experience. This is precisely what the Negro voters showed indubitable signs of doing. First they strove for schools to abolish ignorance, and second, a large and growing number of them revolted against the extravagance and stealing that marred the beginning of Reconstruction, and joined with the best elements to institute reform. The greatest stigma on the white South is not that it opposed Negro suffrage and resented theft and incompetence, but that, when it saw the reform movements growing and even in some cases triumphing, and a larger and larger number of black voters learning to vote for honesty and ability, it still preferred a Reign of Terror to a campaign of education and disfranchised Negroes instead of punishing rascals.

No one has expressed this more convincingly than a Negro who was himself a member of the Reconstruction legislature of South Carolina, and who spoke at the convention which disfranchised him against one of the onslaughts of Tillman. "We were eight years in power. We had built school houses, established charitable institutions, built and maintained the penitentiary system, provided for the education of the deaf and dumb, rebuilt the jails and court houses, rebuilt the bridges, and reëstablished the ferries. In short, we had reconstructed the state and placed it upon the road to prosperity, and at the same time, by our acts of financial reform, transmitted to the Hampton government an indebtedness not greater by more than two and a half million dollars than was the bonded debt of the state in 1868, before the Republican Negroes and their white allies came into power."[16]

So, too, in Louisiana in 1872, and in Mississippi later, the better element of the Republicans triumphed at the polls and, joining with the Democrats, instituted reforms, repudiated the worst extravagance, and started toward better things. Unfortunately there was one thing that the white South feared more than Negro dishonesty, ignorance, and incompetency, and that was Negro honesty, knowledge, and efficiency.

In the midst of all these difficulties the Negro governments in the South accomplished much of positive good. We may recognize three things which Negro rule gave to the South: (1) democratic government, (2) free public schools, (3) new social legislation.

In general, the words of Judge Albion W. Tourgee, a white "carpet bagger," are true when he says of the Negro governments, "They obeyed the Constitution of the United States and annulled the bonds of states, counties, and cities which had been issued to carry on the War of Rebellion and maintain armies in the field against the Union. They instituted a public school system in a realm where public schools had been unknown. They opened the ballot box and the jury box to thousands of white men who had been debarred from them by a lack of earthly possessions. They introduced home rule into the South. They abolished the whipping post, the branding iron, the stocks, and other barbarous forms of punishment which had up to that time prevailed. They reduced capital felonies from about twenty to two or three. In an age of extravagance they were extravagant in the sums appropriated for public works. In all of that time no man's rights of persons were invaded under the forms of law. Every Democrat's life, home, fireside, and business were safe. No man obstructed any white man's way to the ballot box, interfered with his freedom of speech, or boycotted him on account of his political faith."[17]

A thorough study of the legislation accompanying these constitutions and its changes since shows the comparatively small amount of change in law and government which the overthrow of Negro rule brought about. There were sharp and often hurtful economies introduced, marking the return of property to power; there was a sweeping change of officials, but the main body of Reconstruction legislation stood. The Reconstruction democracy brought forth new leaders and definitely overthrew the old Southern aristocracy. Among these new men were Negroes of worth and ability. John R. Lynch, when Speaker of the Mississippi House of Representatives, was given a public testimonial by Republicans and Democrats, and the leading white paper said, "His bearing in office had been so proper, and his rulings in such marked contrasts to the partisan conduct of the ignoble whites of his party who have aspired to be leaders of the blacks, that the conservatives cheerfully joined in the testimonial."[18]

Of the colored treasurer of South Carolina the white Governor Chamberlain said, "I have never heard one word or seen one act of Mr. Cardoza's which did not confirm my confidence in his personal integrity and his political honor and zeal for the honest administration of the state government. On every occasion, and under all circumstances, he has been against fraud and robbery and in favor of good measures and good men."[19]

Jonathan C. Gibbs, a colored man and the first state superintendent of instruction in Florida, was a graduate of Dartmouth. He established the system and brought it to success, dying in harness in 1874. Such men—and there were others—ought not to be forgotten or confounded with other types of colored and white Reconstruction leaders.

There is no doubt that the thirst of the black man for knowledge, a thirst which has been too persistent and durable to be mere curiosity or whim, gave birth to the public school system of the South. It was the question upon which black voters and legislators insisted more than anything else, and while it is possible to find some vestiges of free schools in some of the Southern States before the war, yet a universal, well-established system dates from the day that the black man got political power.

Finally, in legislation covering property, the wider functions of the state, the punishment of crime and the like, it is sufficient to say that the laws on these points established by Reconstruction legislatures were not only different from and even revolutionary to the laws in the older South, but they were so wise and so well suited to the needs of the new South that, in spite of a retrogressive movement following the overthrow of the Negro governments, the mass of this legislation, with elaborations and development, still stands on the statute books of the South.[20]

The triumph of reaction in the South inaugurated a new era in which we may distinguish three phases: the renewed attempt to reduce the Negroes to serfdom, the rise of the Negro metayer, and the economic disfranchisement of the Southern working class.

The attempt to replace individual slavery had been frustrated by the Freedmen's Bureau and the Fifteenth Amendment. The disfranchisement of 1876 was followed by the widespread rise of "crime" peonage. Stringent laws on vagrancy, guardianship, and labor contracts were enacted and large discretion given judge and jury in cases of petty crime. As a result Negroes were systematically arrested on the slightest pretext and the labor of convicts leased to private parties. This "convict lease system" was almost universal in the South until about 1890, when its outrageous abuses and cruelties aroused the whole country. It still survives over wide areas, and is not only responsible for the impression that the Negro is a natural criminal, but also for the inability of the Southern courts to perform their normal functions after so long a prostitution to ends far removed from justice.

In more normal economic lines the employers began with the labor contract system. Before the war they owned labor, land, and subsistence. After the war they still held the land and subsistence. The laborer was hired and the subsistence "advanced" to him while the crop was growing. The fall of the Freedmen's Bureau hindered the transmutation of this system into a modern wage system, and allowed the laborers to be cheated by high interest charges on the subsistence advanced and actual cheating often in book accounts.

The black laborers became deeply dissatisfied under this system and began to migrate from the country to the cities, where there was an increasing demand for labor. The employing farmers complained bitterly of the scarcity of labor and of Negro "laziness," and secured the enactment of harsher vagrancy and labor contract laws, and statutes against the "enticement" of laborers. So severe were these laws that it was often impossible for a laborer to stop work without committing a felony. Nevertheless competition compelled the landholders to offer more inducements to the farm hand. The result was the rise of the black share tenant: the laborer securing better wages saved a little capital and began to hire land in parcels of forty to eighty acres, furnishing his own tools and seed and practically raising his own subsistence. In this way the whole face of the labor contract in the South was, in the decade 1880–90, in process of change from a nominal wage contract to a system of tenantry. The great plantations were apparently broken up into forty and eighty acre farms with black farmers. To many it seemed that emancipation was accomplished, and the black folk were especially filled with joy and hope.

It soon was evident, however, that the change was only partial. The landlord still held the land in large parcels. He rented this in small farms to tenants, but retained direct control. In theory the laborer was furnishing capital, but in the majority of cases he was borrowing at least a part of this capital from some merchant.

The retail merchant in this way entered on the scene as middle man between landlord and laborer. He guaranteed the landowner his rent and relieved him of details by taking over the furnishing of supplies to the laborer. He tempted the laborer by a larger stock of more attractive goods, made a direct contract with him, and took a mortgage on the growing crop. Thus he soon became the middle man to whom the profit of the transaction largely flowed, and he began to get rich.

If the new system benefited the merchant and the landlord, it also brought some benefits to the black laborers. Numbers of these were still held in peonage, and the mass were laborers working for scant board and clothes; but above these began to rise a large number of independent tenants and farm owners.

In 1890, therefore, the South was faced by this question: Are we willing to allow the Negro to advance as a free worker, peasant farmer, metayer, and small capitalist, with only such handicaps as naturally impede the poor and ignorant, or is it necessary to erect further artificial barriers to restrain the advance of the Negroes? The answer was clear and unmistakable. The advance of the freedmen had been too rapid and the South feared it; every effort must be made to "keep the Negro in his place" as a servile caste.

To this end the South strove to make the disfranchisement of the Negroes effective and final. Up to this time disfranchisement was illegal and based on intimidation. The new laws passed between 1890 and 1910 sought on their face to base the right to vote on property and education in such a way as to exclude poor and illiterate Negroes and admit all whites. In fact they could be administered so as to exclude nearly all Negroes. To this was added a series of laws designed publicly to humiliate and stigmatize Negro blood: as, for example, separate railway cars; separate seats in street cars, and the like; these things were added to the separation in schools and churches, and the denial of redress to seduced colored women, which had long been the custom in the South. All these new enactments meant not simply separation, but subordination, caste, humiliation, and flagrant injustice.

To all this was added a series of labor laws making the exploitation of Negro labor more secure. All this legislation had to be accomplished in the face of the labor movement throughout the world, and particularly in the South, where it was beginning to enter among the white workers. This was accomplished easily, however, by an appeal to race prejudice. No method of inflaming the darkest passions of men was unused. The lynching mob was given its glut of blood and egged on by purposely exaggerated and often wholly invented tales of crime on the part of perhaps the most peaceful and sweet-tempered race the world has ever known. Under the flame of this outward noise went the more subtle and dangerous work. The election laws passed in the states where three-fourths of the Negroes live, were so ingeniously framed that a black university graduate could be prevented from voting and the most ignorant white hoodlum could be admitted to the polls. Labor laws were so arranged that imprisonment for debt was possible and leaving an employer could be made a penitentiary offense. Negro schools were cut off with small appropriations or wholly neglected, and a determined effort was made with wide success to see that no Negro had any voice either in the making or the administration of local, state, or national law.

The acquiescence of the white labor vote of the South was further insured by throwing white and black laborers, so far as possible, into rival competing groups and making each feel that the one was the cause of the other's troubles. The neutrality of the white people of the North was secured through their fear for the safety of large investments in the South, and through the fatalistic attitude common both in America and Europe toward the possibility of real advance on the part of the darker nations.

The reaction of the Negro Americans upon this wholesale and open attempt to reduce them to serfdom has been interesting. Naturally they began to organize and protest and in some cases to appeal to the courts. Then, to their astonishment, there arose a colored leader, Mr. Booker T. Washington, who advised them to yield to disfranchisement and caste and wait for greater economic strength and general efficiency before demanding full rights as American citizens. The white South naturally agreed with Mr. Washington, and the white North thought they saw here a chance for peace in the racial conflict and safety for their Southern investments.

For a time the colored people hesitated. They respected Mr. Washington for shrewdness and recognized the wisdom of his homely insistence on thrift and hard work; but gradually they came to see more and more clearly that, stripped of political power and emasculated by caste, they could never gain sufficient economic strength to take their place as modern men. They also realized that any lull in their protests would be taken advantage of by Negro haters to push their caste program. They began, therefore, with renewed persistence to fight for their fundamental rights as American citizens. The struggle tended at first to bitter personal dissension within the group. But wiser counsels and the advice of white friends eventually prevailed and raised it to the broad level of a fight for the fundamental principles of democracy. The launching of the "Niagara Movement" by twenty-nine daring colored men in 1905, followed by the formation of the National Association for the Advancement of Colored People in 1910, marked an epoch in the advance of the Negro. This latter organization, with its monthly organ, *The Crisis*, is now waging a nation-wide fight for justice to Negroes. Other organizations, and a number of strong Negro weekly papers are aiding in this fight. What has been the net result of this struggle of half a century?

In 1863 there were about five million persons of Negro descent in the United States. Of these, four million and more were just being released from slavery. These slaves could be bought and sold, could move from place to place only with permission, were forbidden to learn to read or write, and legally could never hold property or marry. Ninety per cent were totally illiterate, and only one adult in six was a nominal Christian.

Fifty years later, in 1913, there were in the United States ten and a quarter million persons of Negro descent, an increase of one hundred and five per cent. Legal slavery has been abolished leaving, however, vestiges in debt slavery, peonage, and the convict lease system. The mass of the freedmen and their sons have

1. Earned a living as free and partially free laborers.
2. Shared the responsibilities of government.
3. Developed the internal organization of their race.
4. Aspired to spiritual self-expression.

The Negro was freed as a penniless, landless, naked, ignorant laborer. There were a few free Negroes who owned property in the South, and a larger number who owned property in the North; but ninety-nine per cent of the race in the South were penniless field hands and servants.

To-day there are two and a half million laborers, the majority of whom are efficient wage earners. Above these are more than a million servants and tenant farmers; skilled and semi-skilled workers make another million and at the top of the economic column are 600,000 owners and managers of farms and businesses, cash tenants, officials, and professional men. This makes a total of 5,192,535 colored breadwinners in 1910.

More specifically these breadwinners include 218,972 farm owners and 319,346 cash farm tenants and managers. There were in all 62,755 miners, 288,141 in the building and hand trades; 28,515 workers in clay, glass, and stone; 41,739 iron and steel workers; 134,102 employees on railways; 62,822 draymen, cab drivers, and liverymen; 133,245 in wholesale and retail trade; 32,170 in the public service; and 69,471 in professional service, including 29,750 teachers, 17,495 clergymen, and 4,546 physicians, dentists, trained nurses, etc. Finally, we must not forget 2,175,000 Negro homes, with their housewives, and 1,620,000 children in school.

Fifty years ago the overwhelming mass of these people were not only penniless, but were themselves assessed as real estate. By 1875 the Negroes probably had gotten hold of something between 2,000,000 and 4,000,000 acres of land through their bounties as soldiers and the low price of land after the war. By 1880 this was increased to about 6,000,000 acres; in 1890 to about 8,000,000 acres; in 1900 to over 12,000,000 acres. In 1910 this land had increased to nearly 20,000,000 acres, a realm as large as Ireland.

The 120,738 farms owned by Negroes in 1890 increased to 218,972 in 1910, or eighty-one per cent. The value of these farms increased from $179,796,639 in 1900 to $440,992,439 in 1910; Negroes owned in 1910 about 500,000 homes out of a total of 2,175,000. Their total property in 1900 was estimated at $300,000,000 by the American Economic Association. On the same basis of calculation it would be worth to-day not less than $800,000,000.

Despite the disfranchisement of three-fourths of his voting population, the Negro to-day is a recognized part of the American government. He holds 7,500 offices in the executive service of the nation, besides furnishing four regiments in the army and a large number of sailors. In the state and municipal service he holds nearly 20,000 other offices, and he furnishes 500,000 of the votes which rule the Union.

In these same years the Negro has relearned the lost art of organization. Slavery was the almost absolute denial of initiative and responsibility. To-day Negroes have nearly 40,000 churches, with edifices worth at least $75,000,000 and controlling nearly 4,000,000 members. They raise themselves $7,500,000 a year for these churches.

There are 200 private schools and colleges managed and almost entirely supported by Negroes, and these and other public and private Negro schools have received in 40 years $45,000,000 of Negro money in taxes and donations. Five millions a year are raised by Negro secret and beneficial societies which hold at least $6,000,000 in real estate. Negroes support wholly or in part over 100 old folks' homes and orphanages, 30 hospitals, and 500 cemeteries. Their organized commercial life is extending rapidly and includes over 22,000 small retail businesses and 40 banks.

Above and beyond this material growth has gone the spiritual uplift of a great human race. From contempt and amusement they have passed to the pity, perplexity, and fear on the part of their neighbors, while within their own souls they have arisen from apathy and timid complaint to open protest and more and more manly self-assertion. Where nine-tenths of them could not read or write in 1860, to-day over two-thirds can; they have 300 papers and periodicals, and their voice and expression are compelling attention.

Already in poetry, literature, music, and painting the work of Americans of Negro descent has gained notable recognition. Instead of being led and defended by others, as in the past, American Negroes are gaining their own leaders, their own voices, their own ideals. Self-realization is thus coming slowly but surely to another of the world's great races, and they are to-day girding themselves to fight in the van of progress, not simply for their own rights as men, but for the ideals of the greater world in which they live: the emancipation of women, universal peace, democratic government, the socialization of wealth, and human brotherhood.

NOTES

1. The figures given by the census are as follows:
    1850, mulattoes formed 11.2 per cent of the total Negro population.
    1860, mulattoes formed 13.2 per cent of the total Negro population.
    1870, mulattoes formed 12 per cent of the total Negro population.
    1890, mulattoes formed 15.2 per cent of the total Negro population.
    1910, mulattoes formed 20.9 per cent of the total Negro population.
    Or in actual numbers:
    1850, 405,751 mulattoes.
    1860, 588,352 mulattoes.
    1870, 585,601 mulattoes.
    1890, 1,132,060 mulattoes.
    1910, 2,050,686 mulattoes.
2. Cf. "The Spanish Jurist Solorzaris," quoted in Helps: *Spanish Conquest*, IV, 381.
3. Hurd: *Law of Freedom and Bondage*.
4. "Obi (Obeah, Obiah, or Obia) is the adjective; Obe or Obi, the noun. It is of African origin, probably connected with Egyptian Ob, Aub, or Obron, meaning 'serpent.' Moses forbids Israelites ever to consult the demon Ob, i.e., 'Charmer, Wizard.' The Witch of Endor is called Oub or Ob. Oubaois is the name of the Baselisk or Royal Serpent, emblem of the Sun, and, according to Horus Appollo, 'the Ancient Deity of Africa.' "—Edwards: *West Indies*, ed. 1819, II, 106–119. Cf. Johnston: *Negro in the New World*, pp. 65–66; also *Atlanta University Publications*, No. 8, pp. 5–6.
5. *Boston Transcript*, March 24, 1906.
6. Bassett: *North Carolina*, pp. 73–76.
7. Cf. Wilson: *The Black Phalanx*.
8. Wilson: *The Black Phalanx*, p. 108.
9. *American Historical Review*, Vol. XV.
10. Report to President Johnson.
11. *Reconstruction and the Constitution*.
12. Brewster: *Sketches*, etc.
13. McPherson: *Reconstruction*, p. 52.
14. Report to the President, 1865.
15. *American Historical Review*, Vol. XV, No. 4.
16. *Occasional Papers*, American Negro Academy, No. 6.
17. *Occasional Papers*, American Negro Academy, No. 6.
18. *Jackson (Miss.) Clarion*, April 24, 1873.
19. Allen: *Governor Chamberlain's Administration*, p. 82.
20. Reconstruction Constitutions, practically unaltered, were kept in Florida, 1868–85, seventeen years; Virginia, 1870–1902, thirty-two years; South Carolina, 1868–95, twenty-seven years; Mississippi, 1868–90, twenty-two years.

CHAPTER XII

◆

The Negro Problems

It is impossible to separate the population of the world accurately by race, since that is no scientific criterion by which to divide races. If we divide the world, however, roughly into African Negroes and Negroids, European whites, and Asiatic and American brown and yellow peoples, we have approximately 150,000,000 Negroes, 500,000,000 whites, and 900,000,000 yellow and brown peoples. Of the 150,000,000 Negroes, 121,000,000 live in Africa, 27,000,000[1] in the new world, and 2,000,000 in Asia.

What is to be the future relation of the Negro race to the rest of the world? The visitor from Altruria might see here no peculiar problem. He would expect the Negro race to develop along the lines of other human races. In Africa his economic and political development would restore and eventually outrun the ancient glories of Egypt, Ethiopia, and Yoruba; overseas the West Indies would become a new and nobler Africa, built in the very pathway of the new highway of commerce between East and West—the real sea route to India; while in the United States a large part of its citizenship (showing for perhaps centuries their dark descent, but nevertheless equal sharers of and contributors to the civilization of the West) would be the descendants of the wretched victims of the seventeenth, eighteenth, and nineteenth century slave trade.

This natural assumption of a stranger finds, however, lodging in the minds of few present-day thinkers. On the contrary, such an outcome is usually dismissed summarily. Most persons have accepted that tacit but clear modern philosophy which assigns to the white race alone the hegemony of the world and assumes that other races, and particularly the Negro race, will either be content to serve the interests of the whites or die out before their all-conquering march. This philosophy is the child of the African slave trade and of the expansion of Europe during the nineteenth century.

The Negro slave trade was the first step in modern world commerce, followed by the modern theory of colonial expansion. Slaves as an article of commerce were shipped as long as the traffic paid. When the Americas had enough black laborers for their immediate demand, the moral action of the eighteenth century had a chance to make its faint voice heard.

The moral repugnance was powerfully reënforced by the revolt of the slaves in the West Indies and South America, and by the fact that North America early began to regard itself as the seat of advanced ideas in politics, religion, and humanity.

Finally European capital began to find better investments than slave shipping and flew to them. These better investments were the fruit of the new industrial revolution of the nineteenth century, with its factory system; they were also in part the result of the cheapened price of gold and silver, brought about by slavery and the slave trade to the new world. Commodities other than gold, and commodities capable of manufacture and exploitation in Europe out of materials furnishable by America, became enhanced in value; the bottom fell out of the commercial slave trade and its suppression became possible.

The middle of the nineteenth century saw the beginning of the rise of the modern working class. By means of political power the laborers slowly but surely began to demand a larger share in the profiting industry. In the United States their demand bade fair to be halted by the competition of slave labor. The labor vote, therefore, first confined slavery to limits in which it could not live, and when the slave power sought to exceed these territorial limits, it was suddenly and unintentionally abolished.

As the emancipation of millions of dark workers took place in the West Indies, North and South America, and parts of Africa at this time, it was natural to assume that the uplift of this working class lay along the same paths with that of European and American whites. This was the *first* suggested solution of the Negro problem. Consequently these Negroes received partial enfranchisement, the beginnings of education, and some of the elementary rights of wage earners and property holders, while the independence of Liberia and Hayti was recognized. However, long before they were strong enough to assert the rights thus granted or to gather intelligence enough for proper group leadership, the new colonialism of the later nineteenth and twentieth centuries began to dawn. The new colonial theory transferred the reign of commercial privilege and extraordinary profit from the exploitation of the European working class to the exploitation of backward races under the political domination of Europe. For the purpose of carrying out this idea the European and white American working class was practically invited to share in this new exploitation, and particularly were flattered by popular appeals to their inherent superiority to "Dagoes," "Chinks," "Japs," and "Niggers."

This tendency was strengthened by the fact that the new colonial expansion centered in Africa. Thus in 1875 something less than one-tenth of Africa was under nominal European control, but the Franco-Prussian War and the exploration of the Congo led to new and fateful things. Germany desired economic expansion and, being shut out from America by the Monroe Doctrine, turned to Africa. France, humiliated in war, dreamed of an African empire from the Atlantic to the Red Sea. Italy became ambitious for Tripoli and Abyssinia. Great Britain began to take new interest in her African realm, but found herself largely checkmated by the jealousy of all Europe. Portugal sought to make good her ancient claim to the larger part of the whole southern peninsula. It was Leopold of

Belgium who started to make the exploration and civilization of Africa an international movement. This project failed, and the Congo Free State became in time simply a Belgian colony. While the project was under discussion, the international scramble for Africa began. As a result the Berlin Conference and subsequent wars and treaties gave Great Britain control of 2,101,411 square miles of African territory, in addition to Egypt and the Egyptian Sudan with 1,600,000 square miles. This includes South Africa, Bechuanaland and Rhodesia, East Africa, Uganda and Zanzibar, Nigeria, and British West Africa. The French hold 4,106,950 square miles, including nearly all North Africa (except Tripoli) west of the Niger valley and Libyan Desert, and touching the Atlantic at four points. To this is added the Island of Madagascar. The Germans have 910,150 square miles, principally in Southeast and South-west Africa and the Kamerun. The Portuguese retain 787,500 square miles in Southeast and Southwest Africa. The Belgians have 900,000 square miles, while Liberia (43,000 square miles) and Abyssinia (350,000 square miles) are independent. The Italians have about 600,000 square miles and the Spanish less than 100,000 square miles.

This partition of Africa brought revision of the ideas of Negro uplift. Why was it necessary, the European investors argued, to push a continent of black workers along the paths of social uplift by education, trades-unionism, property holding, and the electoral franchise when the workers desired no change, and the rate of European profit would suffer?

There quickly arose then the *second* suggestion for settling the Negro problem. It called for the virtual enslavement of natives in certain industries, as rubber and ivory collecting in the Belgian Congo, cocoa raising in Portuguese Angola, and diamond mining in South Africa. This new slavery or "forced" labor was stoutly defended as a necessary foundation for implanting modern industry in a barbarous land; but its likeness to slavery was too clear and it has been modified, but not wholly abolished.

The *third* attempted solution of the Negro sought the result of the *second* by less direct methods. Negroes in Africa, the West Indies, and America were to be forced to work by land monopoly, taxation, and little or no education. In this way a docile industrial class working for low wages, and not intelligent enough to unite in labor unions, was to be developed. The peonage systems in parts of the United States and the labor systems of many of the African colonies of Great Britain and Germany illustrate this phase of solution.[2] It is also illustrated in many of the West Indian islands where we have a predominant Negro population, and this population freed from slavery and partially enfranchised. Land and capital, however, have for the most part been so managed and monopolized that the black peasantry have been reduced to straits to earn a living in one of the richest parts of the world. The problem is now going to be intensified when the world's commerce begins to sweep through the Panama Canal.

All these solutions and methods, however, run directly counter to modern philanthropy, and have to be carried on with a certain concealment and half-hypocrisy which is not only distasteful in itself, but always liable to be discovered and exposed by some liberal or religious movement of the masses of men and suddenly overthrown. These solutions are, therefore, gradually merging into a *fourth* solution, which is to-day very popular. This solution says: Negroes differ from whites in their inherent genius and stage of development. Their development must not, therefore, be sought along European lines, but along their own native lines. Consequently the effort is made to-day in British Nigeria, in the French Congo and Sudan, in Uganda and Rhodesia to leave so far as possible the outward structure of native life intact; the king or chief reigns, the popular assemblies meet and act, the native courts adjudicate, and native social and family life and religion prevail. All this, however, is subject to the veto and command of a European magistracy supported by a native army with European officers. The advantage of this method is that on its face it carries no clue to its real working. Indeed it can always point to certain undoubted advantages: the abolition of the slave trade, the suppression of war and feud, the encouragement of peaceful industry. On the other hand, back of practically all these experiments stands the economic motive—the determination to use the organization, the land, and the people, not for their own benefit, but for the benefit of white Europe. For this reason education is seldom encouraged, modern religious ideas are carefully limited, sound political development is sternly frowned upon, and industry is degraded and changed to the demands of European markets. The most ruthless class of white mercantile exploiters is allowed large liberty, if not a free hand, and protected by a concerted attempt to deify white men as such in the eyes of the native and in their own imagination.[3]

White missionary societies are spending perhaps as much as five million dollars a year in Africa and accomplishing much good, but at the same time white merchants are sending at least twenty million dollars' worth of European liquor into Africa each year, and the debauchery of the almost unrestricted rum traffic goes far to neutralize missionary effort.

Under this last mentioned solution of the Negro problems we may put the attempts at the segregation of Negroes and mulattoes in the United States and to some extent in the West Indies. Ostensibly this is "separation" of the races in society, civil rights, etc. In practice it is the subordination of colored people of all grades under white tutelage, and their separation as far as possible from contact with civilization in dwelling place, in education, and in public life.

On the other hand the economic significance of the Negro to-day is tremendous. Black Africa to-day exports annually nearly two hundred million dollars' worth of goods, and its economic development has scarcely begun. The black West Indies export nearly one hundred million dollars' worth of goods; to this must be added the labor value of Negroes in South Africa, Egypt, the West Indies, North, Central, and South America, where the result is blended in the common output of many races. The economic foundation of the Negro problem can easily be seen to be a matter of many hundreds of millions to-day, and ready to rise to the billions tomorrow.

Such figures and facts give some slight idea of the economic meaning of the Negro to-day as a worker and industrial factor. "Tropical Africa and its peoples are being brought more irrevocably every year into the vortex of the economic influences that sway the western world."[4]

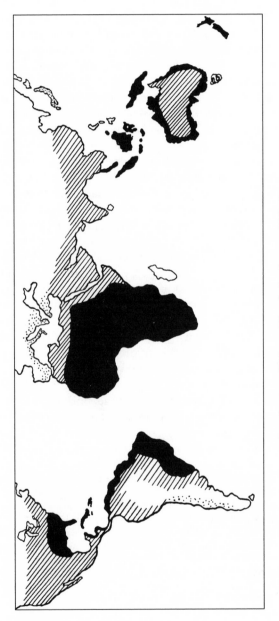

Distribution of Negro Blood, Ancient and Modern

What do Negroes themselves think of these their problems and the attitude of the world toward them? First and most significant, they are thinking. There is as yet no great single centralizing of thought or unification of opinion, but there are centers which are growing larger and larger and touching edges. The most significant centers of this new thinking are, perhaps naturally, outside Africa and in America: in the United States and in the West Indies; this is followed by South Africa and West Africa and then, more vaguely, by South America, with faint beginnings in East Central Africa, Nigeria, and the Sudan.

The Pan-African movement when it comes will not, however, be merely a narrow racial propaganda. Already the more far-seeing Negroes sense the coming unities: a unity of the working classes everywhere, a unity of the colored races, a new unity of men. The proposed economic solution of the Negro problem in Africa and America has turned the thoughts of Negroes toward a realization of the fact that the modern white laborer of Europe and America has the key to the serfdom of black folk, in his support of militarism and colonial expansion. He is beginning to say to these workingmen that, so long as black laborers are slaves, white laborers cannot be free. Already there are signs in South Africa and the United States of the beginning of understanding between the two classes.

In a conscious sense of unity among colored races there is to-day only a growing interest. There is slowly arising not only a curiously strong brotherhood of Negro blood throughout the world, but the common cause of the darker races against the intolerable assumptions and insults of Europeans has already found expression. Most men in this world are colored. A belief in humanity means a belief in colored men. The future world will, in all reasonable probability, be what colored men make it. In order for this colored world to come into its heritage, must the earth again be drenched in the blood of fighting, snarling human beasts, or will Reason and Good Will prevail? That such may be true, the character of the Negro race is the best and greatest hope; for in its normal condition it is at once the strongest and gentlest of the races of men: "Semper novi quid ex Africa!"

NOTES

1. Sir Harry Johnston estimates 135,000,000 Negroes, of whom 24,591,000 live in America. See *Inter-Racial Problems*, p. 335.
2. The South African natives, in an appeal to the English Parliament, show in an astonishing way the confiscation of their land by the English. They say that in the Union of South Africa 1,250,000 whites own 264,000,000 acres of land, while the 4,500,000 natives have only 21,000,000 acres. On top of this the Union Parliament has passed a law making even the future purchase of land by Negroes illegal save in restricted areas!
3. The traveler Glave writes in the *Century Magazine* (LIII, 913): "Formerly [in the Congo Free State] an ordinary white man was merely called 'bwana' or 'Mzunga'; now the merest insect of a pale face earns the title of 'bwana Mkubwa' [big master]."
4. E. D. Morel, in the *Nineteenth Century*.

Suggestions for
Further Reading

There is no general history of the Negro race. Perhaps Sir Harry H. Johnston, in his various works on Africa, has come as near covering the subject as any one writer, but his valuable books have puzzling inconsistencies and inaccuracies. Keane's *Africa* is a helpful compendium, despite the fact that whenever Keane discovers intelligence in an African he immediately discovers that its possessor is no "Negro." The articles in the latest edition of the *Encyclopædia Britannica* are of some value, except the ridiculous article on the "Negro" by T. A. Joyce. Frobenius' newly published *Voice of Africa* is broad-minded and informing, and Brown's *Story of Africa and its Explorers* brings together much material in readable form. The compendiums by Keltie and White, and Johnston's *Opening up of Africa* are the best among the shorter treatises.

None of these authors write from the point of view of the Negro as a man, or with anything but incidental acknowledgment of the existence or value of his history. We may, however, set down certain books under the various subjects which the chapters have treated. These books will consist of (1) standard works for wider reading and (2) special works on which the author has relied for his statements or which amplify his point of view. *The latter are starred.*

THE PHYSIOGRAPHY OF AFRICA

A. S. White: *The Development of Africa*, 2d ed., 1892.
Stanford's Compendium of Geography: *Africa*, by A. H. Keane, 2d ed., 1904–7.
E. Reclus: *Universal Geography*, Vols. X–XIII.

RACIAL DIFFERENCES AND THE ORIGIN AND CHARACTERISTICS OF NEGROES

J. Deniker: *The Races of Man*, etc., New York, 1904.
*J. Finot: *Race Prejudice* (tr. by Wade-Evans), New York, 1907.
*W. Z. Ripley: *The Races of Europe*, etc., New York, 1899.
*Jacques Loeb: in *The Crisis*, Vol. VIII, p. 84, Vol. IX, p. 92.

*Papers on Inter-Racial Problems Communicated to the First Universal Races Congress, etc. (ed. by G. Spiller), 1911.
*G. Sergi: The Mediterranean Race, etc., London, 1901.
*Franz Boas: The Mind of Primitive Man, New York, 1911.
C. B. Davenport: Heredity of Skin Color in Negro-White Crosses, 1913.

EARLY MOVEMENTS OF THE NEGRO RACE

*Sir Harry H. Johnston: The Opening up of Africa (Home University Library).
—— A History of the Colonization of Africa by Alien Races, Cambridge, 1905.
*G. W. Stowe: The Native Races of South Africa (ed. by G. M. Theal), London, 1910.
(Consult also Johnston's other works on Africa, and his article in Vol. XLIII of the Journal of the Royal Anthropological Institute of Great Britain and Ireland; also Inter-Racial Problems, and Deniker, noted above.)

NEGRO IN ETHIOPIA AND EGYPT

(The works of Breasted and Petrie, Maspero, Budge and Newberry and Garstang are the standard books on Egypt. They mention the Negro, but incidentally and often slightingly.)
*A. F. Chamberlain: "The Contribution of the Negro to Human Civilization" (Journal of Race Development, Vol. I, April, 1911).
T. E. S. Scholes: Glimpses of the Ages, etc., London, 1905.
W. H. Ferris: The African Abroad, etc., 2 vols., New Haven, 1913.
E. A. W. Budge: The Egyptian Sudan, 2 vols., 1907.
*Archeological Survey of Nubia.
*A. Thompson and D. Randal McIver: The Ancient Races of the Thebaid, 1905.

ABYSSINIA

Job Ludolphus: A New History of Ethiopia (tr. by Gent), London, 1682.
W. S. Harris: Highlands of Æthiopia, 3 vols., London, 1844.
R. S. Whiteway: The Portuguese Expedition to Abyssinia . . . as narrated by Castanhosa, etc., 1902.

THE NIGER RIVER AND ISLAM

*F. L. Shaw (Lady Lugard): A Tropical Dependency, etc., London, 1906.
(The reader may dismiss as worthless Lady Lugard's definition of "Negro." Otherwise her book is excellent.)
*Es-Sa'di, Abderrahman Ben Abdallah, etc., translated into French by O. Houdas, Paris, 1900.
*F. DuBois: Timbuktu the Mysterious (tr. by White), 1896.
*W. D. Cooley: The Negroland of the Arabs, etc., 1841.
*H. Barth: Travels and Discoveries in North and Central Africa, etc., 5 vols., 1857–58.
*Ibn Batuta: Travels, etc. (tr. by Lee), 1829.
*Leo Africanus: The History and Description of Africa, etc. (tr. by Pory, ed. by R. Brown), 3 vols., 1896.
*E. W. Blyden: Christianity, Islam, and the Negro Race.
*Leo Frobenius: The Voice of Africa (tr. by Blind), 2 vols., 1913.
Mungo Park: Travels in the Interior Districts of Africa, 1799.

THE NEGRO ON THE GUINEA COAST

*Leo Frobenius (as above).
Sir Harry H. Johnston: Liberia, 2 vols., New York, 1906.
H. H. Foote: Africa and the American Flag, New York, 1859.

T. H. T. McPherson: *A History of Liberia*, Baltimore, Johns Hopkins Studies.
T. J. Alldridge: *A Transformed Colony* (Sierra Leone), London, 1910.
E. D. Morel: *Affairs of West Africa*, 1902.
H. L. Roth: *Great Benin and Its Customs*, 1903.
*F. Starr: *Liberia*, 1913.
W. Jay: *An Inquiry*, etc., 1835.
*A. B. Ellis: *The Tshi-speaking Peoples of the Gold Coast*, 1887.
————— *The Ewe-speaking Peoples of the Slave Coast*, 1890.
————— *The Yoruba-speaking Peoples of the Slave Coast*, 1894.
C. H. Read and O. M. Dalton: *Antiquities from the City of Benin*, etc., 1899.
*M. H. Kingsley: *West African Studies*, 2d. ed., 1904.
*G. W. Ellis: *Negro Culture in West Africa* (Vai-speaking peoples), 1914.

THE CONGO VALLEY

*G. Schweinfurth: *The Heart of Africa*, Vol. II, 1873.
*H. M. Stanley: *Through the Dark Continent*, 2 vols., 1878.
————— *In Darkest Africa*, 2 vols., 1890.
————— *The Congo*, etc., 2 vols., London, 1885.
H. von Wissman: *My Second Journey through Equatorial Africa*, 1891.
*H. R. Fox-Bourne: *Civilization in Congoland*, 1903.
Sir Harry H. Johnston: *George Grenfell and the Congo*, 2 vols., London, 1908.
*E. D. Morel: *Red Rubber*, London, 1906.

THE NEGRO IN THE REGION OF THE GREAT LAKES

*Sir Harry H. Johnston: *The Uganda Protectorate*, 2d ed., 2 vols., 1904.
————— *British Central Africa*, 1897.
————— *The Nile Quest*, 1903.
*D. Randal McIver: *Mediæval Rhodesia*, 1906.
The Last Journals of David Livingstone in Central Africa (ed. by H. Waller), 1874.
J. Dos Santos: *Ethiopia Oriental* (Theal's *Records of South Africa*, Vol. VII).
C. Peters: "Ophir and Punt in South Africa" (*African Society Journal*, Vol. I).
De Barros: *De Asia.*
R. Burton: *Lake Regions of Central Africa*, 1860.
R. P. Ashe: *Chronicles of Uganda*, 1894.
    (See also Stanley's works, as above.)

THE NEGRO IN SOUTH AFRICA

*G. M. Theal: *History and Ethnography of South Africa of the Zambesi to 1795*, 3 vols., 1907–10.
————— *History of South Africa since September, 1795*, 5 vols., 1908.
————— *Records of South Eastern Africa*, 9 vols., 1898–1903.
*J. Bryce: *Impressions of South Africa*, 1897.
D. Livingstone: *Missionary Travels in South Africa*, 1857.
*South African Native Affairs Commission, 1903–5, *Reports*, etc., 5 vols., Cape Town, 1904–5.
G. Lagden: *The Basutos*, London, 1909.
J. Stewart: *Lovedale*, 1884.
    (See also Stowe, as above.)

ON NEGRO CIVILIZATION

J. Dowd: *The Negro Races*, 1907, 1914.
*H. Gregoire: *An Inquiry concerning the Intellectual and Moral Faculties and Literature of Negroes*, etc.
    (tr. by Warden), Brooklyn, 1810.

C. Bücher: *Industrial Evolution* (tr. by Wickett), New York, 1904.
*Franz Boas: "The Real Race Problem" (*The Crisis*, December, 1910).
——— *Commencement Address* (Atlanta University Leaflet, No. 19).
*F. Ratzel: *The History of Mankind* (tr. by Butler), 3 vols., 1904.
C. Hayford: *Gold Coast Institutions*, 1903.
A. B. Camphor: *Missionary Sketches and Folk Lore from Africa*, 1909.
R. H. Nassau: *Fetishism in West Africa*, 1907.
*William Schneider: *Die Culturfähigkeit des Negers*, Frankfort, 1885.
*G. Schweinfurth: *Artes Africanae*, etc., 1875.
Duke of Mecklenburg: *From the Congo to the Niger and the Nile* (English tr.), Philadelphia, 1914.
D. Crawford: *Thinking Black.*
R. N. Cust: *Sketch of Modern Language of Africa*, 2 vols., 1883.
H. Chatelain: *The Folk Lore of Angola.*
D. Kidd: *The Essential Kaffir*, 1904.
——— *Savage Childhood*, 1906.
——— *Kaffir Socialism and the Dawn of Individualism*, 1908.
M. H. Tongue: *Bushman Paintings*, Oxford, 1909.
(See also the works of A. B. Ellis, Miss Kingsley, Sir Harry H. Johnston, Frobenius, Stowe, Theal, and Ibn Batuta; and particularly Chamberlain's article in the *Journal of Race Development*.)

THE SLAVE TRADE

T. K. Ingram: *History of Slavery and Serfdom*, London, 1895. (Same article revised in *Encyclopædia Britannica*, 11th edition.)
John R. Spears: *The American Slave Trade*, 1900.
*T. F. Buxton: *The African Slave Trade and Its Remedy*, etc., 1896.
T. Clarkson: *History . . . of the Abolition of the African Slave Trade*, etc., 2 vols., 1808.
R. Drake: *Revelations of a Slave Smuggler*, New York, 1860.
Report of the Lords of the Committee of Council, etc., London, 1789.
*B. Mayer: *Captain Canot or Twenty Years of an African Slaver*, etc., 1854.
W. E. B. DuBois: *The suppression of the African Slave-Trade to the U.S.A.*, 1896.
(See also Bryan Edwards' *West Indies*.)

THE WEST INDIES AND SOUTH AMERICA

Fletcher and Kidder: *Brazil and the Brazilians*, 1879.
*Bryan Edwards: *History . . . of the British West Indies*, 5 editions, Vols. II–V, 1793–1819.
*Sir Harry H. Johnston: *The Negro in the New World*, 1910.
T. G. Steward: *The Haitian Revolution, 1791–1804*, 1914.
J. N. Leger: *Haiti*, etc., 1907.
J. Bryce: *South America*, etc., 1912.
*J. B. de Lacerda: "The Metis or Half-Breeds of Brazil" (*Inter-Racial Problems*, etc.)
A. K. Fiske: *History of the West Indies*, 1899.

THE NEGRO IN THE UNITED STATES

Walker's Appeal, 1829.
*G. W. Williams: *History of the Negro Race in America, 1619–1880*, 1882.
B. G. Brawley: *A Short History of the American Negro*, 1913.
B. T. Washington: *Up from Slavery*, 1901.
——— *The Story of the Negro*, 2 vols., 1909.
The Autobiography of an Ex-Colored Man, 1912.
*G. E. Stroud: *Sketch of the Laws relating to Slavery*, etc., 1827.
The Human Way: Addresses on Race Problems at the Southern Sociological Congress, Atlanta, 1913 (ed. by J. E. McCulloch).

W. J. Simmons: *Men of Mark*, 1887.
*J. R. Giddings: *The Exiles of Florida*, 1858.
W. E. Nell: *The Colored Patriots of the American Revolution*, etc., 1855.
C. W. Chesnutt: *The Marrow of Tradition*, 1901.
P. L. Dunbar: *Lyrics of Lowly Life*, 1896.
Life and Times of Frederick Douglass, revised edition, 1892.
*H. E. Kreihbel: *Afro-American Folk Songs*, etc., 1914.
T. P. Fenner and others: *Cabin and Plantation Songs*, 3d ed., 1901.
W. F. Allen and others: *Slave Songs of the United States*, 1867.
W. E. B. DuBois: "The Negro Race in the United States of America" (*Inter-Racial Problems*, etc.).
———— "The Economics of Negro Emancipation" (*Sociological Review*, October, 1911).
———— *John Brown.*
———— *The Philadelphia Negro*, 1899.
W. E. B. DuBois: "Reconstruction and its Benefits" (*American Historical Review*, Vol. XV, No. 4).
    editor, *The Crisis*: A Record of the Darker Races, monthly, 1910.
    editor, *The Atlanta University Studies*:
    No. 1. *Mortality Among Negroes in Cities*, 1896.
    No. 2. *Social and Physical Conditions of Negroes in Cities*, 1897.
    No. 3. *Some Efforts of Negroes for Social Betterment*, 1898.
    No. 4. *The Negro in Business*, 1899.
    No. 5. *The College Bred Negro*, 1900.
    No. 6. *The Negro Common School*, 1901.
    No. 7. *The Negro Artisan*, 1902.
    No. 8. *The Negro Church*, 1903.
    No. 9. *Notes on Negro Crime*, 1904.
    No. 10. *A Select Bibliography of the Negro American*, 1905.
    No. 11. *Health and Physique of the Negro American*, 1906.
    No. 12. *Economic Co-operation among Negro Americans*, 1907.
    No. 13. *The Negro American Family*, 1908.
    No. 14. *Efforts for Social Betterment among Negro Americans*, 1909.
    No. 15. *The College Bred Negro American*, 1910.
    No. 16. *The Common School and the Negro American*, 1911.
    No. 17. *The Negro American Artisan*, 1912.
    No. 18. *Morals and Manners among Negro Americans*, 1913.
*G. W. Cable: *The Silent South*, etc., 1885.
*J. R. Lynch: *The Facts of Reconstruction*, 1913.
*J. T. Wilson: *The Black Phalanx*, 1897.
William Goodell: *Slavery and Anti-Slavery*, 1852.
G. S. Merriam: *The Negro and the Nation*, 1906.
A. B. Hart: *The Southern South*, 1910.
*G. Livermore: *An Historical Research respecting the Opinions of the Founders of the Republic on Negroes*, etc., 1862.
Hartshorn and Penniman: *An Era of Progress and Promise*, 1910 (profusely illustrated).
*James Brewster: *Sketches of Southern Mystery, Treason, and Murder.*
Willcox and DuBois: *Negroes in the United States* (United States Census of 1900, Bulletin No. 8).

THE FUTURE OF THE NEGRO RACE

*J. S. Keltie: *The Partition of Africa*, 2d ed., 1895.
B. T. Washington: *The Future of the Negro.*
W. E. B. DuBois: "The Future of the Negro Race in America" (*East and West*, Vol. II, No. 5).
———— *Souls of Black Folk*, 1913.
———— *Quest of the Silver Fleece.*
Alexander Crummell: *The Future of Africa*, 2d ed., 1862.

*Casely Hayford: *Ethiopia Unbound*, 1911.
Kelly Miller: *Out of the House of Bondage*, 1914.
—— *Race Adjustment*, 1908.
*J. Royce: *Race Questions*, etc., 1908.
*R. S. Baker: *Following the Color Line*, 1908.
N. S. Shaler: *The Neighbor*.
E. D. Morel: "Free Labor in Tropical Africa" (*Nineteenth Century and After*, 1914).
   (See also Finot, Boas, *Inter-Racial Problems*, and White's *Development of Africa*.)

Index

William Edward Burghardt Du Bois: A Chronology

Compiled by Henry Louis Gates, Jr. and Terri Hume Oliver

1868	Born William Edward Burghardt Du Bois, 23 February, in Great Barrington, Massachusetts—the only child of Alfred Du Bois and Mary Silvina Burghardt. Mother and child move to family farm owned by Othello Burghardt, Mary Silvina's father, in South Egremont Plain.
1872	Othello Burghardt dies 19 September and family moves back to Great Barrington, where Mary Sylvina finds work as a domestic servant.
1879	Moves with mother to rooms on Railroad Street. Mother suffers stroke, which partially paralyzes her; she continues to work despite her disability.
1883–1885	Writes occasionally for *Springfield Republican*, the most influential newspaper in the region. Reports on local events for the *New York Globe*, a black weekly, and its successor, the *Freeman*.
1884	Graduates from Great Barrington High School. Works as timekeeper on a construction site.
1885	Mother dies 23 March at age 54. A scholarship is arranged by local Congregational churches so Du Bois can attend Fisk University in Nashville. Enters Fisk with sophomore standing. Contracts typhoid and is seriously ill in October; after recovering, resumes studies and becomes editor of the school newspaper, the *Fisk Herald*.
1886–1887	Teaches at a black school near Alexandria, Tennessee, for two summers. Begins singing with the Mozart Society at Fisk.
1888	Receives BA from Fisk. Enters Harvard College as a junior after receiving a Price-Greenleaf grant.
1890	Awarded second prize in Boylston oratorical competition. Receives BA *cum laude* in philosophy on 25 June. Delivers commencement oration on Jefferson Davis, which receives national press attention. Enters Harvard Graduate School in social science.

1891	Awarded MA in history from Harvard. Begins work on doctorate. Presents paper on the suppression of the African slave trade at meeting of American Historical Association in Washington, D.C.
1892	Awarded a Slater Fund grant to study in Germany at Friedrich Wilhelm University in Berlin.
1893	Grant is extended for an additional year.
1894	Denied doctoral degree at Friedrich Wilhelm University due to residency requirements. Denied further aid from Slater Fund; returns to Great Barrington. Receives teaching chair in classics at Wilberforce University in Xenia, Ohio.
1895	Awarded a PhD in history; he is the first black to receive a PhD from Harvard.
1896	Marries Nina Gomer, a student at Wilberforce. His doctoral thesis, *The Suppression of the African Slave-Trade to United States of America, 1638–1870*, is published as the first volume of Harvard's Historical Monograph Series. Hired by the University of Pennsylvania to conduct a sociological study on the black population of Philadelphia's Seventh Ward.
1897	Joins Alexander Crummell and other black intellectuals to found the American Negro Academy, an association dedicated to black scholarly achievement. Appointed professor of history and economics at Atlanta University. Begins editing a series of sociological studies on black life, the *Atlanta University Studies* (1898–1914). First child, Burghardt Comer Du Bois, is born in Great Barrington on 2 October.
1899	*The Philadelphia Negro* is published by the University of Pennsylvania. Burghardt Gomer Du Bois dies on 24 May in Atlanta and is buried in Great Barrington. Publishes articles in *Atlantic Monthly* and *The Independent*.
1900	In July attends first Pan-African Congress in London and is elected secretary. In an address to the congress, he declares that "the problem of the twentieth century is the problem of the color line." Enters an exhibit at Paris Exposition and wins grand prize for his display on black economic development. Daughter Nina Yolande born 21 October in Great Barrington.
1901	Publishes "The Freedman's Bureau" in *Atlantic Monthly*.
1902	Booker T. Washington offers Du Bois a teaching position at Tuskegee Institute, but Du Bois declines.
1903	*The Souls of Black Folk* is published in April. Publishes the essay "The Talented Tenth" in *The Negro Problem*.
1904	Resigns from Washington's Committee of Twelve for the Advancement of the Negro Race due to ideological differences. Publishes "Credo" in *The Independent*.
1905	Holds the first conference of the Niagara Movement and is named general secretary. Founds and edits *The Moon Illustrated Weekly*.

1906	Second meeting of the Niagara Movement. *The Moon* ceases publication. The Atlanta riots, in which white mobs target blacks, occur in September; Du Bois responds by writing his most famous poem, *A Litany of Atlanta*. After the riots Du Bois's wife and daughter move to Great Barrington.
1907	Niagara Movement in disarray due to debt and dissension. Founds and edits *Horizon*, a monthly paper that folds in 1910.
1908	Fourth conference of Niagara Movement; few attend.
1909	The National Negro Committee, an organization dominated by white liberals, is formed (it will later be renamed the National Association for the Advancement of Colored People [NAACP]); Du Bois joins. The fifth and last Niagara Conference is held. *John Brown*, a biography, is published.
1910	Appointed director of publications and research for the NAACP; becomes the only black member of the board of directors. Moves to New York City to found and edit *The Crisis*, the official publication of the NAACP.
1911	Attends Universal Races Conference in London. Publishes his first novel, *The Quest of the Silver Fleece*. Joins the Socialist Party.
1912	Endorses Woodrow Wilson in *The Crisis*. Resigns from Socialist Party.
1913	Writes and presents *The Star of Ethiopia*, a pageant staged to commemorate the fiftieth anniversary of emancipation.
1914	Supports women's suffrage in *The Crisis*. Supports the Allied effort in World War I despite declaring that imperialist rivalries are a cause of the war.
1915	Booker T. Washington dies on 14 November. *The Negro* is published. Protests D. W. Griffith's racist film *The Birth of a Nation*.
1917	Undergoes kidney operations early in the year. Supports the establishment of separate training camps for black officers as the only way to insure black participation in combat.
1918	In his July editorial for *The Crisis*, he publishes "Close Ranks," urging cooperation with white citizens. The War Department offers Du Bois a commission as a captain in the army in an effort to address racial issues, but the offer is withdrawn after controversy. Goes to Europe in December to evaluate the conditions of black troops for the NAACP.
1919	Organizes the first Pan-African Conference in Paris, and is elected executive secretary. Returns to the U.S. in April and writes the editorial "Returning Soldiers," which the U.S. postmaster Albert Burleson tries to suppress; the issue sells 106,000 copies, the most ever for *The Crisis*.
1920	Founds and edits *The Brownies' Book*, a monthly magazine for children. Publishes *Darkwater: Voices from within the Veil*, a collection of essays.

1921	The second Pan-African Conference is held in London, Brussels, and Paris. Du Bois signs group protest against Henry Ford's support of the anti-Semitic forgery, *Protocols of the Elders of Zion*.
1922	Works for passage of the Dyer Anti-Lynching Bill, which is blocked by Senate.
1923	Writes "Back to Africa," an article attacking Garvey for encouraging racial division. Organizes the third Pan-African Conference in London, Paris, and Lisbon; declines to attend Paris session due to disproval of French assimilationists. Receives the Spingarn Medal from the NAACP. Travels to Liberia to represent the United States at the Liberian presidential inauguration.
1924	Publishes *The Gift of Black Folk: The Negroes in the Making of America*.
1925	Contributes "The Negro Mind Reaches Out" to Alain Locke's *The New Negro: An Interpretation*, one of the most influential works of the Harlem Renaissance.
1926	Founds the Krigwa Players, a Harlem theater group. Travels to the Soviet Union to examine life after the Bolshevik Revolution. Praises Soviet achievements in *The Crisis*.
1927	The fourth and last Pan-African Conference is held in New York City.
1928	Daughter Yolande weds the poet Countee Cullen in Harlem; the marriage ends within a year. Du Bois's novel, *Dark Princess, A Romance*, is published.
1929	*The Crisis* faces financial collapse.
1930	Awarded honorary Doctor of Laws degree from Howard University.
1932	Du Bois's daughter Yolande and her second husband, Arnett Williams, have a daughter, Du Bois Williams.
1933	Losing faith in the possibilities of integration, Du Bois begins to publicly examine his position on segregation. Accepts a one-year visiting professorship at Atlanta University. Relinquishes the editorship of *The Crisis* but retains general control of the magazine.
1934	Writes editorials encouraging voluntary segregation and criticizing the integrationist policies of the NAACP. Resigns as editor of *The Crisis* and from the NAACP. Accepts the chairmanship in sociology at Atlanta University. Named the editor in chief of the *Encyclopedia of the Negro*, which is never completed or published.
1935	Publishes the revolutionary historical study, *Black Reconstruction*.
1936	Spends five months in Germany on a grant to study industrial education. Travels through Poland, the Soviet Union, Manchuria, China, and Japan.
1938	Receives honorary Doctor of Laws degree from Atlanta University and honorary Doctor of Letters degree from Fisk.
1939	*Black Folk, Then and Now*, a revised edition of *The Negro* is published.

1940	Publishes his first autobiography, *Dusk of Dawn*. Founds and edits *Phylon*, a quarterly magazine examining black issues. Awarded honorary Doctorate of Humane Letters at Wilberforce.
1941–1942	Proposes and then coordinates the study of southern blacks for black land-grant colleges.
1943	Organizes the First Conference of Negro Land-Grant Colleges at Atlanta University. Informed by Atlanta University that he must retire by 1944, he attempts to have the policy reversed.
1944	Named first black member of the National Institute of Arts and Letters. Despite his protests, he is retired by Atlanta University. Although hesitant to work with Walter White, he rejoins the NAACP as director of special research and moves back to New York. Publishes the essay "My Evolving Program for Negro Freedom" in Rayford Logan's collection *What the Negro Wants*.
1945	Writes a weekly column for the *Chicago Defender*. Serves as consultant, with Mary McLeod Bethune and Walter White, at the San Francisco conference that drafts the United Nations charter; criticizes the charter for failing to oppose colonialism. In October he presides at the Fifth Pan-African Conference in Manchester, England. Nina Du Bois suffers a stroke, which paralyzes her left side. Publishes the first volume of *Encyclopedia of the Negro: Preparatory Volume* with coauthor Guy B. Johnson. Publishes an anti-imperialist analysis of the postwar era, *Color and Democracy: Colonies and Peace*. Resigns from the American Association of University Professors in protest of conferences held in segregated hotels.
1946	Invites leaders of twenty organizations to New York to draft a petition to the United Nations on behalf of African Americans; the appeal becomes an NAACP project.
1947	Edits and writes the introduction to *An Appeal to the World*, a collection of essays sponsored by the NAACP to enlist international support for the fight against racial discrimination in America. At the United Nations, the appeal is supported by the Soviet Union but opposed by the United States. Publishes *The World and Africa*.
1948	Fired from the NAACP after his memorandum critical of Walter White and the NAACP board of directors appears in the *New York Times*. Supports Henry Wallace, the Progressive Party candidate for president. Takes unpaid position as vice chairman (with Paul Robeson) of the Council of African Affairs, an organization listed as "subversive" by the U.S. attorney general. Begins writing for the *National Guardian*.
1949	Helps sponsor and addresses the Cultural and Scientific Conference for World Peace in New York City. Attends the First World Congress of the Defenders of Peace in Paris. Travels to the All-Union Conference of Peace Proponents in Moscow.
1950	Nina Gomer Du Bois dies in Baltimore in July; she is buried in Great Barrington. Elected chairman of the Peace Information

Center, an organization dedicated to the international peace movement and the banning of nuclear weapons. Organization disbands under pressure from the Department of Justice. Du Bois is nominated by the American Labor Party for U.S. senator from New York. Receives 4 percent of the vote statewide, 15 percent in Harlem.

1951   Secretly marries Shirley Graham, aged 45, a writer, teacher, and civil rights activist, on Valentine's Day. Indicted earlier that month as an "unregistered foreign agent" under the McCormick Act: Du Bois, along with four other officers of the Peace Information Center, is alleged to be agents of foreign interests. He suffers the indignity of being handcuffed, searched, and fingerprinted before being released on bail in Washington, D.C. National lecture tours and a fundraising campaign for his defense expenses raise over $35,000. The five-day trial in Washington ends in acquittal.

1952   Publishes *In Battle for Peace*, an account of the trial. The State Department refuses Du Bois a passport on grounds that his foreign travel is not in the national interest. Later, the State Department demands a statement declaring that he is not a Communist Party member; Du Bois refuses. Advocacy of leftwing political positions widens the distance between Du Bois and the black mainstream.

1953   Prints a eulogy for Stalin in *National Guardian*. Reads 23rd Psalm at the funeral of Julius and Ethel Rosenberg, executed as Soviet spies. Awarded International Peace Prize by the World Peace Council.

1954   Surprised by the Supreme Court decision in *Brown v. Topeka Board of Education*, which outlaws public school segregation, Du Bois declares "I have seen the impossible happen."

1955   Refused a U.S. passport to attend the World Youth Festival in Warsaw, Poland.

1956   Supports Reverend Martin Luther King Jr. during the Montgomery bus boycott. Refused a passport in order to lecture in the People's Republic of China.

1957   Publishes *The Ordeal of Mansart*, the first volume of the *Black Flame*, a trilogy of historical novels chronicling black life from Reconstruction to the mid-twentieth century. A bust of Du Bois is unveiled at the Schomburg Collection of the New York Public Library. Refused a passport to attend independence ceremonies in Ghana. His great-grandson Arthur Edward McFarlane II is born.

1958   A celebration for Du Bois's ninetieth birthday is held at the Roosevelt Hotel in New York City; 2,000 people attend. Begins writing *The Autobiography of W. E. B. Du Bois*, drawing largely from earlier work. A Supreme Court ruling allows Du Bois to obtain a passport. His subsequent world tour includes England, France, Belgium, Holland, Czechoslovakia, East Germany, and the Soviet Union. He receives an honorary doctorate from Humbolt University in East Berlin, known as Friedrich Wilhelm University when Du Bois attended in 1892–1894.

1959   Meets with Nikita Khrushchev. In Beijing, makes broadcast to Africa over Radio Beijing and meets with Mao Zedong and Zhou Enlai. Awarded the International Lenin Prize. Publishes the second volume of the *Black Flame* trilogy, *Mansart Builds a School.*

1960   Participates in the celebration of Ghana's establishment as a republic. Travels to Nigeria for the inauguration of its first African governor-general.

1961   Du Bois's daughter Yolande dies of a heart attack in March. *Worlds of Color*, the final book in the *Black Flame* trilogy, is published. Du Bois accepts the invitation of Kwame Nkrumah to move to Ghana and direct a revival of the *Encyclopedia Africana* project. Before leaving for Africa, Du Bois applies for membership in the Communist Party.

1962   Travels to China. His autobiography is published in the Soviet Union.

1963   Becomes a citizen of Ghana. Turns ninety-five in February. Dies in Accra, Ghana, on 27 August, on the eve of the civil rights march on Washington. W. E. B. Du Bois is buried in a state funeral in Accra on the 29th.

1968   *The Autobiography of W. E. B. Du Bois* is published in the United States.

1992   Honored by the United States Postal Service with a 29-cent commemorative stamp as part of the Black Heritage Series, and again in 1998, with a 32-cent commemorative stamp.

1999   Du Bois's efforts to produce alternately an encyclopedia of the Negro and of Africa and Africans are realized when *Encarta Africana* is published by Microsoft, and *Africana: The Encyclopedia of the African and African American Experience*, edited by Kwame Anthony Appiah and Henry Louis Gates Jr. is published by Basic Civitas Books. In 2005 a second much-expanded edition of *Africana* is published by Oxford University Press.

Selected Bibliography

WORKS OF W. E. B. DU BOIS

The Suppression of the African Slave-Trade to the United States of America, 1638–1870. New York: Longmans, Green, 1896.

Atlanta University Publications on the Study of Negro Problems. Publications of the Atlanta University Conferences, ed. Du Bois (1898–1913).

The Philadelphia Negro: A Social Study. Boston: Ginn and Company, 1899.

The Souls of Black Folk: Essays and Sketches. Chicago: A. C. McClurg, 1911.

John Brown. Philadelphia: George W. Jacobs, 1909.

The Quest of the Silver Fleece: A Novel. Chicago: A. C. McClurg, 1911.

The Negro. New York: Harcourt, Brace, 1928.

Darkwater: Voices from within the Veil. New York: Harcourt, Brace and Howe, 1920.

The Gift of Black Folk: Negroes in the Making of America. Boston: Stratford, 1924.

Dark Princess: A Romance. New York: Harcourt, Brace, 1928.

Africa—Its Place in Modern History. Girard, Kansas: Haldeman-Julius, 1930.

Africa, Its Geography, People, and Products. Girard, Kansas: Haldeman-Julius, 1930.

Black Reconstruction: An Essay toward a History of the Part Which Black Folk Played in the Attempt to Reconstruct Democracy in America, 1860–1880. New York: Harcourt, Brace, 1935.

Black Folk Then and Now: An Essay in the History and Sociology of the Negro Race. New York: Henry Holt, 1939.

Dusk of Dawn: An Essay toward an Autobiography of a Race Concept. New York: Harcourt, Brace, 1940.

Color and Democracy: Colonies and Peace. New York: Harcourt, Brace, 1945.

Du Bois, W. E. B., and Guy B. Johnson. *Encyclopedia of the Negro, Preparatory Volume with Reference Lists and Reports.* New York: Phelps-Stokes Fund, 1946.

The World and Africa: An Inquiry into the Part Which Africa Has Played in World History. New York: Masses & Mainstream, 1947.

I Take My Stand for Peace. New York: Masses & Mainstream, 1951.

The Ordeal of Mansart. New York: Mainstream, 1957.

In Battle for Peace: The Story of My 83rd Birthday. With Comment by Shirley Graham. New York: Masses & Mainstream, 1952.

Fourty-Two Years of the USSR [sic]. Chicago: Baan Books, 1959.

Worlds of Color. New York: Mainstream, 1961.

An ABC of Color: Selections from over a Half Century of the Writings of W. E. B. Du Bois. Berlin: Seven Seas, 1963.

The Autobiography of W. E. B. Du Bois: A Soliloquy on Viewing My Life from the Last Decade of Its First Century, ed. Herbert Aptheker. New York: International Publishers, 1968.

COLLECTIONS

Aptheker, Herbert, ed. *Creative Writings by W. E. B. Du Bois: A Pageant, Poems, Short Stories, and Playlets.* New York: Kraus-Thomson Organization, 1985.

Aptheker, Herbert, ed. *The Complete Published Works of W. E. B. Du Bois.* 35 vols. Millwood, NY: Kraus-Thomson, 1973.

Aptheker, Herbert, ed. *The Correspondence of W. E. B. Du Bois.* 3 vols. Amherst: University of Massachusetts Press, 1973–1978.

Aptheker, Herbert, ed. *Writings by W. E. B. Du Bois in periodicals Edited by Others.* 4 vols. Millwood, NY: Kraus-Thomson, 1982.

Foner, Philip S., ed. *W. E. B. Du Bois Speaks: Speeches and Addresses 1890–1919.* New York: Pathfinder, 1970.

Huggins, Nathan I., ed. *W. E. B. Du Bois: Writings.* New York: Library of America, 1986.

Lewis, David Levering, ed. *W. E. B. Du Bois: A Reader.* New York: Henry Holt, 1985.

Sundquist, Eric J., ed. *The Oxford W. E. B. Du Bois Reader.* New York: Oxford University Press, 1996.

BIBLIOGRAPHIES

Aphtheker, Herbert. *Annotated Bibliography of the Published Writings of W. E. B. Du Bois.* Millwood, NY: Kraus-Thomson, 1973.

McDonnell, Robert W., and Paul C. Partington. *W. E. B. Du Bois: A Bibliography of Writings About Him.* Whittier, CA: Paul C. Partington Book Publisher, 1989.

Partington, Paul C. *W. E. B. Du Bois: A Bibliography of His Published Writings.* Whittier, CA: Paul C. Partington Book Publisher, 1977.

BIOGRAPHIES

Broderick, Francis L. *W. E. B. Du Bois: A Negro Leader in Time of Crisis.* Stanford: Stanford University Press, 1959.

Du Bois, Shirley Graham. *His Day is Marching On: A Memoir of W. E. B. Du Bois.* Philadelphia: Lippincott, 1971.

Lewis, David Levering. *W. E. B. Du Bois: The Fight for Equality and the American Century, 1919–1963.* New York: Henry Holt, 2000.

Marable, Manning. *W. E. B. Du Bois: Black Radical Democrat.* Boston: Twayne, 1986.

Rudwick, Elliot M. *W. E. B. Du Bois: Propagandist of the Negro Protest.* 1960; reprint. New York: Atheneum, 1968.

CRITICAL WORKS

Appiah, Anthony. "The Uncompleted Argument: Du Bois and the Illusion of Race." *Critical Inquiry* 12 (Autumn 1985): 21–37.

Aptheker, Herbert. *The Literary Legacy of W. E. B. Du Bois.* Whit Plains, NY: Kraus International, 1989.

Ashton, Susanna. "Du Bois's 'Horizon': Documenting Movements of the Color Line." *MELUS* 26.4 (2001): 3–23.

Baker, Houston A. Jr. "The Black Man of Culture: W. E. B. Du bois and *The Souls of Black Folk.*" In *Long Black Song.* Charlottesville: University of Virginia Press, 1972.

Balfour, Lawrie. "Representative Women: Slavery, Citizenship, and Feminist Theory in Du Bois's 'Damnation of Women.'" *Hypatia: A Journal of Feminist Philosophy* 20.3 (2005): 127–148.

Bauerlein, Mark. "Booker T. Washington and W. E. B. Du Bois: The Origins of a Bitter Intellectual Battle." *Journal of Blacks in Higher Education* 46 (Winter 2004–2005): 106–114.

Bell, Bernard, Emily Grosholz, and James Stewart, eds. *W. E. B. Du Bois on Race and Culture: Philosophy, Politics, and Poetics.* New York: Routledge, Chapman, and Hall, 1996.

Bhabha, Homi K. "The Black Savant and the *Dark Princess.*" *ESQ: A Journal of the American Renaissance* 50.1–3 (2004): 137–155.

Blight, David W. "W. E. B. Du Bois and the Struggle for American Historical Memory." In *History and Memory in African-American Culture,* ed. Genevieve Fabre and Robert O'Meally. New York: Oxford University Press, 1994.

Bremen, Brian A. "Du Bois, Emerson, and the 'Fate' of Black Folk." *American Literary Realism* 24 (Spring 1992): 80–88.

Bruce, Dickson D., Jr. "W. E. B. Du Bois and the Idea of Double Consciousness." *American Literature: A Journal of Literary History, Criticism, and Bibliography* 64.2 (June 1992): 299–309.

Byerman, Keith. *Seizing the Word: History, Art, and the Self in the Work of W. E. B. Du Bois.* Athens: University of Georgia Press, 1994.

Castronovo, Russ. "Beauty along the Color Line: Lynching, Aesthetics and the *Crisis.*" *PMLA: Publications of the Modern Language Association of America* 36.2 (2006): 1443–1159.

Crouch, Stanley, and Playthell Benjamin. *Reconsidering the Souls of Black Folk: Thoughts on the Groundbreaking Classic Work of W. E. B. Du Bois.* Philadelphia: Running Press, 2002.

Early, Gerald, ed. *Lure and Loathing: Essays on Race, Identity, and the Ambivalence of Assimilation.* New York: Allen Lane, 1993.

Fisher, Rebecka Rutledge. "Cultural Artifacts and the Narrative of History: W. E. B. Du Bois and the Exhibiting of Culture at the 1900 Paris Exposition Universelle." *MFS: Modern Fiction Studies* 51.4 (2005): 741–774.

Fontenot, Chester J., Mary Alice Morgan, and Sarah Gardner, eds. *W. E. B. Du Bois and Race.* Macon, Georgia: Mercer University Press, 2001.

Frederickson, George. "The Double Life of W. E. B. Du Bois." *New York Review of Books* 48.2 (February 8, 2001): 34–36.

Frederickson, George. *The Black Image in the White Mind: The Debate on Afro-American Character and Destiny, 1817–1914*. New York: Harper and Row, 1971.

Gabiddon, Shaun L. "W. E. B. Du Bois: Pioneering American Criminologist." *Journal of Black Studies* 31.5 (2001): 581–599.

Gooding-Williams, Robert. "Du Bois's Counter-Sublime." *The Massachusetts Review: A Quarterly of Literature, the Arts and Public Affairs* 35.2 (Summer 1994): 202–224.

Herring, Scott. "Du Bois and the Minstrels." *MELUS* 22 (Summer 1997): 3–18.

Hubbard, Dolan, ed. *The Souls of Black Folk One Hundred Years Later*. Columbia, Missouri: University of Missouri Press, 2003.

Jones, Gavin. "'Whose Line Is It Anyway?' W. E. B. Du Bois and the Language of the Color-Line." In *Race Consciousness: African-American Studies for the New Century*, ed. Judith Jackson Fossett and Jeffrey A. Tucker. New York: New York University Press, 1997.

Judy, Ronald A. T., ed. "Sociology Hesitant: Thinking with W. E. B. Du Bois." Special Issue: *Boundary 2: An International Journal of Literature and Culture* 27.3 (2000).

Juguo, Zhang. *W. E. B. Du Bois and the Quest for the Abolition of the Color Line*. New York: Routledge, 2001.

Kirschke, Amy. "Du Bois, *The Crisis*, and Images of Africa and the Diaspora." In *African Diasporas in the New and Old Worlds: Consciousness and Imagination*, ed. Geneviève Fabre and Benesch Klaus. Amsterdam: Rodopi, 2004. 239–262.

Lemke, Sieglinde. "Transatlantic Relations: The German Du Bois." *German? American? Literature? New Directions in German-American Studies*. Ed. Winfried Fluck and Werner Sollors. New York: Peter Lang, 2002. 207–215.

McCaskill, Barbara, and Caroline Gebhard, eds. and introd. *Post-Bellum, Pre-Harlem: African American Literature and Culture*. New York: New York University Press, 2006.

McKay, Nellie. "W. E. B. Du Bois: The Black Women in His Writings—Selected Fictional and Autobiographical Portraits." In *Critical Essays on W. E. B. Du Bois*, ed. William L. Andrews. Boston: G. K. Hall, 1985.

Meier, August. "The Paradox of W. E. B. Du Bois." In *Negro Thought in America, 1880–1915; Radical Ideologies in the Age of Booker T. Washington*. Ann Arbor: University of Michigan Press, 1963.

Miller, Monica. "W. E. B. Du Bois and the Dandy as Diasporic Race Man." *Callaloo* 26.3 (2003): 738–765.

Mizrunchi, Susan. "Neighbors, Strangers, Corpses: Death and Sympathy in the Early Writings of W. E. B. Du Bois." In *Centuries' Ends, Narrative Means*, ed. Robert Newman. Stanford, CA: Stanford University Press, 1996.

Moses, Wilson Jeremiah. *Creative Conflict in African American Thought: Frederick Douglass, Alexander Crummell, Booker T. Washington, W. E. B. Du Bois, and Marcus Garvey*. Cambridge, England: Cambridge University Press, 2004.

Pauley, Garth E. "W. E. B. Du Bois on Woman Suffrage: A Critical Analysis of His *Crisis* Writings." *Journal of Black Studies* 30.3 (2000): 383–410.

Peterson, Dale. "Notes from the Underworld: Dostoyevsky, Du Bois, and the Discovery of the Ethnic Soul." *Massachusetts Review* 35 (Summer 1994): 225–247.

Posnock, Ross. "The Distinction of Du Bois: Aesthetics, Pragmatism, Politics." *American Literary History* 7 (Fall 1995): 500–524.

Rampersad, Arnold. *The Art and Imagination of W. E. B. Du Bois.* Cambridge, MA: Harvard University Press, 1976.

Rampersad, Arnold, and Deborah E. McDowell, eds. *Slavery and the Literary Imagination: Du Bois's* The Souls of Black Folk. Baltimore: Johns Hopkins University Press, 1989.

Rothberg, Michael. "W. E. B. Du Bois in Warsaw: Holocaust Memory and the Color Line, 1949–1952." *Yale Journal of Criticism* 14.1 (2001): 169–189.

Schneider, Ryan. "Sex and the Race Man: Imagining Interracial Relationships in W. E. B. Du Bois's *Darkwater.*" *Arizona Quarterly: A Journal of American Literature, Culture, and Theory* 59.2 (2003): 59–80.

Schrager, Cynthia D. "Both Sides of the Veil: Race, Science, and Mysticism in W. E. B. Du Bois." *American Quarterly* 48 (December 1996): 551–587.

Siemerling, Winfried. "W. E. B. Du Bois, Hegel, and the Staging of Alterity." *Callaloo* 24.1 (2001): 325–333.

Smith, Shawn Michelle. *Photography on the Color Line: W. E. B. Du Bois, Race, and Visual Culture.* Durham: Duke University Press, 2004.

Sundquist, Eric J. "Swing Low: *The Souls of Black Folk.*" In *To Wake the Nations.* Cambridge, MA: Harvard University Press, 1993.

Temperley, Howard, Michael B. Katz, and Thomas J. Sugrue. "W. E. B. Du Bois, Race, and the City." *The Times Literary Supplement.* No. 4996 (1999).

"The Study of African American Problems: W. E. B. Du Bois's Agenda, Then and Now." *Annals of the American Academy of Political and Social Science* 568 (March 2000): 1–313.

Warren, Kenneth W. "Troubled Black Humanity in *The Souls of Black Folk* and *The Autobiography of an Ex-Colored Man.*" In *The Cambridge Companion to American Realism and Naturalism: Howells to London,* ed. Donald Pizer. Cambridge: Cambridge University Press, 1995.

West, Cornel. "W. E. B. Du Bois: The Jamesian Organic Intellectual." In *The American Evasion of Philosophy: A Genealogy of Pragmatism.* Madison: University of Wisconsin Press, 1989.

Williamson, Joel. *The Crucible of Race: Black-White Relations in the American South Since Emancipation.* New York: Oxford University Press, 1984.

Wolters, Raymond. *Du Bois and His Rivals.* Columbia, Missouri: University of Missouri Press, 2002.

Zamir, Shamoon. *Dark Voices: W. E. B. Du Bois and American Thought, 1888–1903.* Chicago: University of Chicago Press, 1995.

Zamir, Shamoon. "'The Sorrow Songs'/'Song of Myself': Du Bois, the Crisis of Leadership, and Prophetic Imagination." In *The Black Columbiad: Defining Moments in African American Literature and Culture.* Cambridge, MA: Harvard University Press, 1994.

Zwarg, Christina. "Du Bois on Trauma: Psychoanalysis and the Would-Be Black Savant." *Cultural Critique* 51 (2002): 1–39.